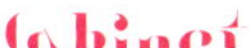

181 Wyckoff Street
Brooklyn NY 11217 USA
tel + 1 718 222 8434
fax + 1 718 222 3700
email info@cabinetmagazine.org
www.cabinetmagazine.org

Fall 2008, issue 31

Editor-in-chief Sina Najafi
Senior editor Jeffrey Kastner
Editors D. Graham Burnett, Christopher Turner
UK editor Brian Dillon
Managing editor Colby Chamberlain
Associate editor & graphic designer Ryo Manabe
Art director Jessica Green
Development director Elizabeth Grimaldi
Website directors Luke Murphy, Ryan O'Toole, Kristofer Widholm
Editors-at-large Saul Anton, Mats Bigert, Brian Conley, Christoph Cox, Jesse Lerner, Jennifer Liese, Frances Richard, Daniel Rosenberg, David Serlin, Debra Singer, Margaret Sundell, Allen S. Weiss, Eyal Weizman, Margaret Wertheim, Gregory Williams, Jay Worthington, Tirdad Zolghadr
Contributing editors Joe Amrhein, Molly Bleiden, Eric Bunge, Pip Day, Charles Green, Carl Michael von Hausswolff, Srdjan Jovanovic Weiss, Dejan Krsic, Roxana Marcoci, Phillip Scher, Lytle Shaw, Cecilia Sjöholm, Sven-Olov Wallenstein
Editorial assistants Amanda Donnan, Alicia Puglionesi
Cabinet National Librarian Matthew Passmore
Founding editors Brian Conley & Sina Najafi

Printed in Belgium by Die Keure, whose professionalism puts us to shame.

Cabinet (USPS # 020-348, ISSN 1531-1430) is a quarterly magazine published by Immaterial Incorporated, 181 Wyckoff Street, Brooklyn, NY 11217. Periodicals Postage paid at Brooklyn, NY and additional mailing offices.

Postmaster:
Please send address changes to Cabinet, 181 Wyckoff Street, Brooklyn, NY 11217.

Subscriptions
1 year (4 issues): US $32, Canada $38, Western Europe $40, Elsewhere $50
2 years (8 issues): US $60, Canada $72, Western Europe $76, Elsewhere $96

Email subscriptions@cabinetmagazine.org or call + 1 718 222 8434.
Subscriptions address: 181 Wyckoff Street, Brooklyn, NY 11217, USA
Please either send a check in US dollars made out to "Cabinet," or mail, fax, or email us your Visa/MC/AmEx/Discover information. Subscriptions are also available online at www.cabinetmagazine.org/subscribe or through Paypal (paypal@cabinetmagazine.org). For back issues, see the last page of this issue.

Institutional subscriptions are available through EBSCO or Swets, or via our website. Different rates apply.

Advertising
Email advertising@cabinetmagazine.org or call + 1 718 222 8434.

Distribution
Cabinet is available in the US and Canada through Disticor, which distributes both using its own network and also through Ingram, Source Interlink, Armadillo News, Ubiquity, Hudson News, DDRS, Small Changes, Last Gasp, Emma Marian Ltd, Cowley Distribution, Kent News, LMPI, MSolutions, The News Group, Newsways, Newbury Comics, Don Olson Distribution, and Chris Stadler Distribution. If you'd like to use one of these distributors, contact Melanie Raucci at Disticor. Tel: + 1 631 587 1160, Email: mraucci@disticor.com

Cabinet is available in Europe and elsewhere through Central Books, London. Email: orders@centralbooks.com

A version of Cabinet printed as a book (and sporting an ISBN) is available through D.A.P./ Distributed Art Publishers. Tel: + 1 212 627 1999, Email: dap@dapinc.com

Email circulation@cabinetmagazine.org or call + 1 718 222 8434 if you need further information.

Submissions
See <www.cabinetmagazine.org/information/submissions.php>. No paper submissions, please.

Cabinet is a non-profit 501 (c) (3) magazine published by Immaterial Incorporated. Our survival is dependent on support from foundations and generous individuals. Please consider supporting us at whatever level you can. Contributions to Cabinet are fully tax-deductible for those who pay taxes to Uncle Sam. All donations are acknowledged online. Donations of $25 or more will be noted in the next possible issue, and those above $100 will be noted for four consecutive issues. Checks should be made out to "Cabinet" and sent to our office address. Please mark the envelope, "This will make you blush."

Cabinet wishes to thank the following visionary foundations and individuals for their support of our activities during 2008. Additionally, we will forever be indebted to the extraordinary contribution of the Flora Family Foundation from 1999 to 2004; without their generous support, this publication would not exist. We would also like to extend our enormous gratitude to the Orphiflamme Foundation for a recent generous donation.

$50,000
The Andy Warhol Foundation for the Visual Arts
The Starry Night Fund of Tides Foundation

$10,000 – $14,999
The New York City Department of Cultural Affairs
The New York State Council on the Arts
The National Endowment for the Arts
Stina & Herant Katchadourian
The Peter Norton Family Foundation

$5,000 – $9,999
The Danielson Foundation
Epson America, Inc.

$1000 or under
Foundation for Contemporary Arts
Martha & Thomas G. Armstrong

$500 or under
Spencer Finch
Brett Littman & Kara Vander Weg
Jason Olin
James Siena

$250 or under
Ann and Jim Chamberlain
Fred Clarke
James D. Cox
Jane Crawford
Jeffrey Cunard
Eshrat Erfanian
Steven Igou
Deborah Lovely
Ben Marcus

Jason Pickleman
Jocelyn Prince & Lucky Leone
Jonathan Rabinowitz
Gretchen I. Schaffner & Alex Reid
Jim Shaw
Linnaea Tillett

$100 or under
Nathalie Angles, Robert Barrick, Regine Basha & Gabriel Perez-Barreiro, Tom Bayley, Thea Bloom, Katherine Bovee, Edward Branigan, Wayne Brenner, Thomas Callahan, Brian Cohen, Matthew Counts, Forrest Darrough, Erika Devries, Scott Duncan, Libby Ellis, Burton Fox, Joseph Fratesi, Jim Frazer, Jay Frazier, William Ganis, Sam Garst, Andrew Green, Lyn Hejinian, Institute of Cultural Inquiry, Judy Jacobson, Robert Jarrel, David Kiehl, Richard Klein, Leah Koransky, Hedi Kyle, William Lofton, Elissa & Mark Loparco, Richard J. March, Richard Maxwell, John Paul Miller, Dee Mitchell, Nina Morgan, Gary Niebuhr, Chris O'Toole, Eugenia Parry, John Parascandola, Marcus Ratliff, Siri von Reis, Ariana Riera, Alison Rossiter, Sara Ryan, Emily & John Sabath, John Sargent, Brian Scanlon, Kathy Soltwedell, Barry Stoltz, Mark Strehlow, Tracy Sunderland, Carolee Thea, Jordi Torrent, Michael Watkins, Alyssa Wendt, Susan West, Bonnie Williams, Jeffry Williams, Emily Wilson, F. Michael Zula, Marina van Zuylen

Cover: A fig leaf, the sole purpose of which seems to be to cover human genitals.

Page 4: How to begin on this one? Braintree Scientific is a company based in Massachussetts that specializes in manufacturing equipment for experimentation on small animals. In the 1980s, they commissioned a series of illustrations as covers for their product catalogues, each image featuring rats in various anthropomorphic poses. This reworking of Botticelli's *Birth of Venus* gave us goosebumps. First, there's the utter faithfulness of the rendition, down to the last flower. And then there is the mind-boggling projection of shame and modesty onto the coy Venus-rat, who, lacking the long golden hair of Venus, resorts to using her tail to hide her genitals. This is an image that we will undoubtedly carry with us to our graves. We toyed with the idea of using this image for the cover but then became anxious that its "challenging" aesthetics might put off potential readers, like you. We wish we had been brave enough to use this on the cover but are ashamed to admit that we were too cowardly.

COLUMNS

MAIN

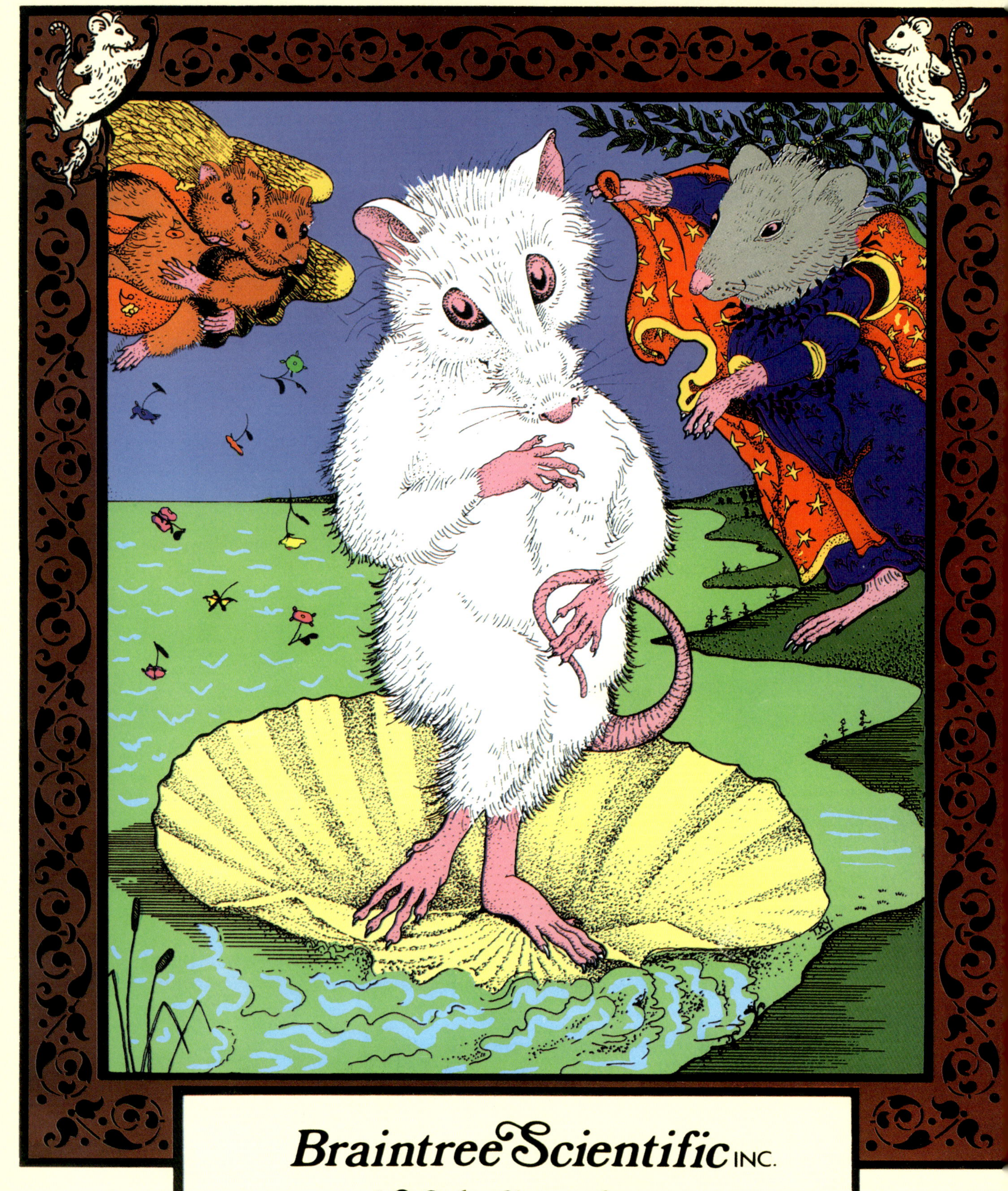

Braintree Scientific INC.
1986 Catalog

CONTRIBUTORS

Jonathan Ames is the author of eight books, including *Wake Up, Sir!* (Scribner, 2004), *The Double Life is Twice As Good* (Scribner, forthcoming), and *The Alcoholic* (DC Comics, 2008), a graphic novel illustrated by Dean Haspiel.

Lauren Berlant teaches English at the University of Chicago. Recent work related to affect, politics, and aesthetics includes *The Queen of America Goes to Washington City* (Duke University Press, 1997), *The Female Complaint* (Duke University Press, 2008), and, as contributor and editor, *Intimacy* (University of Chicago Press, 2000), *Compassion* (Routledge, 2004), and *On the Case*, a special issue of Critical Inquiry (2007). Her book, *Cruel Optimism*, is forthcoming. She can also be found at <supervalentthought.wordpress.com>.

Adam Broomberg and Oliver Chanarin are a photographic team based in London. Together they have produced six books that examine the language of documentary photography. Their most recent book, *Fig.*, was published by Steidl in 2007. More of their work can be seen at <www.choppedliver.info>.

D. Graham Burnett is an editor of *Cabinet*, and a historian of science at Princeton University. He is the author of four books, including *Trying Leviathan: The Nineteenth-Century New York Court Case that Put the Whale on Trial and Challenged the Order of Nature* (Princeton University Press, 2007), which won the 2008 New York City Book Award and the 2008 Hermalyn Prize in Urban History.

Amy Cutler is an artist based in Brooklyn, New York.

Brian Dillon is UK editor of *Cabinet* and the author of a memoir, *In the Dark Room* (Penguin, 2005), which won the Irish Book Awards non-fiction prize. His writing appears regularly in such publications as *Frieze, Art Review, Modern Painters*, the *London Review of Books*, and the *Times Literary Supplement*. His book *Tormented Hope: Nine Hypochondriac Lives* will be published in 2009.

David Dinges is chief of the Division of Sleep and Chronobiology, and Director of the Unit for Experimental Psychiatry in the Department of Psychiatry at the University of Pennsylvania School of Medicine.

Leland de la Durantaye is associate professor in the Department of English at Harvard University. He is the author of *Style is Matter: The Moral Art of Vladimir Nabokov* (Cornell University Press, 2007) and *Giorgio Agamben: A Critical Introduction* (forthcoming from Stanford University Press, 2009). Alongside his scholarly work, he has written for the *Boston Globe, Harvard Review, Rain Taxi, Bookforum*, and the *Village Voice*.

Paul Ekman's books include *Why Kids Lie: How Parents Can Encourage Truthfulness* (Penguin, 1991) and *Emotions Revealed* (Holt, 2007).

Cathy Haynes is a London-based producer, editor, and teacher. She is co-editor of *Implicasphere*, and initiated and co-produced Artangel's "Nights of London" series of artists' projects.

Marilyn Ivy teaches anthropology at Columbia University. She is the author of *Discourses of the Vanishing: Modernity, Phantasm, Japan* (University of Chicago Press, 1995) and has published widely on themes ranging from the obsession with missing children in the United States to the place of Buddhism in late modernity. Her recent work has focused on the complex political and aesthetic agendas that have shaped "Superflat" art in contemporary Japan.

Alan Jacobs teaches English at Wheaton College in Illinois. His most recent book is *Original Sin: a Cultural History* (HarperOne, 2008), and he is currently writing about trees.

Christopher James is an artist based in Los Angeles. He is the co-author of "–gone wild," an ongoing sculpture project that can be seen at <www.thehouseoflazyj.org>. He is currently soliciting sponsorship funding for a journey to Ultima Thule, the recently discovered but as yet untouched northernmost point of land on Earth.

Josh Kun is the author of *Audiotopia: Music, Race, and America* (University of California Press, 2005) and co-author of *And You Shall Know Us By The Trail Of Our Vinyl* (Crown, 2008), an album cover history of Jews in America. He is a professor in the Annenberg School for Communication and the Department of American Studies and Ethnicity at the University of Southern California.

David Levine works in theater and visual art. His installations, videos, and performances have been seen at the Sundance Theater Lab, Gavin Brown@ Passerby, Galerie Magnus Mueller, and Documenta XII (with *Cabinet*). He is the recipient of a Kulturstiftung des Bundes grant for *Bauerntheater* (2007) and an Étant Donnés Grant for *Venice Sav'd: A Seminar*, which will premiere at P.S. 122 in March 2009. Portions of his archive of headshots, featured in this issue, will be exhibited in 2009 at Galerie Feinkost in Berlin.

Aaron Levy is executive director and a senior curator at Slought Foundation, and lecturer in English at the University of Pennsylvania. Publications edited include *Blood Orgies: Hermann Nitsch in America* (2008) and *Cities Without Citizens* (2004), and a series of DVD publications with Alain Badiou, Dennis Oppenheim, Vito Acconci, and Werner Herzog (all published by Slought Foundation). He is co-curator of "Into the Open: Positioning Practice," the US representation at La Biennale di Venezia, 11th International Architecture Exhibition.

Florian Maier-Aichen is a German artist working in Cologne and Los Angeles. He received his MFA in 2001 from the University of California, Los Angeles. He recently exhibited at the Museo Thyssen-Bornemisza, Madrid, and his second solo exhibition at 303 Gallery, New York, opens in spring 2009.

George Makari is the director of the Institute for the History of Psychiatry and associate professor of Psychiatry at Weill Medical College of Cornell University. He is the author of *Revolution in Mind: The Creation of Psychoanalysis*, which was published by HarperCollins in 2008.

Daniel Joseph Martinez is an artist based in South Los Angeles. He is currently building a doomsday device and a time machine, an attempt to change the past in order to affect the future. He looks forward to the end of the world, as we know it.

Sina Najafi is editor-in-chief of *Cabinet*.

Sally O'Reilly is a London-based writer, lecturer, and producer of performance-based events, as well as co-editor of *Implicasphere* and co-founder of Brown Mountain College of the Performing Arts.

George Pendle has written for the *Times*, the *Financial Times*, the *Los Angeles Times*, and the New York City Department of Parks and Recreation. He is the author of *Strange Angel: The Otherworldly Life of Rocket Scientist John Whiteside Parsons* (Harcourt, 2005), *The Remarkable Millard Fillmore: The Unbelievable Life of a Forgotten President* (Three Rivers Press, 2007), and the recently published *Death: A Life* (Three Rivers Press, 2008). He is currently writing an in-depth study of airport carpeting.

Cara Phillips is a Brooklyn-based photographer. She is also the co-founder and co-curator of the online exhibition project "Women in Photography." Her work can be seen in New York this fall in New York in a group show curated by the Humble Arts Foundation and in "Art in Odd Places." See <www.cara-phillips.com> and <www.wipnyc.org> for more information.

Paul Ramirez Jonas is an artist based in New York. His work is currently on view at the Aldrich Contemporary Art Museum, Ridgefield, Connecticut, and at the 28th São Paulo Biennial.

Daniel Rosenberg is not related to Julius or Ethel Rosenberg. He is associate professor of history in the Robert D. Clark Honors College at the University of Oregon, an editor-at-large of *Cabinet*, and great-grandson of Edward Kuntz.

Renata Salecl is a researcher based in Ljubljana, Slovenia. Her books include *On Anxiety* (Routledge, 2004), *(Per)versions of Love and Hate* (Verso, 2000), and *The Spoils of Freedom: Psychoanalysis and Feminism After the Fall of Socialism* (Routledge, 1994).

David Serlin is associate professor of communication and science studies at the University of California, San Diego, and an editor-at-large for *Cabinet*. He is the author of *Replaceable You: Engineering the Body in Postwar America* (University of Chicago Press, 2004).

Eluned Summers-Bremner is senior lecturer in English at the University of Auckland, New Zealand. She has published *Insomnia: A Cultural History* (Reaktion Books, 2008) and is currently writing *A History of Wandering* (Reaktion Books). Her book *Ian McEwan: Sex, Death and History* is forthcoming (Cambria Press) and she is working on studies of trauma, the affective work of love and reading, and a project on mid-century British fiction and World War II.

Christina Tarnopolsky teaches political science at McGill University. Her interests include emotions, aesthetics and politics. She is the author of *Prudes, Perverts and Tyrants: Plato and the Politics of Shame*, which will be released by Princeton University Press in winter 2010.

Christopher Turner is an editor of *Cabinet*. His book, *Adventures in the Orgasmatron: How the Sexual Revolution Came To America*, is forthcoming from Farrar, Straus and Giroux.

Aleksandra Wagner teaches sociology at The New School for General Studies, works as a psychoanalyst in Manhattan, and harbors passionate interest in other types of oral traditions. *Considering Forgiveness*, a book she has co-edited with Carin Kuoni, will be released in early spring 2009.

LEFTOVERS / THE ORIENTING STONE
D. GRAHAM BURNETT

The black granite Ka'ba, the cubical structure that stands as the holiest center of Islam, features at its eastern vertex a small black stone about the size of a grapefruit, the *al-hajar al-aswad*, which may or may not have fallen to earth in the time of Adam and Eve. Supported in a silver frame, this obsidian-like cipher structures space for some billion Muslims, standing as it does at the culminating point known as the *qibla*— the direction to which devout followers of Mohammed address their five daily obeisances. Tradition has it that the rock was once snowy white, and has darkened over time through exposure to human sin.

A snowy white stone that gives shape to the universe: as it happens, we all carry within our skulls the vestige of such a thing, a kind of existentially reversed *qibla* (this one perspectival, the other metaphysical) that gives us our sense of being at the center of things, the sense that we are upright at the origin point of a three-dimensional space. The "otolithic organs," as they are known, are a pair of sensors—the utricle and the saccule—nestled in the labyrinthine architecture of the inner ear. Grossly speaking, each consists of a bunch of tiny pebbles (of the white rock known as calcium carbonate) embedded in a gooey wad that sits atop a carpet of delicate hairs. The saccule is roughly vertical in our heads, and the utricle more or less horizontal. Together they orient us in the world, since they work as tiny inertial references: raise your head suddenly (or get in a jerky elevator), and the pebbles of the saccule get momentarily left behind as your skull starts upward; this bends down the hairs against which those pebbles lay, and the sensitive hairs function like switches, sending signals to your brain that you register as a feeling of ascent. The utricle does the same work for motion from side to side, and between them these tiny organs generate the neurological data that give us our normal sense of being in the world. What would it feel like not to have those pebbles? Delete them from a mouse and it spends a lot of time falling over.

Both the utricle and the saccule contain what I have called "pebbles," but they are little more than mineral crystals really, microscopic sand bound together into a mass by a matrix of protein. Not so the homologous structures in fish, our evolutionary ancestors. They retain, inside their skulls, quite clearly defined, and

overleaf: Twelve otoliths (not to scale) from various fresh and saltwater fish. Courtesy Doug Ferrell, New South Wales Department of Primary Industries.

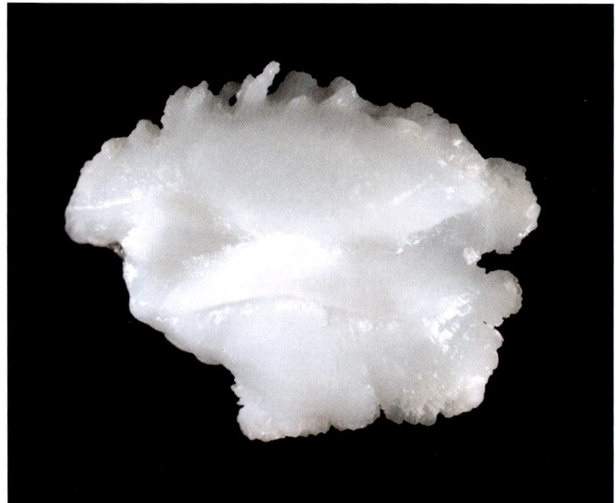

Branchiostegus wardi (Ward's tilefish)

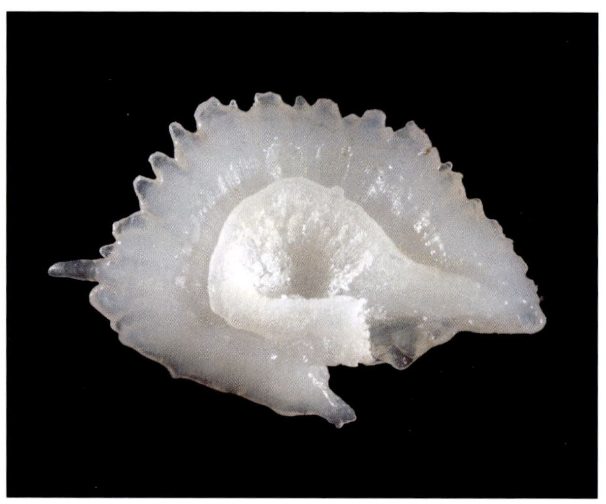

Cyprinus carpio (Common carp)

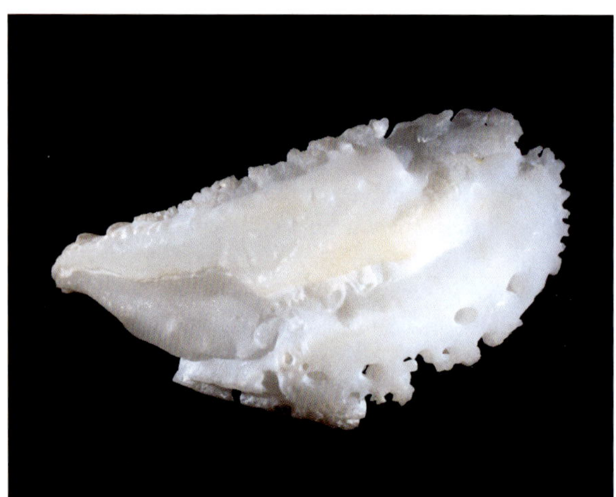

Epinephelus lanceolatus (Giant grouper)

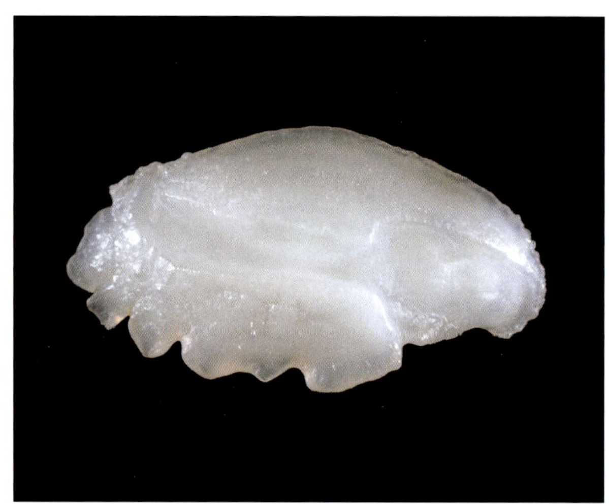

Macquaria ambigua (Golden perch)

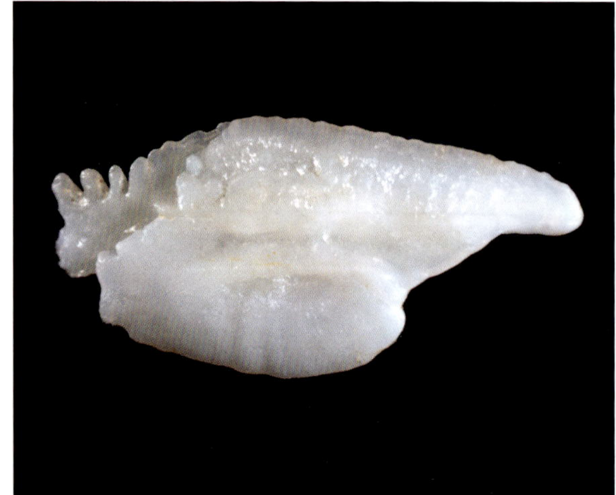

Helicolenus barathri (Bigeye sea perch)

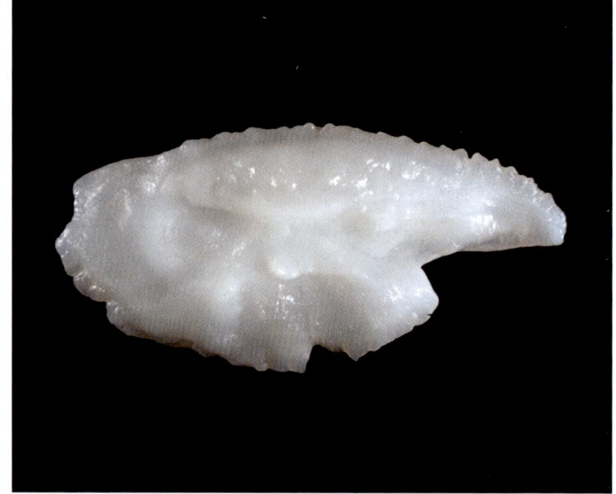

Helicolenus percoides (Red gurnard perch)

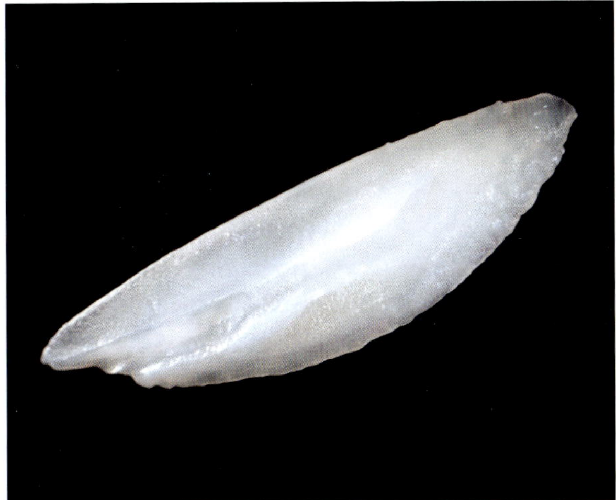

Platycephalus caeruleopunctatus (Blue-spotted flathead)

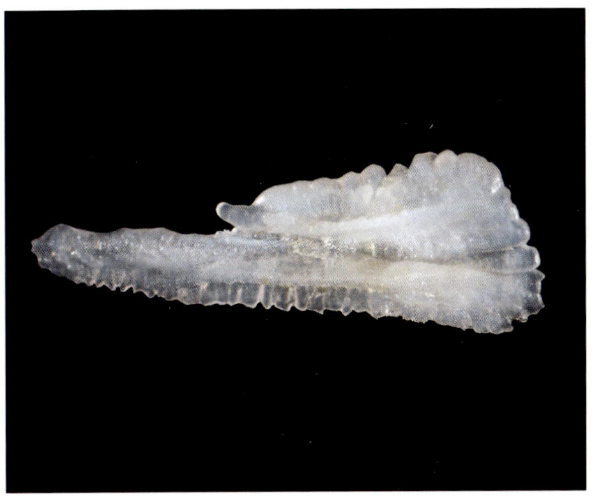

Sarda australis (Australian bonito)

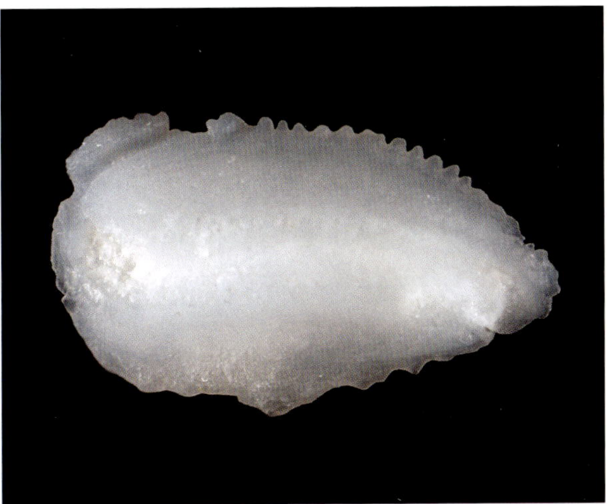

Hyporhamphus australis (Eastern sea garfish)

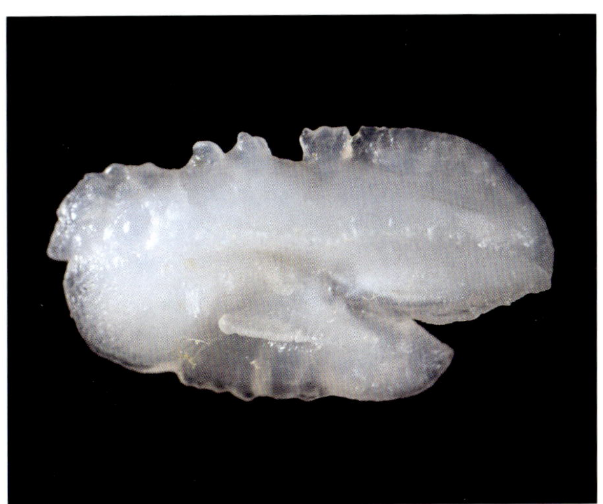

Nematalosa erebi (Australian river gizzard shad)

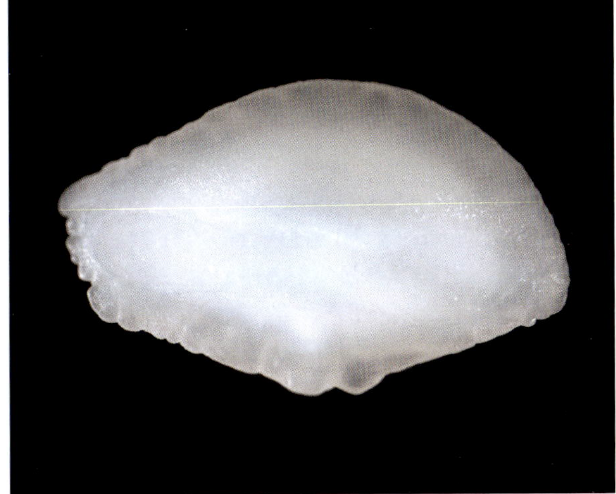

Sillago flindersi (Flinders' sillago)

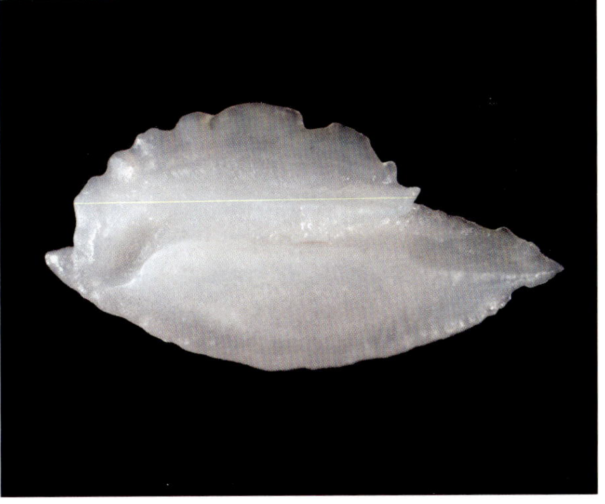

Trachurus novaezelandiae (Yellowtail horse mackerel)

nearly always large enough to see (and sometimes as large as marbles), healthy little rocks known as otoliths, or "ear stones." The minute pebbles of our otolithic organs would appear to be the powdered remains of these ancestral lithic pips. It is in this sense that I said we carry within us the "vestiges" of an orienting stone; only our oceanic kin secrete such a thing in an intact form. It is as if, in the course of evolutionary time, our inner *al-hajar al-aswad* came under the hammer of an angry god. We are, as it were, hanging on after this blow, but our sense of the center may not hold quite as it should.

Fish otoliths are among the strangest and most wonderful bits of vertebrate anatomy. They are strikingly sculptural, and their clean surfaces tend to display an alluring opalescent sheen. No one is absolutely sure about all their functions (which would seem to vary from species to species), but it is safe to say that they generally serve in a sensory system very much like the saccule/utricle: they sit atop a mat of sensitive hairs and their sloshing around gives the fish information about its movement in space. Fish that have to deal with complicated spatial environments (reefs, kelp beds) usually have bigger otoliths; those open water predators that stick to swimming fast in straight lines (tuna, billfish) tend to have relatively small ones. Otoliths also seem to play a role in underwater hearing in many species: because they are stone (and therefore of a different specific gravity than the rest of the fish), their vibrations in response to sound waves are out of phase with those of the animal's body; these differences can be translated into acoustic information. (Interestingly, although hearing in mammals is now handled by a very different system, it has recently been shown that human beings can "hear" very high frequency sounds by means of their otolithic organs, which appear to retain some acoustic sensitivity, despite having been converted almost entirely into sensors for movement and orientation).

There are several thousand researchers around the world who spend their whole working day looking at fish otoliths. This has nothing to do with their physiological functions, however, and everything to do with their structure and the staggering amount of information they contain. In the first place, each species of fish has a unique otolith shape. Couple this with the fact that they are stone (and therefore comparatively resistant to decomposition), and their utility as a biological marker becomes clear. Interested in the food habits of bottlenose whales? Pump their stomachs and you will end up with relatively few bones but lots of otoliths. Find an otolith expert and he or she will be able to give you a menu. Similar work has been done to reconstruct the ecology of seabirds or to determine, using kitchen middens from archaeological sites, the diet of early coast-dwelling humans.

But the true wonder of these peculiar pearls lies within. Should you have occasion to tonsure a snapper or sea-bass, slicing off the top of its skull just above the eyes, you might take a moment to remove the two largest otoliths (there are, as a rule, six in all, three on each side) from their velvet seats to the right and left of the brain stem. With the heel of a knife you should be able to snap one of them in two, and then, holding it to the light, you will discern a set of concentric bands. These are growth rings—annuli—which, properly counted, will give the age of your fish in years. This in itself is interesting, and enormously valuable to those who wish to understand the life-cycles and population structure of commercial species. But about thirty years ago a curious geologist, tinkering with an otolith (it was a rock, after all), made the truly shocking discovery that those annual layers can be further resolved, microscopically, down to *daily* layers, layers that contain, in their chemical composition and size, information about the temperature and the salinity of the water through which the fish moved, the food that it ate, and various environmental contaminants it encountered. The result is a stratigraphy unprecedented in the organic world: the diligent student can peruse the otolith of a long-lived deep sea fish, and reconstruct not merely its age, but (and I am barely exaggerating) what it had for breakfast on 6 March 1964, or roughly where it was on the occasion of a particular nuclear test. Not for nothing have those who gather at the biennial "Otolith Olympics" (the insiders' name for the scientific conference of dedicated otolith researchers) taken to calling the ear stone the "flight recorder" of the piscine world.

And that's not all. Ever inclined to make an inscription, human beings have figured out how to write their own messages in the heart of the pearl. By sequentially altering the temperature of the water in which salmon fry are hatched and raised, researchers can lay a distinctive "batch label" into the chemical layers of the otolith—a kind of barcode, inscribed in stone, and indelibly preserved within the maturing adult fish (a puckish early student of this technique used it to write "hi mom" in binary inside his experimental animal). Later, when these free-swimming creatures are captured at sea, each can be traced unfailingly to its hatchery of origin. Some five billion Pacific salmon have now been marked in this way, their inner *qibla* reconfigured to refer to their point of origin, and thus the point to which they seek return.

INGESTION / EDIBLE OBJECT 114868-7(34)
DANIEL ROSENBERG

Archives are meant to be indiscriminate—to receive and not to select. As a consequence, they are full of unstrange objects of all varieties. Occasionally, such objects embody an exceptional unstrangeness, as in the case of Object 114868-7(34) in Record Group 118 of the United States National Archives and Records Administration—Northeast Region (New York).[1] At a glance, Object 114868-7(34) looks more interesting than it really is. But looks are deceiving. Students of history know that the famous espionage trial of Julius and Ethel Rosenberg in 1951 turned on the question of whether Julius Rosenberg had arranged a meeting between two communist spies, one of whom had confessed to stealing atomic secrets from the military compound at Los Alamos, the other to delivering them to his Soviet controller. To the bitter end, the Rosenbergs protested their ignorance. According to the prosecution, led by Irving Saypol and Roy Cohn, Julius Rosenberg set up the meeting from New York (he himself never went to New Mexico) and gave each of the spies a key that would allow him to recognize the other. The prosecution alleged that Rosenberg took the side of an ordinary box of Jell-O, cut it into two jagged pieces, and gave one half to each spy. Then, when the spies met in Albuquerque in June 1945, each was able to confirm the other's identity by fitting the two fragments together like puzzle pieces. But the object preserved in the National Archives that appears to be the famous Jell-O box is, in fact, nothing of the sort. It is an original facsimile, an ordinary Jell-O box purchased by the Department of Justice in 1951 for display as Exhibit 4 at the trial.[2]

At the trial, the term used to characterize the box was "substantially identical," which seems to have meant something like "not identical at all, but you get the idea." On this point, the prosecution was crystal clear: Exhibit 4, now archived as Object 114868-7(34), was not the same box that Julius Rosenberg had cut up and handed out—but a Jell-O box is just a Jell-O box, after all. David Greenglass, one of the confessed spies who had turned witness for the prosecution, testified that the fragments of the box shown in the courtroom were just like the ones that his wife, Ruth, had received from Julius Rosenberg in January 1945 and that the Soviet courier, Harry Gold, had presented to him in Albuquerque in June of that year. Though he testified that he had not paid attention to how the original box looked or what was written on it (adding that he was color blind), he maintained that the boxes looked about the same.

Moreover, he knew, because everyone knows, what a box of Jell-O with its big red letters looks like.

That's the thing about Jell-O. In the beginning, in 1897, its inventors, Pearle and May Wait, had heady ideas, and, right off the bat, the ad men called Jell-O "America's most famous dessert." Eventually, they wouldn't be far wrong. But it wasn't the special qualities of Jell-O that made for its success; it was its very lack of qualities. In 1897, gelatin desserts were not new. Peter Cooper had patented his process for deriving gelatin a half-century earlier, in 1845, and by the turn of the century most of the uses to which Jell-O would later be put were already in practice in kitchens all over. But before Jell-O, there was still the soaking, and the waiting, and the adding of flavors. There was still, as the Jell-O ads were apt to point out, an indefinable animal scent. "Ooh, what a smell!" went one ad. And pictures enhanced the text; as Carolyn Wyman observes, "It's hard to find a women's magazine from 1934 or 1935 that does not contain an ad of a woman with a Royal, Knox, or Jell-O gelatin box up her nose."[3] The innovations of Jell-O were to simplify the preparation, to integrate the dessert flavors into the mix (initially, strawberry, raspberry, orange, and lemon), and to neutralize the taste and special fragrance of the gelatin.

Jell-O rarely staked its claim on tastiness *per se*, only on its likeability and its inoffensiveness. Jell-O was a dessert that you could eat to infinity. As the old slogans put it, "People who like to eat like Jell-O gelatin," and, "There's always room for Jell-O." When Jell-O eventually introduced an unflavored variety to compete with Knox and Royal, it promoted the new Jell-O as having "a lack of flavor all its own." In Jell-O, we are in the realm of food with no qualities, matter without form (ready to be molded), medium without content (avoid raw pineapple, which will sink), neither raw nor cooked (no refrigerator needed either, contrary to the popular misconception). Trying to define its special character is, as the saying goes, like "trying to nail Jell-O to the wall." And none of this even comes close to touching the metaphysical complexity by which Jell-O, derived from the bones, skins, and other leftovers of cows, horses, and pigs, ends up outside the domain of meat, and, by some arcane Maimonidean logic attested by orthodox rabbis, turns out not only kosher, but kosher for Passover.

By 1951, imitation raspberry flavor Jell-O had achieved a nearly unparalleled degree of unremarkableness. Admittedly, the use of the term "imitation" on the box was a bit of a boast, in the same way that "virtual" is today. It was meant to give the product a little gee-whiz appeal. But the gee-whiz gesture, too, was entirely regular in the gee-whiz 1950s. It would be another twenty

JELL-O

BRAND

GELATIN DESSERT

SUGAR · GELATIN · CITRIC ACID
NATURAL RASPBERRY FLAVOR ENHANCED WITH ARTIFICIAL FLAVOR
SODIUM CITRATE AND/OR PHOSPHATE · SALT · U·S·CERTIFIED COLOR

IMITATION RASPBERRY FLAVOR

3 OZ. NET WEIGHT · 85 GRAMS

MANUFACTURED BY GENERAL FOODS CORPORATION
ADDRESS: NEW YORK · N·Y· MADE IN U·S·A

JELL-O IMITATION RASPBERRY

JELL-O IMITATION RASPBERRY

FLAVOR

FLAVOR

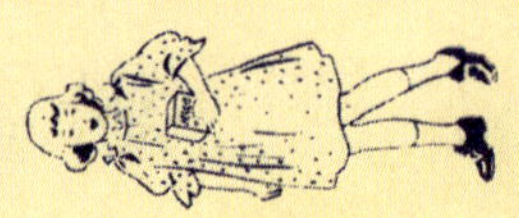
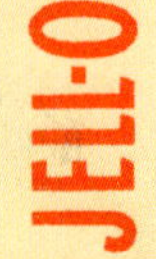

JELL-O

AMERICA'S MOST FAMOUS DESSERT

SIX DELICIOUS FLAVORS

Directions for the New Improved Jell-O

Pour 2 standard measuring cups (1 pint) hot water over contents of this package. Stir until completely dissolved. Pour into mold. Place in refrigerator or other cold place; let stand until firm. Makes 4 to 6 servings.

To unmold, loosen firm Jell-O around edge of mold with small knife, warmed in water. Then quickly dip mold just to the rim in warm water. Shake slightly to loosen Jell-O. Cover with plate and turn mold and plate together. Lift off mold.

To add fruits, nuts, etc., fold them in after Jell-O has thickened slightly. They will then remain evenly distributed. Raw, cooked, or canned fruit may be used except fresh pine-apple. (Use only cooked or canned pineapple for jellied dishes.)

To whip Jell-O, chill dissolved Jell-O until slightly thick-ened. Set bowl of Jell-O in a larger bowl partly filled with ice and water. (Be sure it rests firmly on the bottom of larger bowl.) Whip Jell-O with rotary egg beater until fluffy and thick like whipped cream.

COCONUT BAVARIAN CREAM—Dissolve 1 package Raspberry Jell-O in 2 cups hot water. Chill until slightly thickened. Fold in ¾ cup cream, whipped, and ¾ cup fine-ly cut Baker's Shredded Coconut. Turn into large mold or individual molds. Chill until firm. Unmold. Serves 8. (All measurements are level.)

years before a Soviet scientist noticed that some lab rats that had ingested Red Dye No. 2—the very coloring used in raspberry Jell-O—were dying of cancer, and the claim of artificiality would finally lose its luster. It was the Rosenberg trial itself that Irving Saypol called a "necessary by-product of the atomic age," but the same words might equally apply to the star Exhibit 4 presented by the prosecution, the imitation box of imitation raspberry flavor Jell-O, a fabrication of a fabrication at once satisfying the highest standards of food science and evidentiary procedure.

According to David Greenglass, there had been an actual Jell-O transaction in 1945 (with a box, he said, "much darker in color"). Problem was, no one had the box. Both Greenglass and Gold testified to having disposed of their pieces immediately after their contact. But problems are made to be solved, and in the Rosenberg case, the prosecution was nothing if not inventive. On the morning of 12 March 1951, prosecutor Roy Cohn entered into evidence as Exhibit 4 a brand new box of imitation raspberry flavor Jell-O. He then asked Greenglass to cut it up in just the same way that Julius Rosenberg had. Greenglass removed one side of the Jell-O box—the side with instructions for making a coconut Bavarian Cream, not the side "with the picture of the little girl"—and snipped it into two pieces, which were then marked Government's Exhibit 4-A for the piece similar to the one kept by his wife and 4-B for the one similar to the one kept by Julius Rosenberg to pass along to his Soviet contact.

The defense made no objection to entering the two pieces of cardboard into the trial. Just the opposite; the move was such an obvious piece of courtroom theater that it appeared as likely as not to blow up on the prosecution. When it came time for cross-examination, Julius Rosenberg's defense attorney, Emanuel Bloch, went on the offensive. The prosecution's reliance on exhibits 4-A and 4-B was a clear demonstration of the *lack* of material evidence of a crime, he said. Bloch returned again and again to the point. David Greenglass was not present for the cutting of the box. He had no clear memory of what the box looked like. He did not know what color the box was or what was written on it. Gold's testimony was even more vague. Initially, he referred to the Jell-O side as only a "piece of cardboard." Then, with prompting, he became more specific, but not much more, saying it "appeared to have been cut from a packaged food of some sort."

And even Exhibit 4 itself seemed to cry out for doubt. As Bloch noted in his cross-examination, this was not just any Jell-O but *imitation* flavor Jell-O. The whole thing was just too weird to let pass without comment. But Judge Kaufman, who indulged the prosecution in its box-cutting skit, was less lenient with the defense, closing the 12 March session by chiding Bloch for posing so many detailed questions about an exhibit that, after all, was not actually evidence, and for his "facetious" reference to the imitation character of the Jell-O. The judge was, he said, looking forward to turning the page on the whole "Jell-O situation."

But, as defense attorney Edward Kuntz argued, none of this was a matter of humor, and the next morning, to the annoyance of the court, Bloch picked up right where he left off, reading directly from the imitation imitation Jell-O box, and sparring again with a grinning Greenglass. "Did you ever hear of the words 'coconut Bavarian cream'?" Bloch asked. "Did I ever hear of the words?" Greenglass replied. "I have heard them around, sure." The defense reasoned that the more the jury got to see the non-evidence of the Jell-O box, the more absurd the whole thing would seem. But, in the matter of Jell-O box, the prosecution won the day.

What the jury saw in the Jell-O box presented to them was something that didn't need to be original. It didn't even need to look like the original. The cleverness of the device, as Ruth Greenglass said on the witness stand, lay in its simplicity and modesty. The fact that the box was unremarkable was what made it so very useful. Who could suspect that such a thing would be the key to the secret of the atom bomb? Who could deny it? And the genius of the jury passed into the archives. Here in a place that claims to be entirely transparent, a medium without a message, here, enshrined as Object 114868-7(34), is a Jell-O box, not *the* Jell-O box, but one substantially identical to a Jell-O box of great historical interest.

1 Jell-O Box Exhibit, Case File 114868, Box 7, Item 34; Significant Case Files; United States Attorney for the Southern District of New York; Records of United States Attorneys, Record Group 118; National Archives and Records Administration—Northeast Region (New York).
2 In the extensive and argumentative literature, see, Bernice Schrank, "Reading the Rosenbergs after Venona," *Labour/Le Travail* 49 (2002): 189-210; Ivy Meeropol, dir., *Heir to An Execution: A Granddaughter's Story* (HBO/Blowback Productions, 2004). A complete trial transcript may be found online at <www.law.umkc. edu/faculty/projects/ftrials/rosenb/ROS_TRIA.HTM>. It appears likely that new revelations are now forthcoming. On 7 April 2008, Ruth Greenglass died, and, in June 2008, under pressure from the non-profit National Security Archive and the American Historical Association, federal prosecutors agreed to release some grand jury testimony from the Rosenberg case, still under seal fifty years later.
3 Carolyn Wyman, *Jell-O: A Biography* (San Diego: Harcourt, 2001), p. 32. See also <www.kraftfoods.com/jello/explore/history/>.
4 Marjorie Garber, "Jell-O," in Marjorie Garber and Rebecca L. Walkowitz, eds., *Secret Agents: The Rosenberg Case, McCarthyism, and Fifties America* (New York: Routledge, 1995), p. 17.

opposite: The Jell-O box admitted as evidence during the espionage trial of the Rosenbergs and Morton Sobell, 6–29 March 1951. Courtesy National Archives and Records Administration.

Will posterity remember us for our successes or our mistakes? Will our legacy be the result of a life's dedicated application, or a moment's half-forgotten accident? Years can be spent chasing chimeras without realizing that our claim to enduring fame was forged in the blink of an eye in the heat of pursuit. Such is the tale of Johann Konrad Dippel, whose ineradicable achievement—the creation of Prussian Blue—was of little interest to him when placed beside his grand magical dreams.

Dippel was born in Castle Frankenstein in 1673. It is not known whether lightning attended his birth, but certainly it would not have been an overly dramatic sign for a man who seemed determined to blaze his way into history. His father intended him to be a minister, but from an early age Dippel sought astonishment and argument rather than concord and conformity. He openly questioned the Catechism when he was nine years old, before spending his youth aggressively defending, then mercilessly attacking, orthodox Lutheranism. While attending theological college in Giessen he began to publish satirical religious tracts under the name Christianus Democritus. These were written with a vehemence that many found unseemly.

His religious contrariness brought him minor infamy. He was labeled "ein indifferentistischer Schwarmer" ("an indifferent fanatic"), and found himself persecuted by the clergy and threatened by the mob. Perhaps it was little surprise that within two years of moving to Strasbourg, where he had hoped to make his name in theological study, he had killed a man in a duel and fled back to Giessen.

This setback did not humble Dippel's vaulting ambition. His unorthodox interests had by now broadened to include palmistry and astrology, and after reading the writings of Ramon Llull, the medieval Spanish mystic, Dippel came to believe in his own ability to transmute lead into gold. He bought a small estate, on credit, where he might work in peace, but after eight months of continuous heating, his crucible cracked. Pressure from his creditors forced him to go into hiding.

Moving to Berlin, he created a palatial laboratory in which he sought to achieve that other alchemical dream: a universal remedy. Dippel believed that the secret to this lay in the oil created by the destructive distillation of animal parts. Leather, hoofs, and horns were boiled down into a malodorous treacle that became known as "Dippel's Oil" and which he claimed could cure fevers, colds, and epilepsy. Dippel's Oil gained a certain notoriety as a medicine—Diderot would later openly question its worth—but its success as a sheep dip and insecticide was unchallenged.

Soon the sheer pitch of his ambition attracted the attention of King Frederick I. The Prussian court was, at the time, besieged by alchemists who promised the possibility of limitless wealth in exchange for royal patronage. Dippel was asked to act as referee to their claims. A lesser man might have taken this post as a sinecure, but Dippel was no cynic. He did not seek wealth, only gold, and as such was a conscientious judge. He unmasked pretenders but also sought to learn the secrets of those he thought were genuine. In particular, he waxed rhapsodic about meeting the mysterious Lascaris, who was believed to have performed a double transmutation, changing mercury into gold and gold into silver.

It seems only fitting that a man who believed so utterly in the efficaciousness of alchemy should find the fulfillment of his genius as a direct, albeit unwarranted, result of his fevered alchemical research. In 1704, a dye-maker named Diesbach, who shared Dippel's laboratory, was in the midst of creating a batch of cochineal lake—a deep red—formulated by the boiling of insects and the addition of alum, green vitriol, and potash. Discovering that he had no potash to hand, he borrowed some from his colleague and added it to his heavily pestled insects. As he mixed and mingled he discovered, to his astonishment, that what he was creating was not a deep red, but instead a dark, ungodly blue.

Upon being informed of this uncalled-for transmutation, Dippel tried to piece together the reason for it. The potash Diesbach had used had previously been employed in the creation of Dippel's Oil. It was thus contaminated with animal blood. When mixed with the green vitriol (iron sulfate), this blood caused a reaction, and a blue that had never before been seen on Earth was brought into existence. One can imagine Dippel, the pale student of unhallowed arts, kneeling beside the thing he had put together, quite uncomprehending that this, rather than his alchemy, would be his greatest legacy. He named the newborn color Berlin Blue.

At the time, blue was a particularly difficult color to create and work: azurite turned green when mixed with water; smalt and woad tended to fade; indigo was not colorfast; and ultramarine could only be made from the crushed lapis lazuli mined in the mountains of Badakhshan and cost more than gold. But Dippel's blue had a steadfastness, a vividness, and a simplicity of creation that surpassed them all. Unlike its creator, it was immediately welcomed by the world.

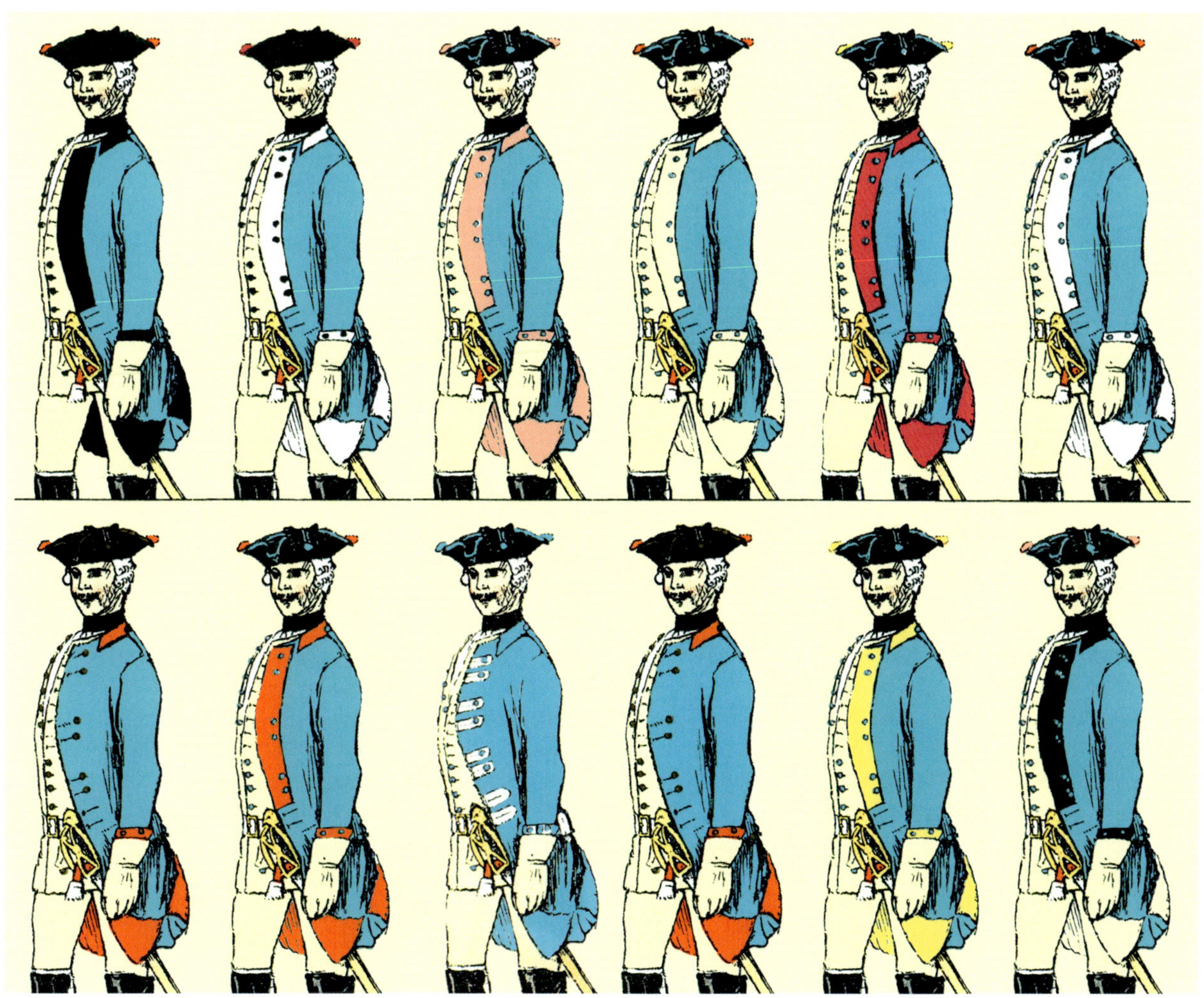

A guide to Prussian military uniforms from 1746 to 1756, undated. From the
Hendrik Jacobus Vinkhuijzen Collection of Military Costume Illustration.
Courtesy the New York Public Library.

Fittingly for a mixture of blood and iron, one of its first uses was to dye the uniforms of the Prussian Army, from which it gained its more familiar name. As the army expanded under Frederick the Great, Prussian blue became a symbol of Teutonic aggression, although after that army's decisive intervention at the Battle of Waterloo calling someone "my Prussian blue" also became a term of endearment in England.

Meanwhile the color's complex molecular structure (which was not fully described until 1977) allowed it adapt to a number of quite different environments. Prussian blue became an indelible mainstay of Victorian innovation, providing the blue in blueprints and the tincture in the early photographs known as cyanotypes. Artists flocked to use it. Japanese printmakers dismissed their beloved indigo for it, while in France the Impressionists used it lavishly in their *plein air* compositions (only Renoir abstained, declaring he was "horrified" by the color). Soon Prussian Blue was working its way into every nook and cranny of society, becoming a pigment in printing inks, typewriter ribbons, and cosmetics.

Yet Prussian Blue's success was not confined to the visible, exterior world. It slowly began to move inside us, inveigling its way into our bodies and displaying far more efficaciousness than Dippel's Oil ever had. It became an antidote to heavy metal poisoning and remains the pathologist's leading tool in detecting lead poisoning. Encroaching onto the microscopic world, it revealed itself as a natural molecule-based magnet.

There was a solitary blip in its relentless evolution when, in 1958, Crayola renamed their "Prussian Blue" crayon "Midnight Blue," following schoolteachers' complaints that explaining the causes of the Thirty Years' War severely retarded their pupils' attempts to color-by-numbers. But otherwise the color's spread has been inexorable. It has even gained a role—as Dippel himself had—as an important arbiter of truth. Its appearance in paintings made before 1704 is one of the key ways to detect a forgery. Similarly, its absence from the gas chambers at Auschwitz has been used as a speculative crutch by Holocaust deniers who claim it should have appeared there as the byproduct of the interaction between cyanide, a substance found in both Zyklon-B and Prussian Blue, and the iron in the chambers' walls. A neo-fascist teen folk group recently named themselves after the color.

But while Prussian Blue has rampaged across time and space, its popularity assured by its constant revelation of new characteristics, Johann Konrad Dippel remained fatefully trapped within his own time and antagonistic personality. In 1707, after years of luckless alchemical experimentation, he left Berlin and became a student of medicine in Leyden. For reasons unknown, he was jailed for seven years on the Danish island of Bornholm, where he spent his incarceration convincing himself that ancient Egyptians had once inhabited the same land. European royalty's well-known weakness for alchemists saw him freed after seven years, and he became physician to the Swedish court in Stockholm, but once again his argumentative character brought this role to a premature end. His last years were spent as a guest at the Castle Wittgenstein where he engaged in further theological controversies and alchemical research. In 1733, he predicted that he would live until he was 135 years old. With characteristic exactitude, he was found dead in his bed the following spring.

Posterity has been no kinder to Dippel than the age in which he lived. Recent attempts to recognize the alchemist who was born in Castle Frankenstein, who worked with animal parts, and who attempted to defy the laws of nature, as the inspiration for Mary Shelley's *Frankenstein* have been deemed highly improbable by scholars. Yet one thing is immutable: Dippel's most successful creation—a blue deeper than any God had chosen to create for Himself—could not have come into being without his fiery, misguided, and ill-fated excesses.

TOP TEN SHAMEFUL MOMENTS

JONATHAN AMES

1. I am apolitical and do nothing to help the world.

2. I am often impatient with my mother who is nothing but generous and loving and kind to me.

3. I have hurt and disappointed some women who have fallen in love with me.

4. During college, I cheated, out of desperation, at least twice.

5. I have had several incidences of adult incontinence.

6. I am so lazy that I have used coffee filters when I've run out of toilet paper.

7. When my son was very young, I yelled at him when he would not fall asleep and it was getting very late.

8. Another time, when my son was very young, I said something that made him cry.

9. I've been sexually insane.

10. Due to fear and laziness, I've not lived as full a life as possible.

(Most of these moments have been repeated numerous times. Also, the order of this list is of no great meaning; I simply wrote down ten shameful things as they came to me.)

F PAST THINGS

ld at the beginning
Caligula led her to

ityahu was born.
of 66–73, he was
his soldiers. They
by one, counting
re were only
e other man to
position of the
now known as the
He died in the

wn as Faustina the
arriage to Roman
her as a goddess

s a bureaucrat during
e made some bad
committed suicide

born. She was
death he married
insisted that Lady
ously. She was per-
been poisoned by

as born. During
Christians, the
the bodies of two
en stoned to death,
g on earth, that I
She was immediately

icinius was born. A
order of Emperor
had the next per-
ed in 325, ...

stantius Gallus was
h soft blond hair. He

... when Saint Augustine was born. He wrote a fitting addition to this timeline: "There are three tenses or times: past, present and future ... These are three realities in the mind, but nowhere else as far as I can see, for the present of past things is memory, the present of present things is attention, and the present of future things is expectation." He died as the Vandals were tearing down the walls of Hippo, Algeria, in 430, ...

... when Julius Nepos was born. He was the last legitimate Western Roman Emperor. He ruled for about a year, and was murdered by his own soldiers either on April 25, May 9, or June 22 in 480, ...

... the year that Anicius Manlius Severinus Boethius was born. While tortured and imprisoned, he somehow found time to write the most influential Latin book of the Middle Ages. "A cord was twisted round his head many times for a very long period so that his eyeballs started from their sockets; blows from a club finished off the shattered wreck." He died in 524, ...

... the year that He Shikai was born. Did Gao Yan have him murdered because he was incompetent and corrupt? Or did he have him killed because he was a lover to Empress Wu, wife of Emperor Wucheng, Gao Yan's father?! We'll never know. The murder took place in 571, ...

... the year that Wang Gui, advisor to Li Jiacheng, was born. Li Shimin, the emperor's younger son, killed Li Jiancheng, the heir, and became emperor instead. He retained Wan Gui, knowing him to be an honest and blunt advisor. Talking back to the royal family sometimes pays off. Wang Gui died a duke in 639, ...

... the year that Bishop Aldhelm was born. It is said that his people were slow to come to church, and so to attract them, he would stand by a bridge, sing in the vernacular, gather a crowd, and exhort them to sacred subjects. He died doing his rounds in 709, ...

... the year the Mayan king Yaxun B'alam IV, also called Bird Jaguar IV, was born. He died after a reign of seventeen years in 768, ...

... when the poet Han Yu was born. A religious skeptic, he wrote: "Although your servant is stupid, he cannot help knowing that Your Majesty is not misled by this Buddha, and that you do not perform these devotions to pray for good luck. ... How could a sublime intelligence like yours consent to believe in this sort of thing?"

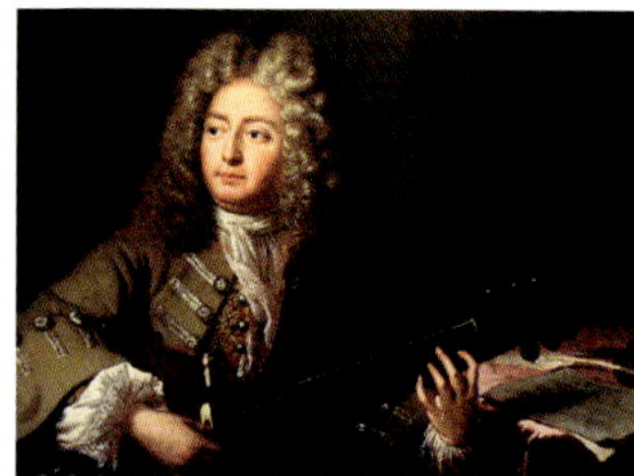

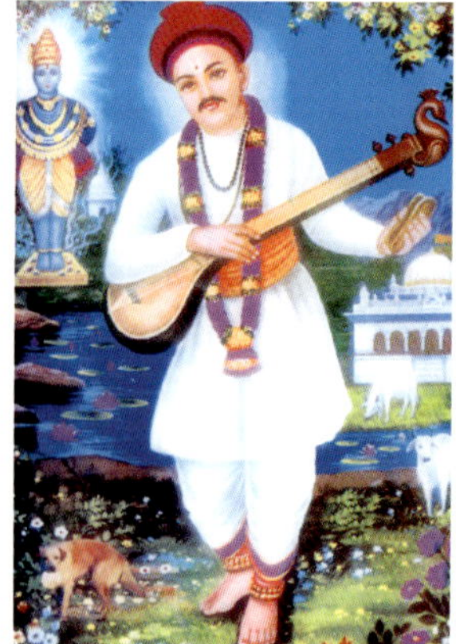

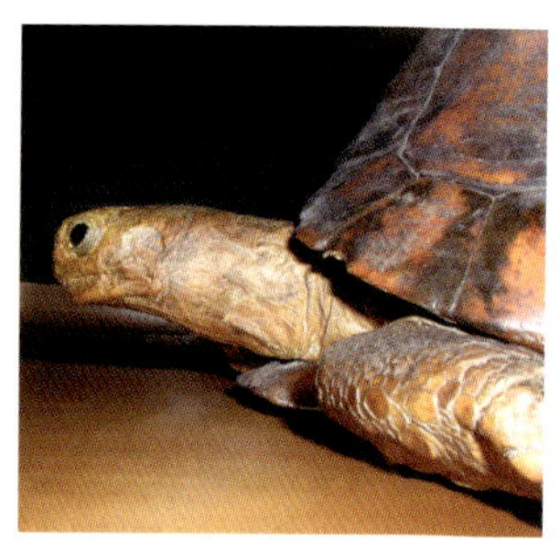

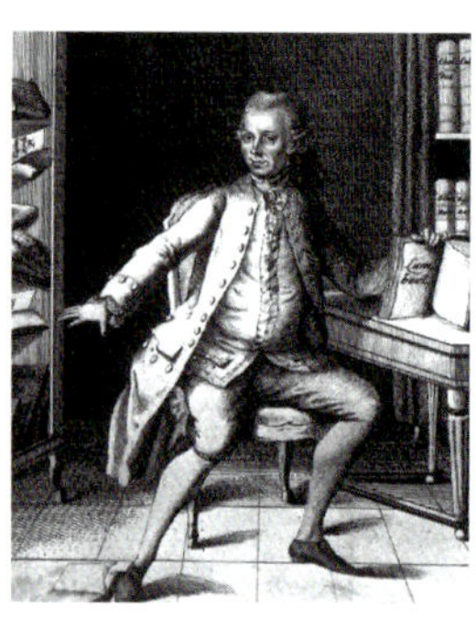

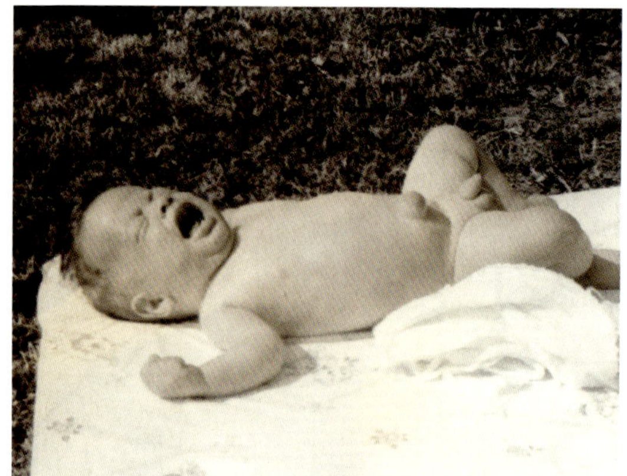

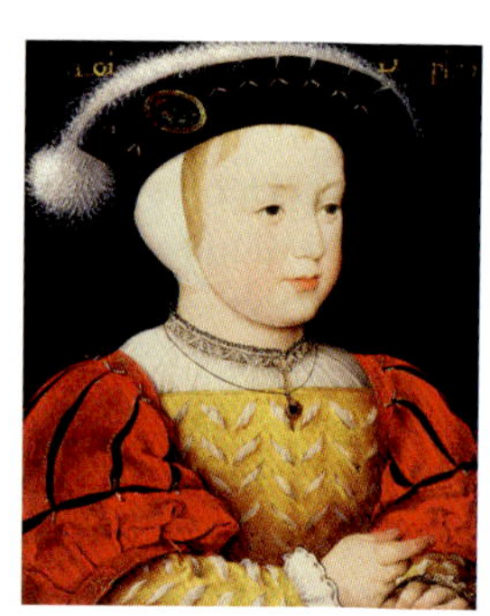

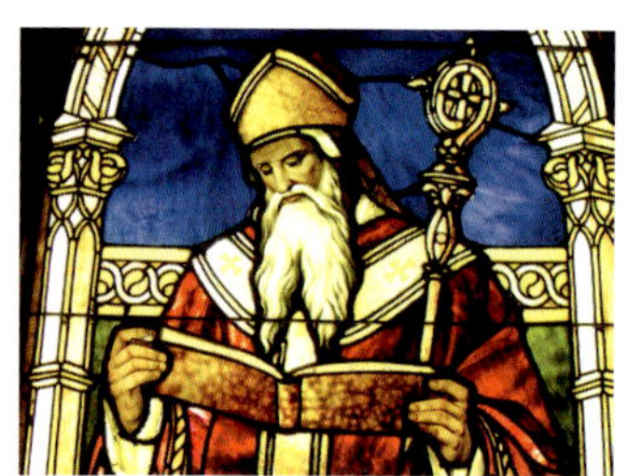

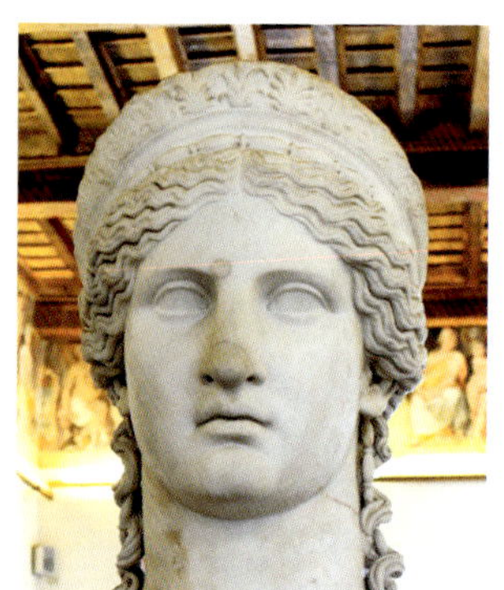

from top left, clockwise: Marin Marais, Namdev, Tu'I Malila, Jean
Clouet, Antonia Minor, Saint Augustine, and Johann Heinrich Lambert.
center: Paul Ramirez Jonas.

Talking back to the royal family sometimes doesn't pays off—he was fired. He died in 824, ...

... the year that Al-Hakim Al-Tirmidhi was born. He wandered the world but had returned to his birthplace by the time of his death in 892, ...

... the year that Ai was born. Ai, The last emperor the Tang Dynasty, noticed something tasted funny in his food and fell dead in 908, ...

... just as the short life of Thankmar began. He asked for trouble his entire life. By the age of thirty, he was bleeding to death on the altar of the church of Saint Peter in Eresburg. The year was 938, ...

... when Abu Aamir Muhammad Ibn Abdullah Ibn Abi Aamir was born. He sacked Barcelona, razed León, destroyed the city of Santiago de Compostela, stole its bells, but left the tomb of Saint James untouched. He died in 1002, ...

... when Mei Yaochen came to this world. A terrible bureaucrat but a fantastic poet, he left more than 3,000 poems behind. Realizing he could not surpass the poets of the past, he decided to write about his own lack of ambition, focusing on the pedestrian. He died in 1060, ...

... while in India, Brahmadeva, son of Candrabudha, was being born. He knew *pi* up to four decimal places: 3.1415. He died in 1130, ...

... when the Confucian scholar Zhu Xi was born. Thousands attended his funeral in 1200, ...

... the year Isaac ben Moses of Vienna, one of the greatest rabbis of the Middle Ages, was born. He witnessed the Jews of France forced to wear a yellow badge, the Jews of Frankfurt massacred, and the Jews of Austria extorted by the nobles. He left his long troubled life in 1270, ...

... the year that Namdev, Marathi saint and poet, came into this world. As a child, he took a food offering to Vithoba in the Pandharpur temple. He waited for the deity to eat the food. The statue did not budge. Upset, he declared that unless accepted, he would kill himself. A miracle then took place and the god ate the offering. Namdev died in 1350, ...

... the year that Andrew of Wyntoun, Scottish chronicler, was born. His *Orygynale Cronykil of Scotland* contains an early mention of Robin Hood. He died the year that construction began on the Temple of Heaven in Beijing, in 1420, ...

... as Nicolaas Jenson was entering this world. That was 588 years ago, and yet as recently as 1996 the fonts he developed where still used as the basis for contemporary typefaces. He died in 1480, ...

... the year that Jean Clouet was born. As an artist, it disturbs me that we know so much about Jean but that there are no surviving paintings we can be sure are his. He died in 1541, ...

... when Hattori Hanzo, a ninja and famous Samurai nicknamed "Devil Hanzo," was born. His battle helmet, spears, and body are still at rest in the Sainen-ji temple cemetery in Shinjuku. He died in 1596, ...

... as Jan Van Goyen was born to this world. He was not a very successful artist, his paintings rarely selling for much. He made up for it by painting quickly (1,200 paintings!), using thin paint and inexpensive pigments. He also speculated in tulips and real estate. Nothing worked. He died 18,000 guilders in debt in 1656, when ...

... French viol player and composer Marin Marais was born. Books: 5, still in print. Children: 19, now all dead. Titles: 1, Ordinaire De La Chambre Du Roy Pour La Viole. Died: 1728, ...

... when Johann Heinrich Lambert was born. He proved that Pi is irrational. He died in 1777, ...

... the year that Tu'I Malila, the longest living animal in history, was born. The tortoise died of natural causes in 1965, ...

... when I, Paul Ramirez Jonas, was born.

***STUDIES IN CLASSIC AMERICAN LITERATURE
BY RITA KAMINS***
JOSH KUN

The reader became the book…
—Wallace Stevens

1.

In December of 1964, Viking Press published the second printing of D. H. Lawrence's 1923 *Studies in Classic American Literature*. Less than a year later, my mother bought a copy for $1.45 at the textbook store of UCLA, where she was just beginning classes as an undergraduate. The book was assigned for an American history lecture course. She wrote her name, "Rita Kamins," on the title page in thick blue ink, in a flowing cursive that is still instantly identifiable as her own. She underlined her name and below it wrote her phone number, "VE 95890," a number that, if anyone had called it, would have rung in the house where she grew up, the house only fifteen minutes east of campus where she was still living.

The book has 177 pages of which my mother read 21. They are the only pages that are marked, and they are marked vigorously, in black ballpoint pen, red marker, and pencil, in a personalized code of underlines, double underlines, triple underlines, five-sided stars, circled words and phrases, brackets, braces, arrows, and margin notes. The markings are traces of her interaction with the text. They are her re-write of Lawrence.

Lawrence's foreword ran for nearly two pages. This is my mother's version:

But equally no good asserting him merely … Because all that is visible to the naked European eye, in America, is a sort of recreant European. We want to see this missing link of the next era. … So the only thing to do is to have a look for him under the American bushes. The old American literature, to start with … Some insisting on the plumbing, and some on saving the world: these being the two great American specialties. … You can't save yourself before you are born. … Two bodies of modern literature seem to me to have come to a real verge: the Russian and the American. … The European moderns are all trying to be extreme. The great Americans I mention just were it. Which is why the world has funked them, and funks them to-day. The great difference between the extreme Russians and the extreme Americans lies in the fact that the Russians are explicit and hate eloquence and symbols, seeing in these only subterfuge, whereas the Americans refuse everything explicit and always put up a sort of double meaning. … subterfuge …

She was eighteen when she read Lawrence and this is what she found important. This is what she decided she should know, what she decided was valuable about what he'd written. It's as close to a portrait of her as a young adult as I will ever get, her mind revealed in marginalia.

When we read books that have been underlined, it's hard not to read them as the reader did. As much as we may resist it, our eyes naturally skip over the original typesetting and focus on the underlined sentences and words. We make instant jump cuts. We are drawn into unconscious remixes. When I read this copy of Lawrence, I read my mother reading him. There is no way for children to truly know their parents, but this might be a place to start—a locked diary rescued from beneath a mattress, a incomplete codex never meant for anyone else to see.

I am not reading D. H. Lawrence. *This is Studies in Classic American Literature*, written by Rita Kamins in the fall of 1965.

2.

Books are beefsteaks. In his 1940 argument for writing in books, "How to Mark a Book," Mortimer J. Adler works the analogy for half a paragraph. "You buy a beefsteak and transfer it from the butcher's icebox to your own. But you do not own the beefsteak in the most important sense until you consume it and get it into your bloodstream." Books don't do us any good, he says, until we eat them up (cut, slice, chew, swallow), get their sinew and fat and muscle and flesh into the mix with our own. Good readers cut up their books to digest them better. Swallow them whole and you won't taste them. Or worse, they'll hurt going down.

Adler doesn't trust people who labor under a "false reverence for paper, binding, and type" and kowtow to an author's genius. Who wants to go through life without getting things dirty, without leaving a trace? Reading is a conversation and if you don't mark your book, you are not adding much to it.

That's the premise of most marginalia buffs, who are pretty sure that Roland Barthes copped his "Death of the Author" idea—once the reader reads, the author stops being the author—from all those anonymous and everyday eighteenth- and nineteenth-century readers who scribbled in the margins with fever and conviction. For every Samuel Johnson publishing a celebrated *Plan of a Dictionary of the English Language* in 1747, there was an average reader like Samuel Maude who thought so much, or so little, of Johnson's book that he used its margins to keep an elaborate personal diary. His curling, swooping handwriting dwarfs the printed type, urging you to read Maude, not Johnson.

home, the homeland. Different places on the face of the earth have different vital effluence, different vibration, different chemical exhalation, different polarity with different stars: call it what you like. But the spirit of place is a great reality. The Nile valley produced not only the corn, but the terrific religions of Egypt. China produces the Chinese, and will go on doing so. The Chinese in San Francisco will in time cease to be Chinese, for America is a great melting pot.

There was a tremendous polarity in Italy, in the city of Rome. And this seems to have died. For even places die. The Island of Great Britain had a wonderful terrestrial magnetism or polarity of its own, which made the British people. For the moment, this polarity seems to be breaking. Can England die? And what if England dies?

Men are less free than they imagine; ah, far less free. The freest are perhaps least free.

Men are free when they are in a living homeland, not when they are straying and breaking away. Men are free when they are obeying some deep, inward voice of religious belief. Obeying from within. Men are free when they belong to a living, organic, *believing* community, active in fulfilling some unfulfilled, perhaps unrealized purpose. Not when they are escaping to some wild west. The most unfree souls go west, and shout of freedom. Men are freest when they are most unconscious of freedom. The shout is a rattling of chains, always was.

Men are not free when they are doing just what they like. The moment you can do just what you like, there is nothing you care about doing. Men are only free when they are doing what the deepest self likes.

And there is getting down to the deepest self! It takes some diving.

Because the deepest self is way down, and the conscious self is an obstinate monkey. But of one thing we may be sure. If one wants to be free, one has to give up the illusion of doing what one likes, and seek what IT wishes done.

But before you can do what IT likes, you must first break the spell of the old mastery, the old IT.

Perhaps at the Renaissance, when kingship and fatherhood fell, Europe drifted into a very dangerous half-truth: of liberty and equality. Perhaps the men who went to America felt this, and so repudiated the old world together. Went one better than Europe. Liberty in America has meant so far the breaking away from *all* dominion. The true liberty will only begin when Americans discover IT, and proceed possibly to fulfil IT. IT being the deepest *whole* self of man, the self in its wholeness, not idealistic halfness.

That's why the Pilgrim Fathers came to America, then; and that's why we come. Driven by IT. We cannot see that invisible winds carry us, as they carry swarms of locusts, that invisible magnetism brings us as it brings the migrating birds to their unforeknown goal. But it is so. We are not the marvellous choosers and deciders we think we are. IT chooses for us, and decides for us. Unless, of course, we are just escaped slaves, vulgarly cocksure of our ready-made destiny. But if we are living people, in touch with the source, IT drives us and decides us. We are free only so long as we obey. When we run counter, and think we will do as we like, we just flee around like Orestes pursued by the Eumenides.

And still, when the great day begins, when Americans have at last discovered America and their own wholeness, still there will be the vast number of escaped slaves to reckon with, those who have no cocksure, ready-made destinies.

Which will win in America, the escaped slaves, or the new whole men?

The real American day hasn't begun yet. Or at least, not yet sunrise. So far it has been the false dawn. That is, in the progressive American consciousness there has been the one dominant desire, to do away with the old thing. Do away with masters, exalt the will of the people. The will of the people being nothing but a figment, the exalting doesn't count for much. So, in the name of the will of the people, get rid of masters. When you have got rid of masters, you are left with this mere phrase of the will of the people. Then you pause and bethink yourself, and try to recover your own wholeness.

So much for the conscious American motive, and for democracy over here. Democracy in America is just the tool with which the old master of Europe, the European spirit, is undermined. Europe destroyed, potentially, American democracy will evaporate. America will begin.

In *Marginalia*, H. J. Jackson's study of the Samuel Maudes of the world (in an inevitable irony, my library copy is spotless), he divides the history of marginalia into three "kingdoms" of authorial defacement: the Kingdom of Competition (up to 1700), the Kingdom of Sociability (1700–1820), and the Kingdom of Subjectivity (1820–present). For Jackson, it's what happens in 1819 that really tips the scales: Samuel Coleridge admits that he too marks up books and publishes a whole volume of his writings in other people's books to prove it. This forever changed the cultural capital bestowed on the margin scribe. Readers were writers, writing in books was a subjective act of creation and intellectual dialogue, and Coleridge was as tempted by blank parchment inches as any other mortal.

As for my mother, squarely in the Kingdom of Subjectivity, she was re-writing Lawrence, who was re-writing eighteenth and nineteenth-century American writers like Benjamin Franklin and Herman Melville. *Studies in Classic American Literature* may have been published as its own book, but wasn't it really just a more formal version of Lawrence's own marginalia in books by Franklin and Melville? Surely Lawrence was a beefsteak guy. In *Studies*, Lawrence famously has a field day with Franklin's stiff-upper-lip list of virtues (Temperance, Moderation, Chastity), countering with his own guide to better American living —"Eat and carouse with Baachus," "There are many Gods," "Follow your passional impulse." Surely, Lawrence would have filled the pages of Franklin's autobiography with angry scribbles and outraged exclamation points.

Of the two lists, my mother liked Lawrence's virtues. She didn't mark Franklin's list, but starred Lawrence's three times, drawing a curved arrow from top to bottom to make sure she re-read all of them. That she would choose Lawrence over Franklin is surprising. The mother I know now is no friend of Baachus, no yoga mat polytheist, and gave up on the "passional" impulses of experience after a bout with leukemia turned her into a careful, guarded taster of life's offerings.

"The world fears a new experience more than it fears anything," she underlined. "Because a new experience displaces so many old experiences." Lawrence was showing her who she would soon be: a protector of old experiences, a reluctant adaptor, a friend of fear.

But it's nice to know that at eighteen, Lawrence's vision of America still looked damn good, even to a girl who would grow up not to drive freeways and only like movies shot in the bright, smiling sunshine of friendly daylight.

3.

Why come to America?, she thought. *It's a great question, the question. What does your leaving there for here say about who you wish to be?* She thought about her grandparents. *Why did the Swedes leave? Why did the Russians leave? They didn't just come to America, they came to North Dakota of all places. America needs to be masterless, but how? Were they the "extreme Russians" Lawrence is talking about? Do we hate eloquence and symbols too? My grandpa didn't talk much—always a little stern, a little grumpy. Nana was the sweet one, but even she was tough, and big, and pillow-like, which I guess makes her extreme. Not very symbolic, just there, present and material, fully themselves. Did grandpa know what Lawrence is talking about? Did he know people like that back in Russia? I wonder how much of Russia he remembers now, what it tasted like, what it smelled like when the winds blew past open kitchen windows, what the earth looked like after his booths walked over it.* She turned the page. *I wonder about this one: the world fears a new experience more than it fears anything, because a new experience displaces so many old experiences.*

She thought about that line, and then thought about it again, and again, and again, until it became a part of her, until the words were hers.

4.

Until she got TiVo, my mother was a reader. She was always a TV watcher— always went through the TV guide that came with the Sunday paper with a pencil, circling shows to watch and marking others to tape on the VCR, serving us dinner during episodes of *CHiPs* or *60 Minutes*, archiving favorite *Oprah* episodes on VHS. But TiVo turned a universe of programming choices into a graspable infinity. Now she circles, marks, and watches more, and reads fewer and fewer books, even those that Oprah recommends.

She used to have a soft spot for historical novels and biographies, especially anything Teddy Roosevelt, anything Aztec or Mayan. Before she had us, there were archaeology dreams, visions of a life of digs and pith helmets, baked crumbling hillsides that when sifted revealed lost worlds. She held on for a while, leading grammar school field trips to California canyons rich in ancient sediment—the basement is still full of flaking mollusk shells and cracked tusks filed delicately in plastic cases meant for action figures—and then volunteering as a tour guide at the La Brea Tar Pits.

My mother, the saber-toothed tiger. My mother, the ground sloth. My mother, the dire wolf. My mother, the mammoth rising from the sticky black sea alongside Wilshire Boulevard. I always figured the books were prosthetics for the amputated limbs of deferred archaeological dreams, turning paper not dirt, handling spines not fossils, excavation time-travel undertaken from the comfort of an armchair with a cup of hot Earl Grey tea and a paper towel sprinkled with almonds and Hershey's kisses.

There are no more beefsteaks. If reading was once her way of living vigorously, what happens when the books stay closed?

You can't save yourself before you are born, she underlines, *but you can after you are born.*

This is where her marginalia starts to get me down.

5.

Studies in Classic American Literature is about the birth of a nation through the birth of its literature. When my mother read it, it wasn't about that at all—it was about a child becoming an adult. Her underlines, stars, and brackets turn it into a secret coming-of-age story, a Judy Blume saga hiding between interpretations of Nathaniel Hawthorne and Edgar Allan Poe. It was an early archaeological move. She took a pick to the hillside of Lawrence and uncovered things she didn't even know were there.

She was most intrigued by Lawrence's interest in the question of America's political, cultural, and literary independence from the yoke of Europe. "Whatever else you are," Lawrence wrote, "be masterless." My mother underlined it and starred it, and when Lawrence quotes Caliban's refrain from *The Tempest* ("Ca Ca Caliban / Be a new master, be a new man"), she underlined *new* and circled *master*. She was taken by Lawrence's feverish attachment to a pure, true freedom and brought out the red marker for his declaration, "Men are free when they are in a living homeland, not when they are straying and breaking away." There is red for his riff on "escaped slaves" versus "new whole men," red for his idea that American liberty is really synonymous with breaking away from the dominion of Europe, red for his fantasy of some "deepest whole self" just waiting to be discovered in the confused American soul. Then, in the midst of Lawrence's critique of Franklin, there is red for my mother's own margin notes: *free to do only as soc. wishes "fenced in" restricted freedom is contradiction.*

Why this interest in freedom? My mother was a daughter in the midst of leaving home and in the throes of re-examining her relationship to her own masters, her

parents. They may not have been from the Old World of Europe and she was certainly not one of Lawrence's "escaped slaves," but her masters were from the wide-open flats of North Dakota, a strange planet of farmhouses, general stores, barn dances, and sunflower harvests that couldn't have been further removed from her life as a girl in 1960s Los Angeles. Her mother was a former nurse and high school basketball player with a soft spot for romance novels. Her father owned a men's clothing store with its own putting green and kept the Dakotas alive in his mind by devouring Louis L'Amour paperbacks like only a Russian Jew from the Badlands could. How to leave them without leaving them? How to be masterless and still be able to go home for spaghetti marinara and clean laundry?

More than anything else, America was like a child seeking freedom. "Like a son escaping from the domination of his parents," Lawrence wrote and my mother underlined. "The escape is not just one rupture. It is a long and half-secret process." Children never escape their parents. It is indeed a long and half-secret process.

Lawrence treats eighteenth- and nineteenth-century America as a literary son, but as more than one scholar has pointed out, America was more of a literary daughter. Perhaps the difference stems from whom Lawrence focuses on—writers, not readers. In her wonderful history of the American novel, *Revolution and the Word*, Cathy Davidson emphasizes that it was not only writers who wrote America into cultural independence. The readers of their novels—and especially all those who wrote in the margins—also helped shape the character of the emergent republic through their judgments and opinions.

The eighteenth century witnessed a shake-up of social hierarchies, thanks in large part to the rise of the American novel. By reading books and writing in them, common readers fought their own war for egalitarianism and democracy. The most common of common readers were women, so much so that the threats the novel was believed to pose to the ruling order of America were very often seen as female— women reading and commenting their way into the boys' club of nationalism, shaping themselves as literate subjects. The threat they posed was quickly met with the invention of a gendered pathology: "Novel Reading, a Cause of Female Depravity" as an 1802 diatribe put it. "I have seen two poor disconsolate parents drop into premature graves," it read, "miserable victims to their daughter's dishonour, and the peace of several relative families wounded, never to be healed again in this world."

My mother saw herself in Lawrence's America. A daughter facing her own independence from her parents' mastery, had she also become one of Davidson's readers, two centuries too late, a daughter afraid of dishonor?

These are the questions I want to write in the margins of her margins, but I resist. I remember what she underlined in the foreword: "The great difference between the extreme Russians and the extreme Americans lies in the fact that the Russians are explicit and hate eloquence and symbols, seeing in these only subterfuge, whereas the Americans refuse everything explicit and always put up a sort of double meaning … subterfuge." If my mother reads this essay, she will undoubtedly get Russian on me. She will accuse her son of eloquence and symbolism. She will cry subterfuge. It would be the same war of independence, the Russian parent and the American child tussling over words.

6.

She does not underline explanations or details or examples. She underlines the big points, the grand claims. She is a good reader. She condenses. She comments. The wildness of life, the unruliness of experience, refined to a palette of reds and blacks, refined to a series of lines, curves, and stars, pages and pages of stars.

The first headshots appeared in the 1950s.[1] By *head-shots*, I mean photographs of actors looking for work rather than publicity portraits of stars. The latter, which have been in circulation since at least the 1860s, emerged from the tradition of portraiture, and the former seem to have emerged from the latter. But clearly the headshot is not a portrait, or if it is, it's a very particular kind of portrait. Indeed, it routinely disregards conventions of portraiture—no environment, no professional emblems, no trace of social context, and no sideways glance. The subject is always looking dead at you. This blankness, however, has nothing in common with the stripped-down psychological portraiture of the late-nineteenth and twentieth centuries, which similarly depends on empty backgrounds and forthright stares.

A better way to analyze headshots might be to consider what *is* there. A smile, a look, a lack of self-sufficiency you very rarely see in conventional portraiture. It is neither the smile of a celebrity sharing beatitude nor the steady gaze of the burgher or aristocrat. Instead, it is a smile that beseeches your understanding, a look that solicits your complicity, and almost always suggests, unlike a conventional portrait, that the experience is incomplete without you. The phrase that headshot photographers use for this is "the light behind the eyes." Unlike the eyes of a portrait in a haunted house, which follow you around the room, headshot eyes fix you in place, attempting to disable your judgment with a look as titillating as it is meaningless.

These photographs need the viewer because the actors they depict are not celebrities yet. They just *want* to be, and your complicity is needed because "you" are the casting agent, actor's agent, manager, or director to whom these photos are addressed. Theater scholar Meron Langsner suggests that the headshot should actually be considered a B2B marketing tool, where B_1 is the actor and B_2 is "the industry." The practical and aesthetic differences between the headshot and the celebrity portrait then become clear: the latter is designed to promote a pre-existing commodity to the public, while the former is designed to market a not-yet commodity to the institutions that could accord it full status. Hence the non-specificity of the photos: whereas a celebrity portrait might show the subject in a specific role or locale, in a headshot such detail is rejected out of hand by casting agents as "too theatrical." You could say that headshot subjects lack individuality because they have not yet been given a *role*; or that they suppress it in order to demonstrate their suitability for all roles.

Pick up any actor's manual and you will find a chapter on headshots: how to shoot them, how to choose them, and where to send them. Indeed, headshot photography comprises an entire industry ancillary to entertainment. An actor will, on average, spend $1,180 each year on photo sessions, prints, and mailings. An agent receives between thirty and sixty unsolicited submission envelopes per week, depending on the size and prestige of the agency. These contain between one and three headshots, depending on how many "looks" the actor wants to show the agent. According to *Ross Reports*, the mailing list bible for actors, there are seventy-nine agencies in New York City, each employing between one and twelve agents, which means that during any given week there are roughly 10,000 headshots circulating through the city. This represents 4.8 tons, and roughly 5,700 acres, of photo paper per year—enough to bury the streets of Manhattan's theater district to a depth of six feet. Ninety-nine percent of these submissions are perfunctorily thrown out; the remaining one percent are put on file and occasionally get the actors an audition and, in very rare cases, a job.

My own archive is culled from the discards, which I catalogue according to pose, paper quality, postage, font style, cover letter etiquette, and other criteria, some more subjective than others. This archive is part of a larger project of tracking, and ultimately memorializing, unsolicited submissions across the entire cultural field. The Culture Industry does generate waste. What's the ecological impact of this rejected material? How much money is lost in its production? How much waste—trashed image CDs, demo tapes, slides, and manuscripts—does the industry need to generate in order to maintain its meritocratic reputation?

Of course, unsolicited material must be thrown out—there is too much of it, and the cultural gatekeepers have no choice. And of course it makes everyone feel awkward: when you send in your unsolicited slides, poems, or headshots, they become tools for scaling a wall, in the hope that, once on the other side, they can go back to being your art, writing, or face, though in a transcendent new way. In the moment of rejection, however, the submission is forever frozen in a state of mere instrumentality. From the trash, it stares up at you hopefully—unsolicited, and still soliciting.

---

1 According to Meron Langsner, whose unpublished paper, "Personal Iconography, the Business of Making Art, and Art for Doing Business: The Actor's Headshot and its Place In and Out of the Theater World, An Overview" is the only critical treatment of the subject I have come across.

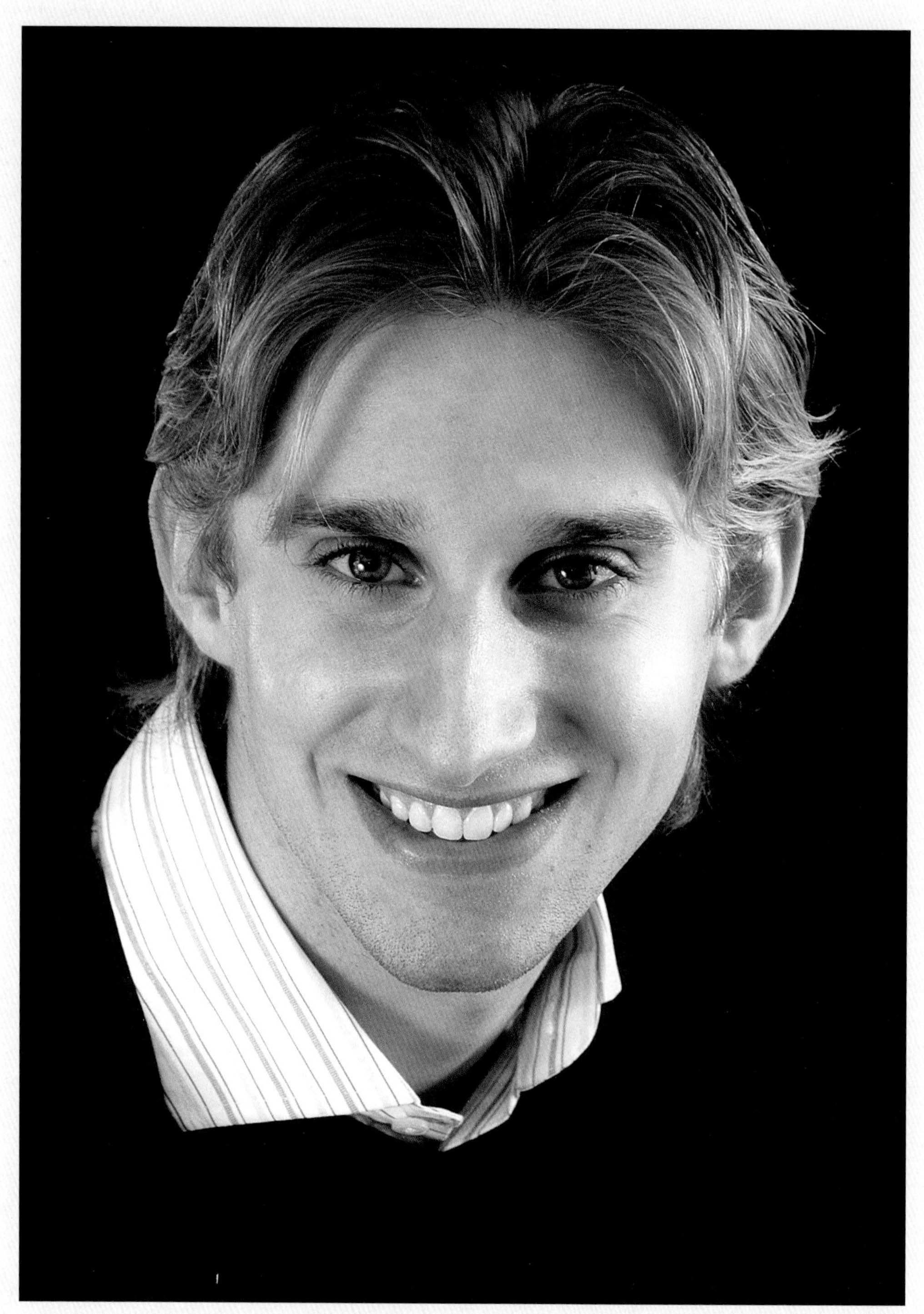

Bill Army

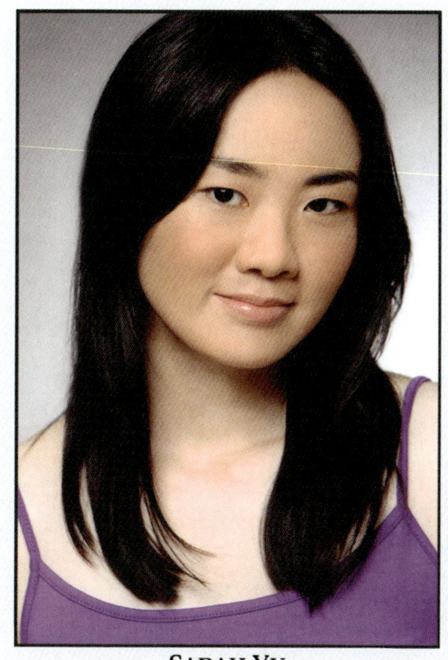

SARAH YU

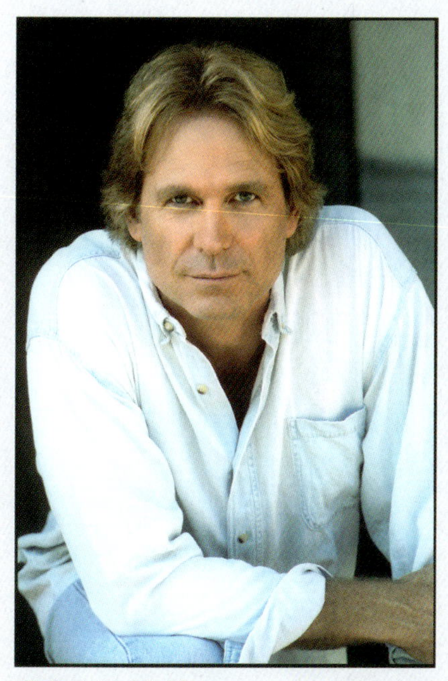

Coleman McClary

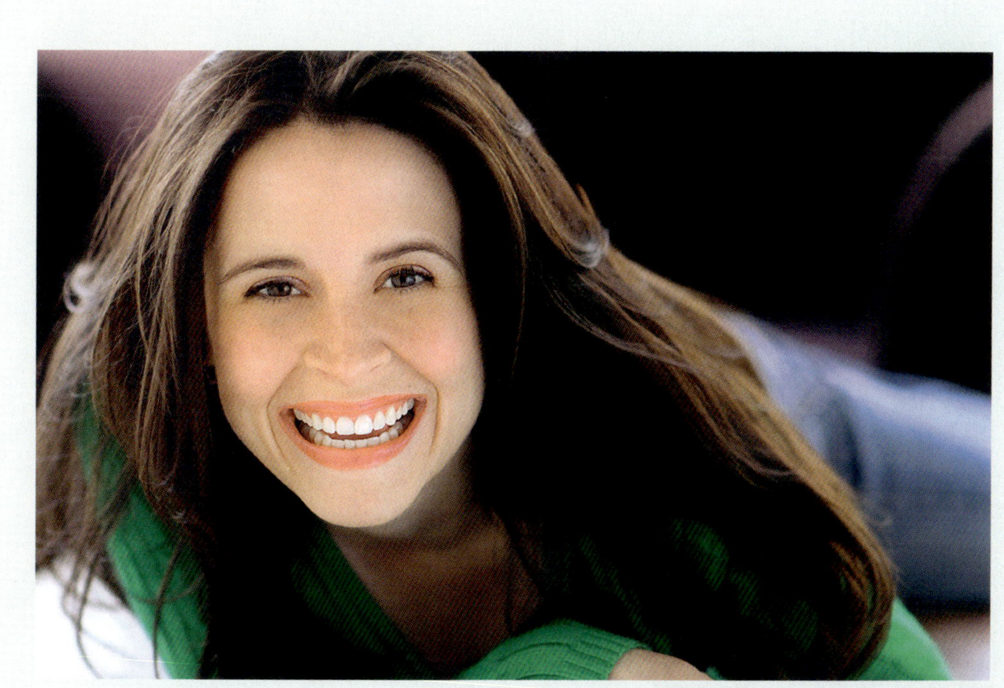

Jennifer Zimmerman

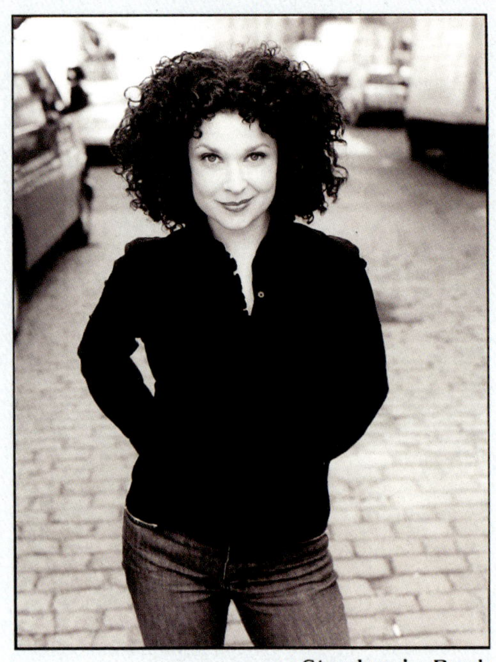

Stephanie Bush

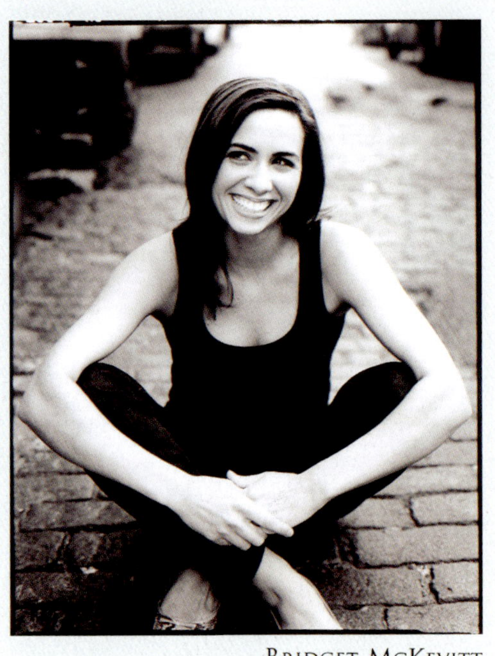

Bridget McKevitt

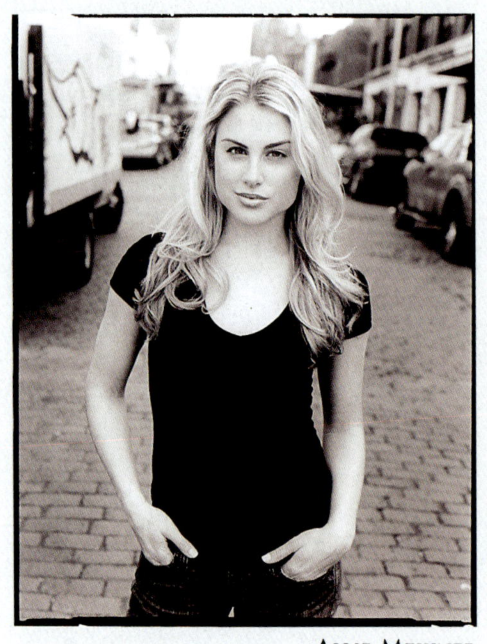

Allie Meixner

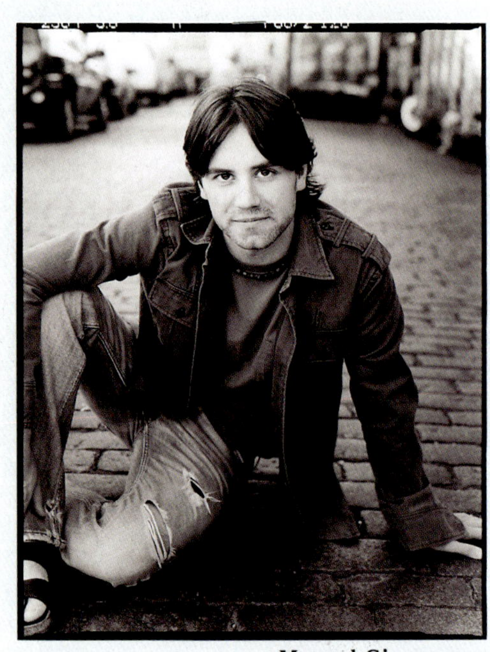

Marcel Simoneau

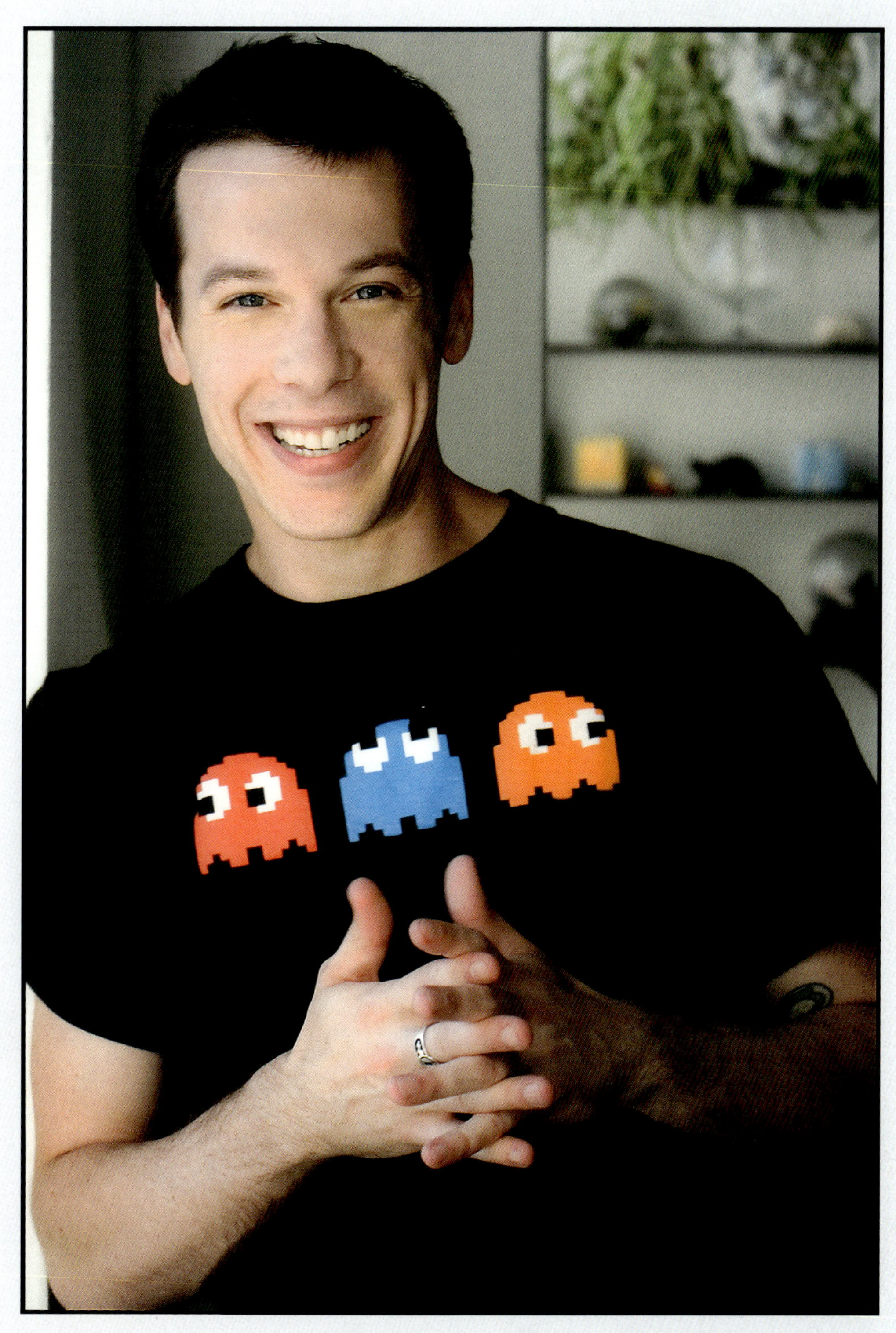

Ross A. McIntyre

I went to photograph this arch off the California coast last winter to use as a reference in a painting I was working on. It's named after the first European to explore the coast. When he passed this point in the autumn of 1542, he saw an apparition through the arch that persuaded him to turn the ship around and abandon any further exploration. Due to a phenomenon involving the sunlight, the angle of the water, the sea spray, and the shape of the arch, you can sometimes see a reflection in the opening, which apparently Cabrillo did.

Recently, I was nearby and went to see the arch again. When I arrived, it was no longer there; it had collapsed. Then I recalled having seen it collapse on my first visit. I don't know why I forgot having seen it collapse. Here are photographs of the before and after. I tried basically to get the same shot the second time for comparison.

I now remember hearing the loud crack while I had the camera up to my eye, and then seeing the thing collapse partially through the viewfinder. I must have taken this one just a second before, because I remember at the time being concerned whether or not I had gotten it in time. As it turned out, I did and was able to use it to paint from. So this is the last photograph taken of Cabrillo's Arch.

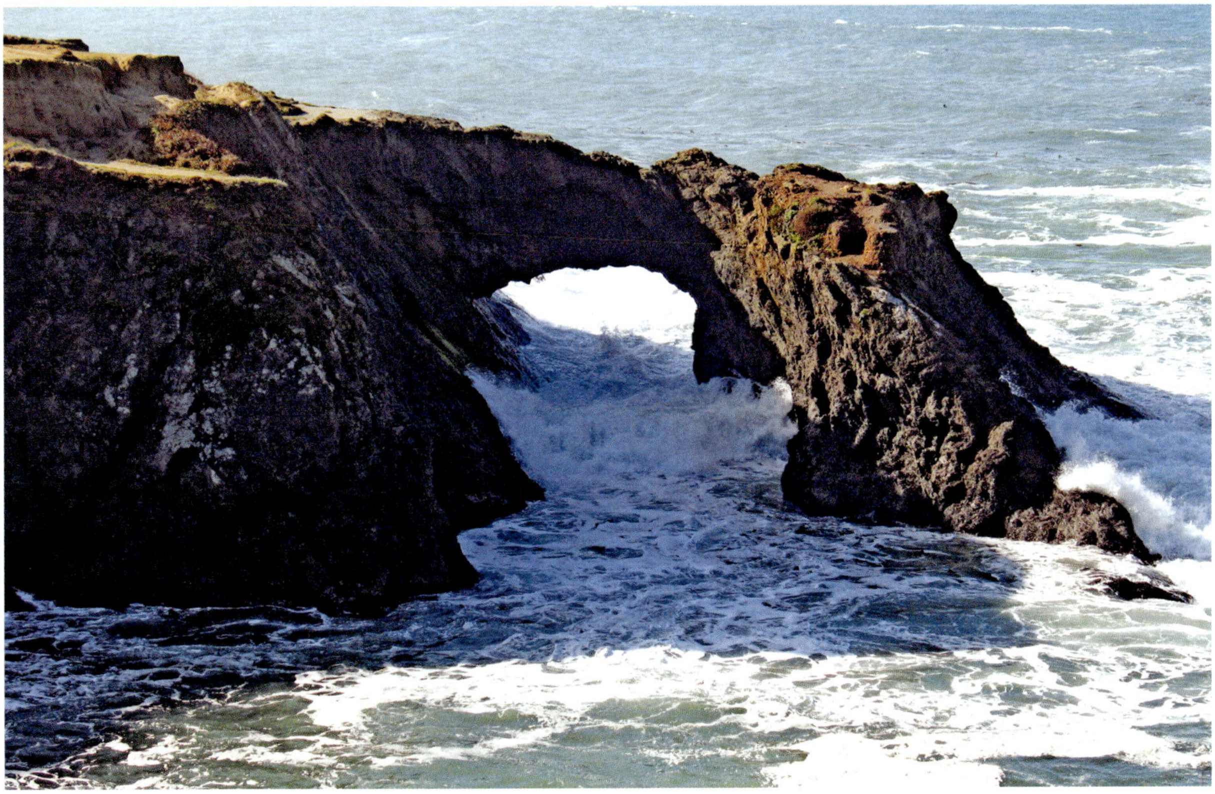

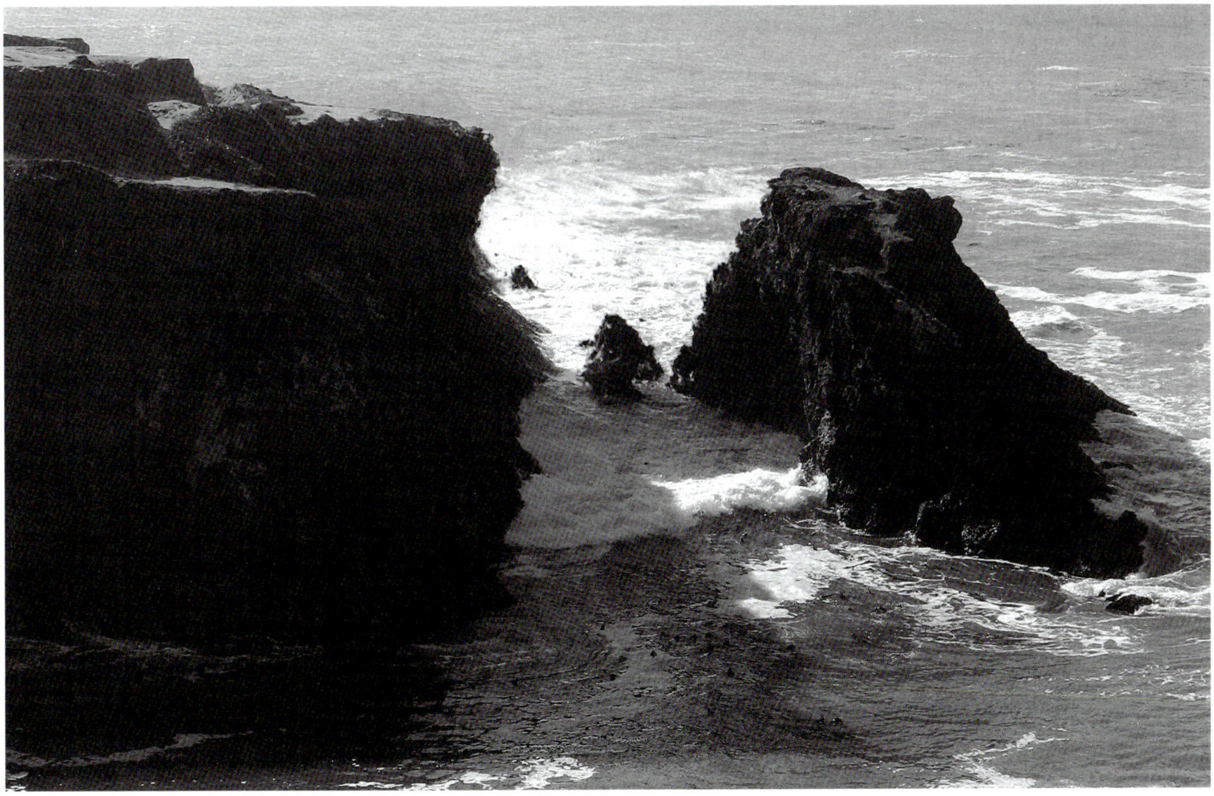

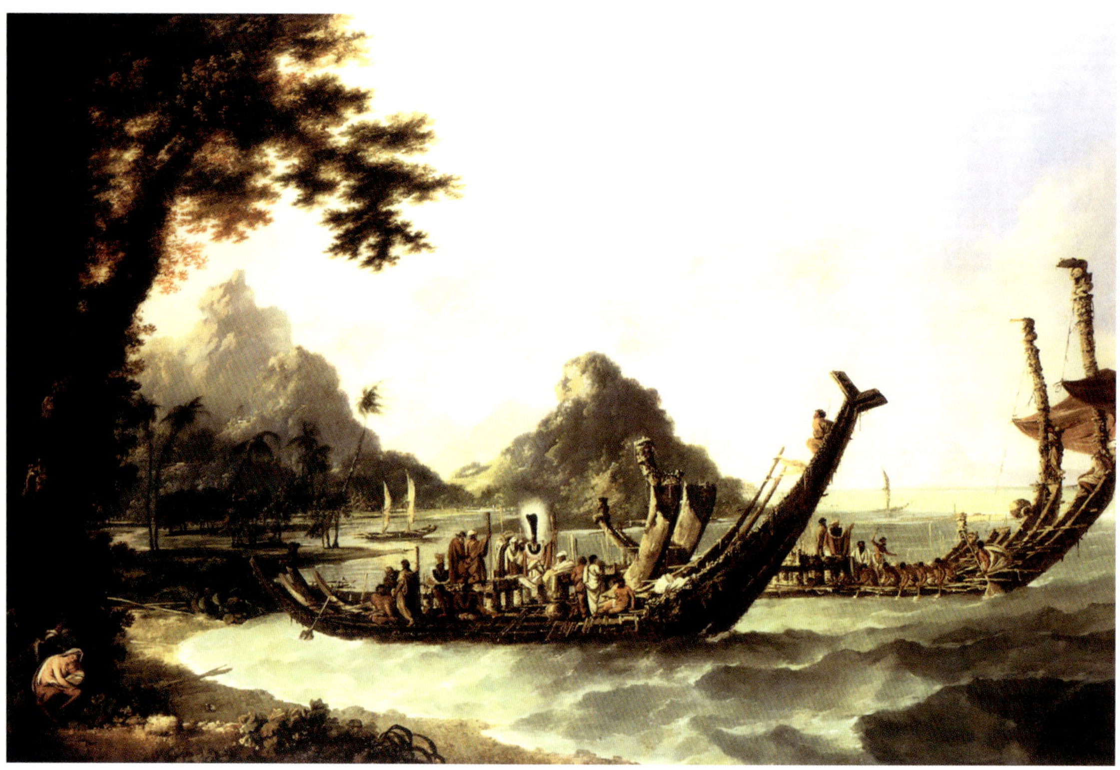

William Hodges, *The War-Boats of the Island of Otaheite* [Tahiti]*, and the Society Islands, with a View of part of the Harbour of Ohameneno, in the Island of Ulietea, one of the Society islands,* 1777.

OTHERWISE

LELAND DE LA DURANTAYE

In November of 1766, the French explorer and man of letters Louis-Antoine de Bougainville set sail for the South Seas. The passage was long and arduous. On April 6th, 1768, Bougainville's ship, aptly named *La Boudeuse* ("The Pouting Woman"), stinking of bilge water and excrement, laid anchor in the shimmering bay of a lush green island. Canoes soon surrounded the ship. A girl climbed aboard from one of them, walking through a crowd of sailors to the quarterdeck. With a single graceful motion she let fall the cloth which covered her and, in Bougainville's words, "appeared to the eyes of all beholders, such as Venus herself to the Phrygian shepherd." More from shock than discipline, the sailors stood frozen. Taking their immobility for disinterest, she was offended and climbed haughtily from the ship.

Despite strict orders to the contrary, one man went ashore later that day. This was not Bougainville but, instead, his cook. As soon as he set foot upon the beach, a great crowd encircled him. They then proceeded to undress him—in Bougainville's opinion, for the purposes of comparative anatomy. After gently examining him, they returned his clothes and invited him to go off with the girl of his choice to "content his desires." To the approbation of his cook, Bougainville named the island "New Cythera," after the island where the goddess of love first emerged from the waves.

During their stay both Bougainville and his cook had a new idea in mind. Fourteen years earlier, Jean-Jacques Rousseau had offered Europe the "noble savage." Voltaire had said that institutions without a rational foundation corrupted human nature, but Rousseau went farther. In his *Discourse on the Origin of Inequality Amongst Men* (1754), he proclaimed that all institutions did so—that society corrupted man. And so he sung the praises of the "noble savage" in the "state of nature." In that blessed state, so Rousseau believed, there was no servitude and no domination. Even sexual desire was not grasping and acquisitive—it remained simple and pure, with, in his words, "everyone peacefully await[ing] the impulsion of nature."

Bougainville had read Rousseau's book and found its account of noble savages illuminating. After the military campaigns he had led in French Canada, however, he had ceased to believe in the nobility of savages. Upon reaching New Cythera—or *Tahiti* as its inhabitants called it—he changed his mind again. These savages seemed to him noble indeed. They seemed to know neither jealousy nor war. For reasons unknown, some of Bougainville's soldiers killed three Tahitians. Instead of rising up against the French forces they outnumbered, the islanders came to their guests with an enormous banana leaf as a sign of peace. Sexual desire appeared neither violent nor acquisitive, and husbands were often the first to persuade their wives to give themselves to visitors. The island so abundantly provided for the needs of its inhabitants that it seemed to Bougainville that they hardly had to work to satisfy them. And yet despite this perpetual lassitude, the Tahitians possessed a great physical beauty—the men strong and well-proportioned, and the women, graceful and attractive.

Bougainville's journal entry for the last day his ship remained anchored in Tahiti ended: "I shall never recall without pleasure the brief time I spent in your midst and as long as I live will extol the happy isle of Cythera: it is the true Utopia." The more sober Englishman James Cook laid anchor in this same bay a few years later and immediately compared it to Arcadia. Upon hearing this, Voltaire wrote, "When the French and English are in agreement, we can be sure that they have not deceived us." Tahiti was paradise and the noble savage lived there.

· · ·

The noble savage was soon in every home. It was perhaps the first philosophical idea outside of the teachings of the church to be actively discussed by Europeans of all social classes. Aspects of Tahitian culture, like human sacrifice and rigid divisions in social rank, were overlooked in favor of alluring images of simplicity and harmony. To satisfy growing curiosity, two Tahitians, four Indian kings, a handful of Eskimos, and several people from the French countryside believed to have been more or less raised by wolves were paraded through Europe's capitals. The Tahitians stole the show. Ahutoru and Omai arrived in 1769 and 1774 in Paris and London, respectively. Both were pleasant, polite, well-spoken, and good-natured. They danced beautifully, had a fine sense for music, played chess and backgammon, learned to ride horses and to ice-skate, met the kings of France and England,

and were popular with the ladies. The great French naturalist Buffon praised the strength of Ahutoru's pulse and his "highly developed sense of smell." Sir Joshua Reynolds painted Omai's portrait (incongruously wearing an Arab turban). Before long, the rage for Tahiti and its noble savages was in full swing.

In 1788, the *HMS Bounty* laid anchor in Tahiti under the command of William Bligh. She returned a year later under the command of Fletcher Christian (blood; sex; fire). Things began moving faster on Tahiti as more visitors came in search of the paradise that had lured Christian back. Representatives of church and state came to insure that both were well-represented. Certain ancestral dances, such as the legendarily lascivious *upaupa* which Paul Gauguin was to paint, but never see, were outlawed. A dress code was established and rigidly enforced. Bibles and preachers arrived in abundance. By 1802, the French writer and statesman Chateaubriand lamented Tahiti's golden era having already run its course. "The lovely women of New Cythera," he wrote, "pass their time reading the Scriptures with Methodist ministers, and deploring the excessive gaiety of their mothers." The Tahitians seemed ever less noble and ever less savage.

In the coming years, Victor Hugo wrote about a Tahitian woman and her European lover. A young whaler named Herman Melville stayed (and was imprisoned) on the island, and wrote two novels about his experiences in French Polynesia. Rimbaud read and reread the tales of Cook's *Voyages* and wove their images into lyric evocations of freedom and savagery. By the end of the nineteenth century, it seemed that the nobly savage Tahiti which Bougainville had marveled at a century earlier was no longer to be found anywhere but in art.

· · ·

During the visit of the two Tahitians to London, Boswell said to Dr. Johnson, "I do not think the people of Tahiti can be reckoned savages," to which Johnson sharply retorted, "Don't cant in defense of savages!" By June 1880, this was a standard response. France annexed Tahiti. The children of Tahiti were forced to abandon native dress, to sing the *Marseillaise*, and to demand the return of the Alsace and the Lorraine.

In 1891, forty-four-year-old Paul Gauguin, a successful businessman turned unsuccessful painter, arrived in Tahiti just as its last king, Pomare the Fifth, was dying. Gauguin could not have been more disappointed by what awaited him. The noble savagery he had dreamed of was nowhere to be found. Brick buildings with roofs of corrugated iron had replaced traditional dwellings. The island's green was covered over by grime and soot. AWOL sailors and escaped convicts filled the ports. Venereal disease was rampant. Life was expensive, dirty, and violent; colonial repression brutal and open. Two days after he arrived, French officials offered Gauguin the honor of decorating the room of the recently deceased king. He declined.

Gauguin was not long in regretting this as he soon found himself broke. He could not afford to eat the island's abundant fresh food and subsisted on canned goods, white bread, and macaroni. He called the natives "savages," leaving off the "noble." You couldn't fall over drunk, he claimed, without bumping into a parish priest or a colonial gendarme, and so he decided to leave the corrupt coast. What he found was another story. The exotic interior of the island was unblemished, and breathtakingly beautiful. Gauguin soon adopted native dress. He noted with pleasure that his feet had hardened from going barefoot, and that through constant exposure his skin "no longer suffered from the sun." He declared himself a "savage." In 1893, he was forced, however, to return to France. From the deck of the boat he cried, "Farewell, land of welcome, land of pleasures! Farewell, home of liberty and beauty!"

Back in Paris, the paintings he brought back from his *atelier des tropiques* were as little in demand as those he had painted before his departure in the *atelier du sud* he had formed with Vincent Van Gogh in Arles, and which had savagely ended two days before Christmas in 1888 when Van Gogh threatened Gauguin with a razor before cutting off his own ear with it. The show of works Gauguin managed to mount in Paris upon his return was, from a financial perspective, an unconditional failure (although Degas kindly bought eleven canvases so as to hide its full extent). Mallarmé marveled at how one could "load such bright colors with such dark mystery," but painters such as Cézanne and Pissarro turned haughtily from his naïve works. The following year Gauguin received a small inheritance. Instead of dedicating it to the urgent needs of his wife and children in Copenhagen, he rented a studio in Paris and began supporting a Javanese mulatto named Annah Martin and her pet monkey Taoa. Later that year he got into a fight with sailors who mocked Annah and/or her monkey (accounts vary) and severely injured his leg. He decided to sail for Tahiti—this time never to return.

Gauguin's second arrival in 1895 disappointed him even more than his first. In his absence, the port of Papeete had acquired electric lighting and a merry-go-round had been installed in the governor's front garden.

Gauguin left the port immediately, returning to savagery and to his work. He varied his media, making ceramics, wood carvings, and experimenting with the ephemeral materials of wax and mud. He lived in a fertile creative chaos. In 1897, word reached him of the death of his daughter Aline. He was overcome by guilt and despair, and began work on a painting which was to be his testament. The mural-sized *Where Do We Come From? What Are We? Where Are We Going?* is an allegory of uncertain meaning. Read from right to left, as Gauguin once recommended, the figures proceed from virgin innocence to corrupt experience, from the infancy of culture to the decadence of civilization. If read, left to right, however, the painting points towards a new innocence. After completing the mysterious painting, Gauguin retreated to the island's interior to take his own life. But this too went differently than he planned. The dose of cyanide he brought with him was too powerful and he became violently ill before it could take fatal effect. He literally crawled back to life.

By 1901, reconciled to continue a life so full of such diverse failure, Gauguin could take no more of a Tahiti that even in its interior showed distressing signs of civilization, and left for the remote island of Hiva-Oa in the Marquesas chain. He hoped "to see no more Europeans," built a house that he baptized "Maison du jouir" ("house of pleasure"), and continued to work. In January 1903, a hurricane hit the island. Gauguin's house was spared, but he didn't have long to remain in it. A few months later, he was convicted by the colonial government of inciting "indigenous anarchy" through speeches criticizing the colonial system. His sentence was a fine of 1000 francs—ruining his finances—and three months in jail—ruining his health. A few days later, he wrote to a friend in Paris, "I am exhausted, but I am not beaten. Is the Indian who is able to laugh through his torture beaten? The savage is better than are we. You once said that I had no right to call myself a savage. You were wrong—I am one! What the civilized public see and feel in my works, and what surprises and unsettles them, is my savagery." Less than a month later, he died.

· · ·

As Gauguin lay dying, a twenty-four-year-old French doctor named Victor Segalen arrived in Tahiti. He had come to meet Gauguin. Redirected to the distant island to which Gauguin had retreated so as "to see no more Europeans," he arrived too late. He visited the "Maison du jouir" and as Gauguin's ramshackle estate had not yet been liquidated, his final works still lay where he had left them. Segalen

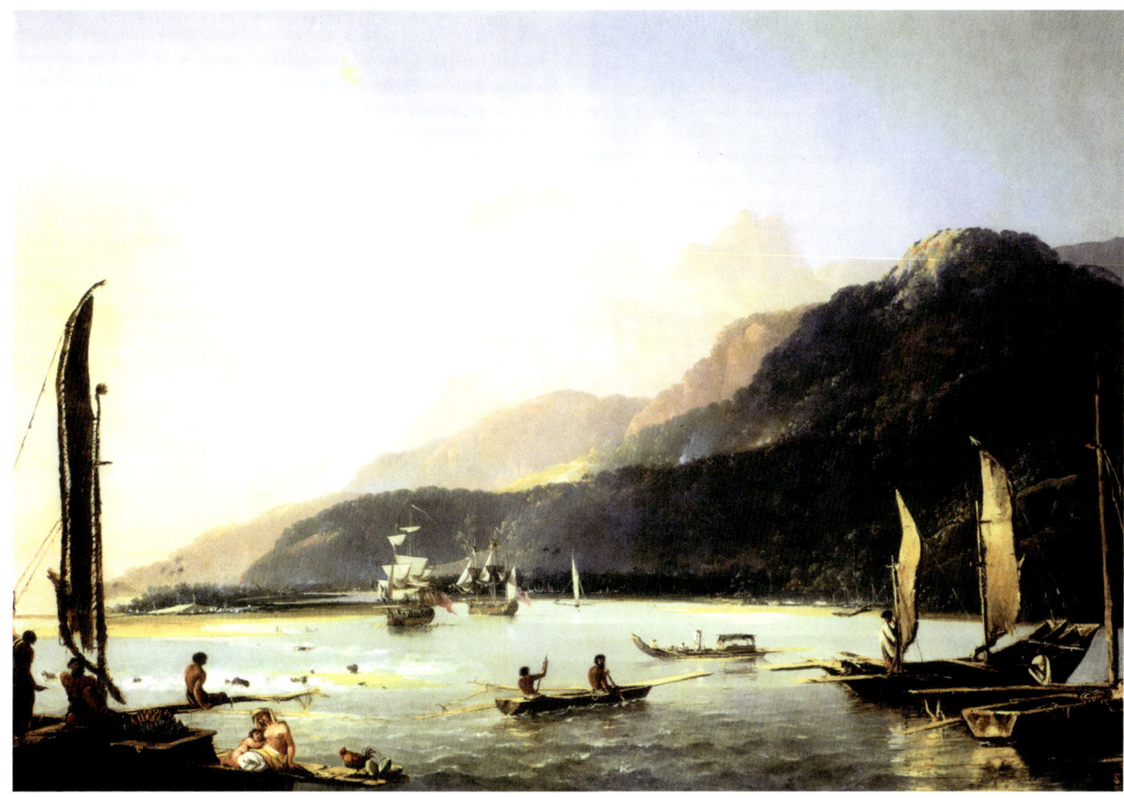

William Hodges, *A View of Maitavie Bay, Otaheite* [Tahiti], 1776.

was inspired by their wild colors and exotic forms. He wrote back to France that "before looking at—or should I not say, before living through—Gauguin's final sketches, I had not really *seen* anything of the land of the *Maori*."(The term Maori was used loosely in the nineteenth century by the French to indicate all Polynesian cultures.)

Segalen began writing articles both about Gauguin and the ravaged state of Polynesian society. Alongside these public projects, he began a private one: a novel. It was exotic in subject, but was to break with the exotic literature of the day—picturesque accounts of what awaited visitors on the sensuous islands of the South Pacific. Segalen's ambition was to travel through this colonial looking-glass and tell the story of the Maori from their side, and thereby create a truly exotic literature.

In 1907, Segalen published *Les immémoriaux* at his own expense and dedicated it to "the Maori of forgotten times." Its composition was equal parts savage and civilized. The civilization lay in the immense archival research that went into his writing of the work, and the savagery in the form he chose for it. Segalen tried, in his own words, to "write" the people of Tahiti in the same way that Gauguin had painted them. This meant inventing a French shot through with flashes of Maori. The idea was of course not to reproduce the broken French that the Maori used to translate their culture. Instead, he shaped French to reflect the innermost forms of Maori thought, language, and culture, to bend and twist the French language until it began to convey something of authentic Maori experience.

Les immémoriaux tells of the "civilizing" of Tahiti during the first period of colonization (1798–1819). It begins with a young *Haere-Po*, or "keeper of genealogies," named Terii who forgets a line of his recitation—an extremely bad omen. Terii soon makes another such error and narrowly escapes from the wrath of the listeners with his life. After unsuccessfully trying to turn himself into a tree, a miracle meant to redeem him in the eyes of his fellow islanders, he flees the island in the company

overleaf: Drawing of Tahiti by Victor Segalen, undated. Courtesy Bibliothèque nationale de France.

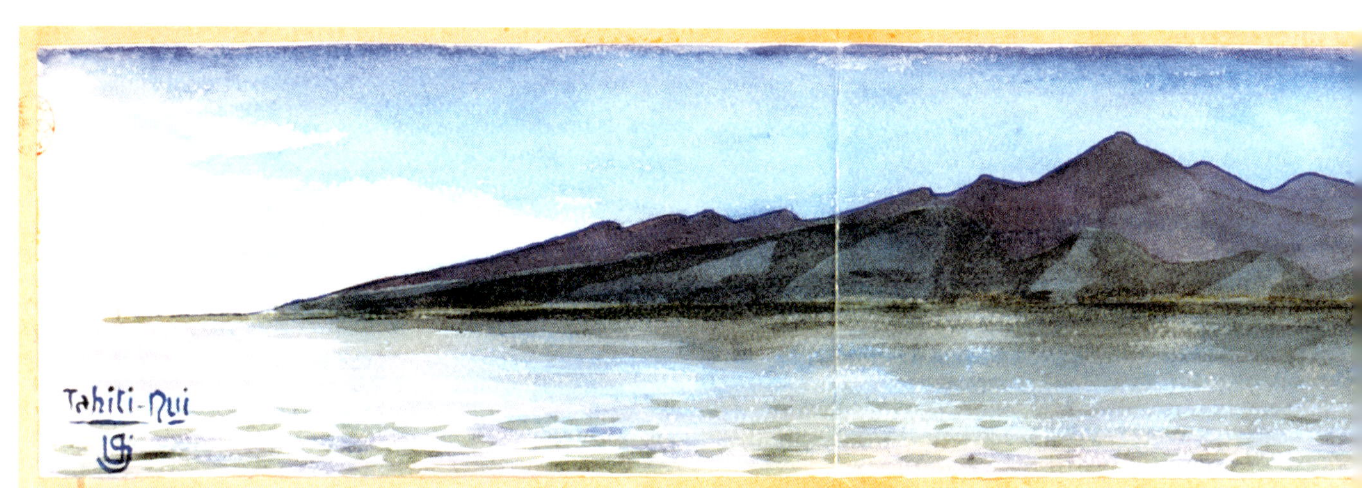
Tahiti-Nui

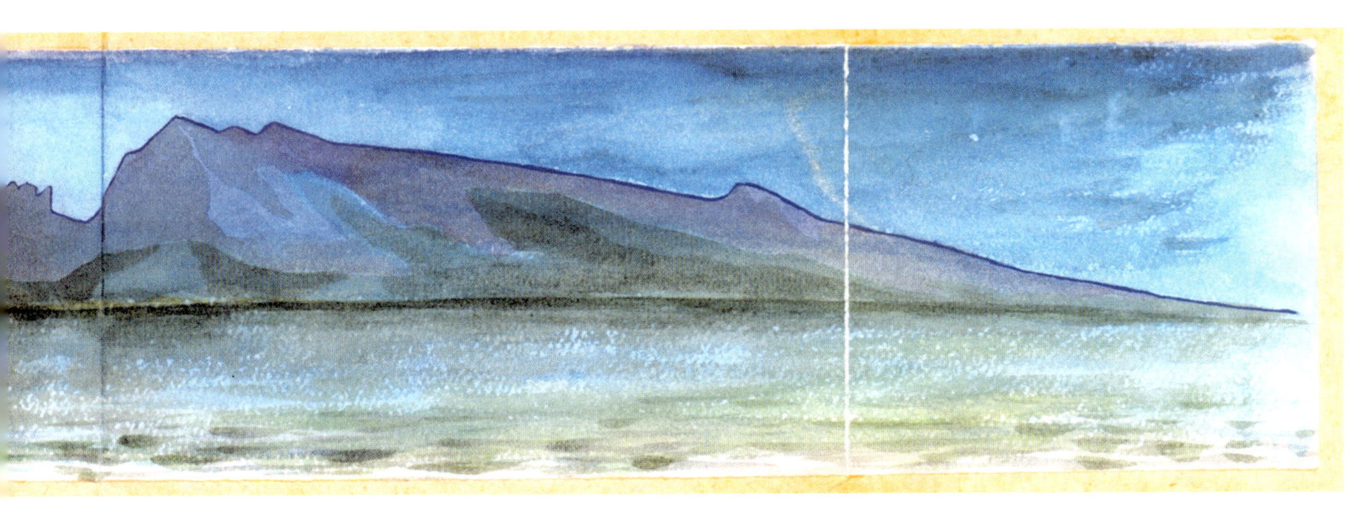

of his mentor. The two circle Polynesia in search of "the origin of things." They make a pilgrimage to one island to hear a great orator, but Terii falls asleep during what turns out to be the man's final speech. A visit to Rapa Nui (Easter Island) is equally frustrating. Their trip lasts twenty years. Failing to find the lost origin, they return to Tahiti to find a society more changed than they could have ever imagined. Terii's companion and mentor refuses to meet the demands of this new society and is soon sentenced to death. Terii proves more flexible. He changes his name to Iakoba, and his religion to Christianity. There, where he had failed in the stringent society into which he was born (his poor memory disqualifying him from the priesthood), he succeeds in the new colonial society whose many books compensate for such lapses. Terii-Iakoba sells his daughter for two bags of nails with which to build a church and decides that the new society is to his liking. So ends Europe's first anti-colonial novel.

· · ·

While working on *Les immémoriaux*, Segalen began another project—one that he would work on for the rest of his life and that in recent years has attracted increasing interest. It is not a novel but instead an "Essay on Exoticism." It was to consolidate the sentimental education that Segalen's travels imparted to him. When he died fifteen years later, the essay was at his side—and still unfinished.

The editors of a recent edition have chosen to order the fragments chronologically. Fittingly, the first entry is written at sea—"within sight of Java," and the work's program is clearly laid out therein. Segalen aspires to bring into relief a parallel between receding in time—"historicism"—and advancing in space—"exoticism." After this ambitious statement of purpose, he seems to have found himself at a loss as to how to continue. The notes quickly taper off as the boat approaches Java, not to be taken up for another four years.

Having completed *Les immémoriaux*, in the second entry Segalen clarified his intention in that work: "Not the effect of the environment on the traveler, but the effect of the traveler on the environment is what I sought to express in writing about the Maori." He continues: "Why should I not do the same thing to express what I will see: a temple, a Chinese crowd, an opium eater, an ancestral ceremonial, a city of millions of inhabitants ... do this for everything that would otherwise become part of a worn exoticism, but which would thereby take on a completely new appearance." Here, too, Segalen strives for an analytic definition of a very

synthetic experience. *Exoticism*, as he conceives of it then, indeed involves contact with exotic material, with the far away and the strange. But this *exotic* material is seen with an eye both more disciplined and more adventurous than the average one. Segalen formulates an approach we have since come to call anthropological. He studies the foreign not simply as it appears to us, but as we appear to it. For Segalen, the uncertainty principle that conditions anthropology's enterprise—the effect of the observer upon the behavior of the observed—is not to be effaced by objective observation. It is to be creatively explored and exploited.

As he continued to travel to more and more exotic places (he had taken up residence in China), it became increasingly clear to Segalen that his exoticism wasn't other people's exoticism—that his sense of the word had little in common with what others understood by it. In his first note, he had defined exoticism as a function of spatial distance. It became more and more clear to him, however, that "movement in space" was not an essential component of the exoticism he was trying to describe. This led him to a singular conclusion.

Following his revised program, "exoticism" is to be "extended ... to Everything." Realizing this was a stretch for his readers, he enlarged the name, calling it "Universal Exoticism" and defining it as "the ability to *conceive otherwise*." This was a decisive formulation, one that both allowed him to continue to write and prevented him from ever finishing his essay. His task in exploring exoticism was nothing less than, "defining ... the sensation of Exoticism, which is nothing other than the notion of difference, the perception of Diversity."

As exoticism became for Segalen the exploration of a "sensation" or "perception" of "Diversity," the "geographic" component ceased to play a central role. The exotic was no longer foreign or far away. Making love to Tahitian princesses or being initiated into the secrets of the Forbidden City were, for him, only "exotic" if they conveyed a sense and sensation of this "Diversity." Distance and strangeness were still essential to an experience of the exotic, but they migrated inwards. "For the child," Segalen wrote, "exoticism comes into being along with the external world."

As a final move in what ultimately becomes a philosophical treatise, Segalen writes: "After discussing Universal Exoticism, we will arrive at an Essential Exoticism." This concerns something else again—the fact that, "the conscious being knows that in conceiving of himself he cannot but conceive of himself as *other* than he is. And he rejoices in his Diversity [*Et il s'éjouit de sa Diversité*]." This curious final phrase—"And he rejoices

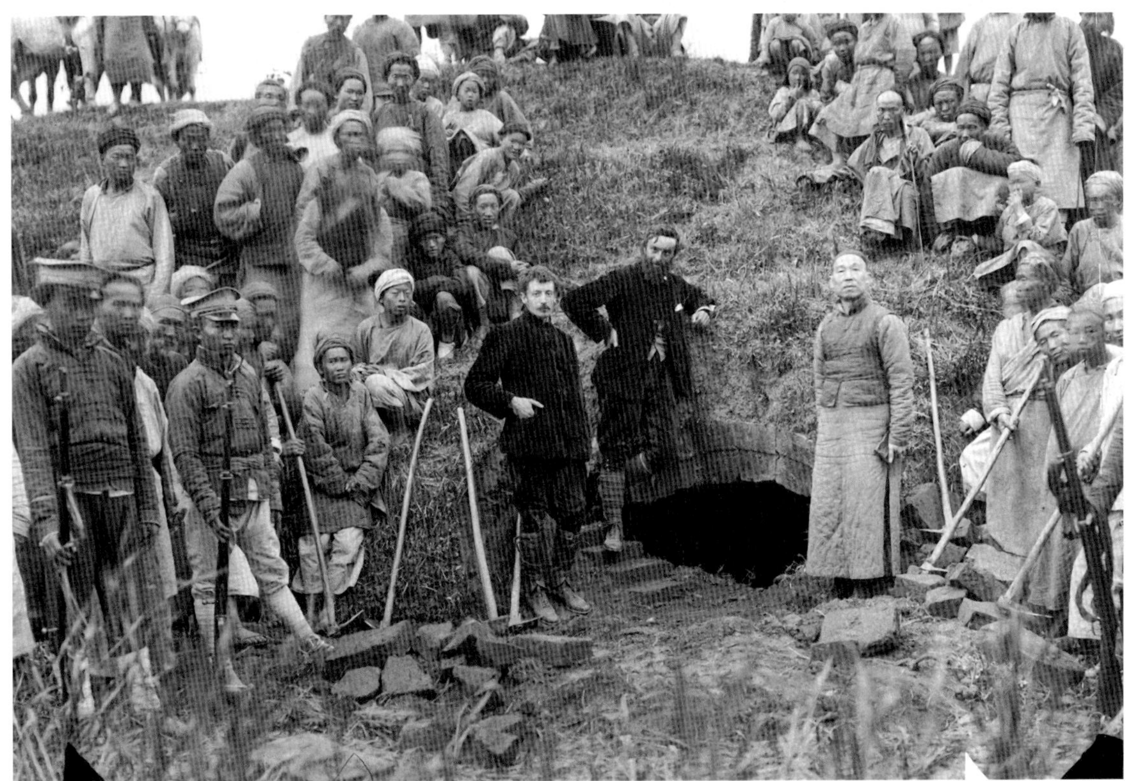

Segalen (with right hand in pocket) at the site of Bao Sanniang's tomb in Sichuan province, 1914. Collection Musée des Arts Asiatiques-Guimet, Paris, France. Courtesy Réunion des Musées Nationaux / Art Resource, NY.

in his Diversity"—is the one with which his unfinished essay ends. Though Segalen does not indicate this, it is a quotation—and one from a singularly unexotic source.

. . .

Gustave Flaubert was born in Normandy, grew up in Normandy, hated Normandy. Hearing of life in exotic places France was then conquering, such as Egypt and Algeria, he declared at twenty that he was "born to live" in such environments. His young mind filled with oriental imaginings, he wrote *The Temptation of Saint Anthony*. He invited his two closest friends to his home in Normandy in September 1849 and during the next four days read his book aloud to them for eight hours each day. Every page burned with a bright oriental fire. When he finished his marathon recitation, his friends retired. They came back with a unanimous verdict: burn the book and travel to take your mind off it. He did not take their advice about burning but he did about traveling, and set off for exotic lands.

A year later, standing astride the border between Upper and Lower Nubia with the second cataract of the Nile at his feet, an idea came to him. During his year and a half in Egypt, Palestine, Rhodes, Asia Minor, Constantinople, Greece, and Italy, he had been captivated by the bright colors, strange sounds, and new sensations of his travels. As soon as he returned home, he began a work far more strange and unfathomable than *The Temptation of Saint Anthony*. The revelation that had come to him on the Nile was the least exotic work in the history of French literature: *Madame Bovary*. Instead of describing the pyramids by moonlight, reproducing the rhythm of travel by camel, or mixing with nomads, pirates, and courtesans, he described what he knew best and liked least—his native Normandy. The flash of the scimitar was replaced by the dull glow of an inept surgeon's scalpel, oriental sunsets by Norman fog, and the reality of travel and adventure by an insatiable longing for travel and adventure. At the center of his story lay a woman so seduced by works of exotic literature that she found herself unable to reconcile herself to the unexotic life she found herself leading. Like a doomsday machine set in motion, this inability slowly destroys her life and those around her.

Forty years later, Segalen's favorite philosopher published a serious book with a seemingly light-hearted title—*Le Bovarysme* (1902). The word was not completely new and had already been used as an insult, but Jules de Gaultier lent the awkward term metaphysical wings. In *Le Bovarysme*, he argued that "the flaw that marks Flaubert's characters points to a fundamental human faculty: the power granted to man to conceive himself as other than he is." Segalen's *Essay on Exoticism* contains many references—to Gauguin, to Pierre Loti, to Nietzsche, and to others. More frequent and more decisive than any other, however, are those to de Gaultier. Though the majority of the quotations from de Gaultier are without quotation marks, Segalen makes no secret of the debt he owes the eccentric philosopher. When he introduces his distinction between "Universal Exoticism" and "Essential Exoticism," he writes, "I am obviously proceeding straight from Jules de Gaultier's thought." Segalen repeatedly wrote to de Gaultier to express his admiration and even copied out passages from this correspondence directly into the text.

What defines de Gaultier's *bovarysme* ("*conceiving otherwise*") also defines Segalen's *exoticism* ("*conceiving otherwise*"). Emma Bovary did what Flaubert did, and what we all do: she conceived of herself other than as she was. De Gaultier frees this trait from its pejorative context and extends it to all of humanity. *Bovarysme* is what makes us what we are, and makes us think we are something else. *Exoticism*, for Segalen, was a method for making a virtue of this necessity.

Segalen's text ends on an enigmatic note, with a phrase which, like an invocation in a fairy tale, is repeated three times: "And he rejoices in his Diversity." The reader might well wonder who "he" is—and to what this "Diversity" refers. The singular phrase is from de Gaultier and designates the product of *bovarysme*: ever-expanding, ceaselessly multiplying, endlessly ramifying "Diversity." "I will call 'Diverse,'" Segalen writes, "all that up until now has been called foreign, strange, unexpected, surprising, mysterious, amorous, superhuman, heroic, and even divine, everything that is '*Other*.'" That is quite a lot—even for a capitalized substantive to bear. In the primary place it accords to a constantly developing "otherness," it anticipates an idea which will resurface two generations later at the fore of French philosophy via the advocates of alterity—Lévinas, Bataille, Blanchot, Lacan, Foucault, Derrida, Irigaray, and Cixous, to name a few. No term enjoyed such currency in the philosophy of the late twentieth century as this "Other," which has raised its curious head to face every new form of identity.

During the years when Segalen began writing the work that was to occupy him for the rest of his life, *exoticism* was a suspicious word. It had become both a commonplace and a marketing strategy, and it was with this exoticism that Segalen wanted to break. He did not want, however, simply to jettison the term—he wanted to retain the freshness and the strangeness it contained, but to do so he needed to recast it. It should come as no surprise that Segalen never finished his essay. How could he have? In seeking to account for the perception of difference in repetition, of alterity in identity, his project asked of him that he do nothing less than develop a philosophy of perception. Segalen writes at one point of "the exoticism of nature," defined as nature viewed in a "non-anthropomorphic" fashion. This is tantamount to analyzing how and why we make the foreign and unfamiliar (the natural world, in this instance) bear our features and turn a reassuring face towards us. Bataille's efforts in this unchartable area also remained incomplete, as did Heidegger's more systematic ones in *Being and Time*. Freud's remarks in his most speculative and outlandish work, *Beyond the Pleasure Principle*, describe but a single moment in such perception and even then are unable to accurately describe the genesis of the mechanisms which protect us from too much exotic stimuli. Aristotle claimed that philosophy proceeded from *wonder*—from wondering at the near and the far, the foreign and the familiar, from ceasing to take the given for granted. It would seem that for Segalen to accomplish his goal—and thereby finish his essay—he would have needed to do no less than account for the birth of wonder in the mind of man.

Ultimately, however, the question Segalen posed himself could not to be answered in conceptual terms. What remained to be done was nothing less than to write—to express his own individual sense of wonder, the effect of the exotic upon him. It is not without irony that the most intelligent and influential treatise on exoticism of its time was inspired as much by the sensual wonders of Tahiti as by what was for a Frenchman of Segalen's day the least exotic place on earth—Normandy. The bright colors, intricate tattoos, rich sensuality, and living myths of Gauguin's Tahiti shaped Segalen's work, but so too did the sleepy and stifling Norman countryside and the frustrations it brought to the fore.

In the same years as Segalen was traveling the world and writing his essay, a singularly sedentary writer reached a similar conclusion. "You need not leave your room," wrote Franz Kafka. "Remain sitting at your table and listen. You need not to even listen. Just wait. Be quiet and still. The world will freely offer itself to you to be unmasked. It will roll in ecstasy at your feet."

From the Latin *ex voto suscepto*, meaning "from the vow undertaken," an "ex-voto" object or image is one produced to express publicly an individual's gratitude for divine assistance in overcoming a difficult or dangerous situation. The ex-voto form was familiar in classical antiquity—the Latin phrase *votum solvit libens merito* ("willingly and deservedly in fulfillment of a vow") was so frequently used to designate Roman objects created to commemorate survival through the decisive intercession of a god or goddess that it is typically abbreviated as "v.s.l.m" on artifacts from the period—and by the Middle Ages had become a commonplace within the Christian tradition, as well. Ranging from painted images of harrowing circumstances endured to sculptural replicas of body parts cured of illness, ex-votos were brought to the New World by the Spainards, and were by the eighteenth century established throughout Latin America, where they are still produced today, as they are in southern Europe.

The four images on the following pages depict mid-twentieth-century examples of the *tavolette*, or "little tablet," form of painted ex-voto, from an area of Sicily near the volcanic Mount Etna, made to give thanks for providential outcomes of accidents involving falling. Created, like most ex-votos, by unknown painters, they are taken from *Fig.* (Steidl, 2007), a book of photographs by the London-based artist team of Adam Broomberg & Oliver Chanarin.

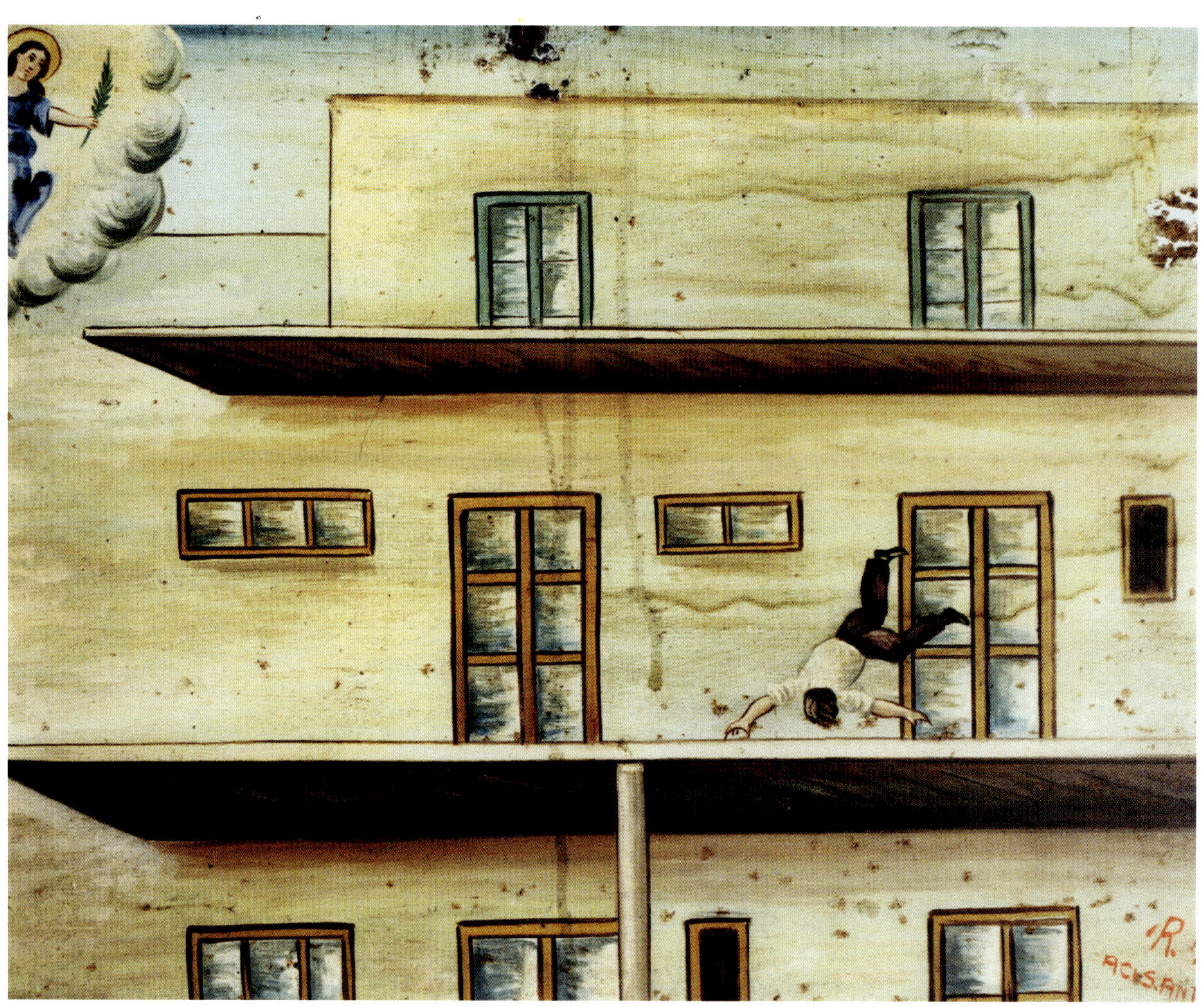

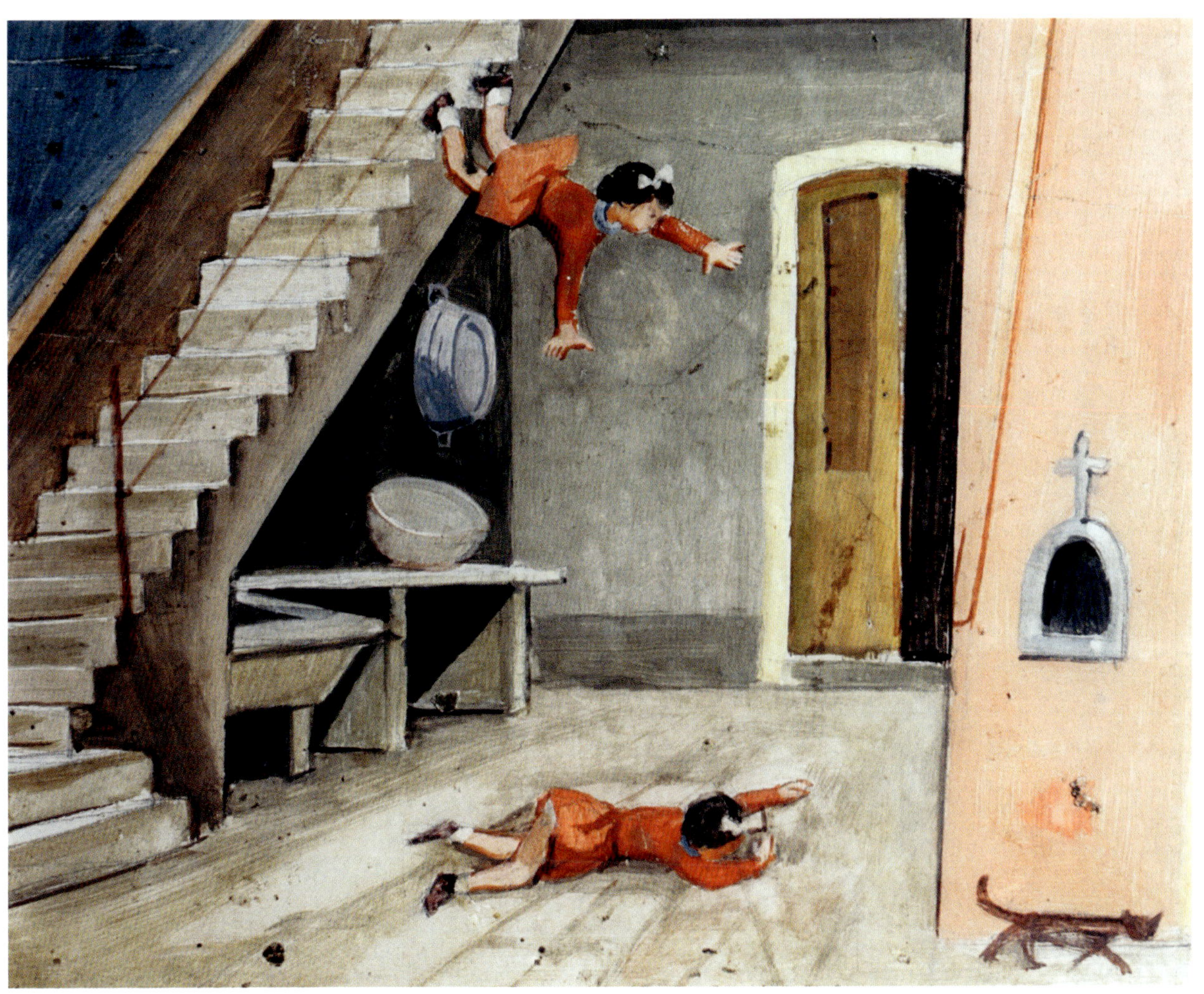

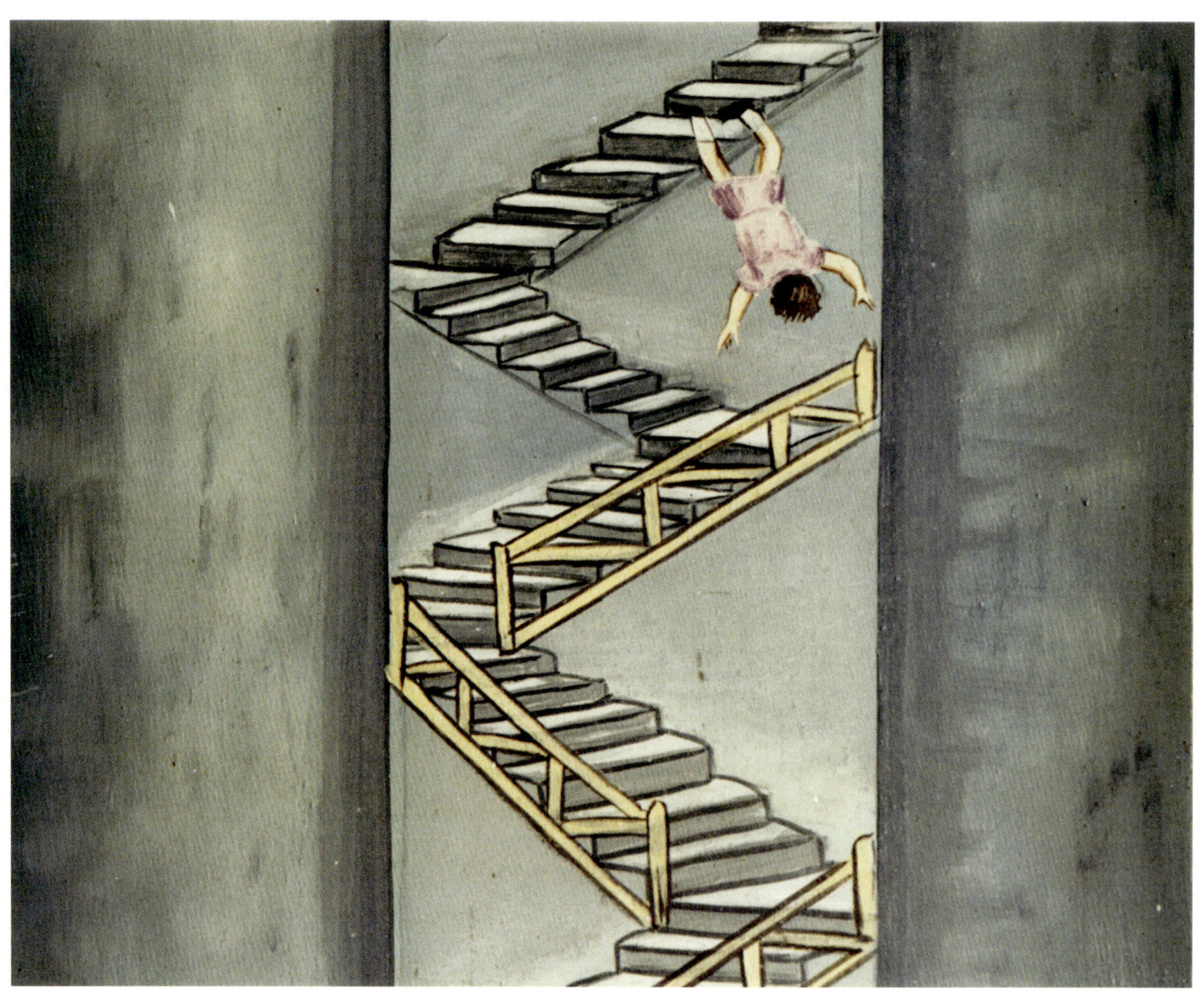

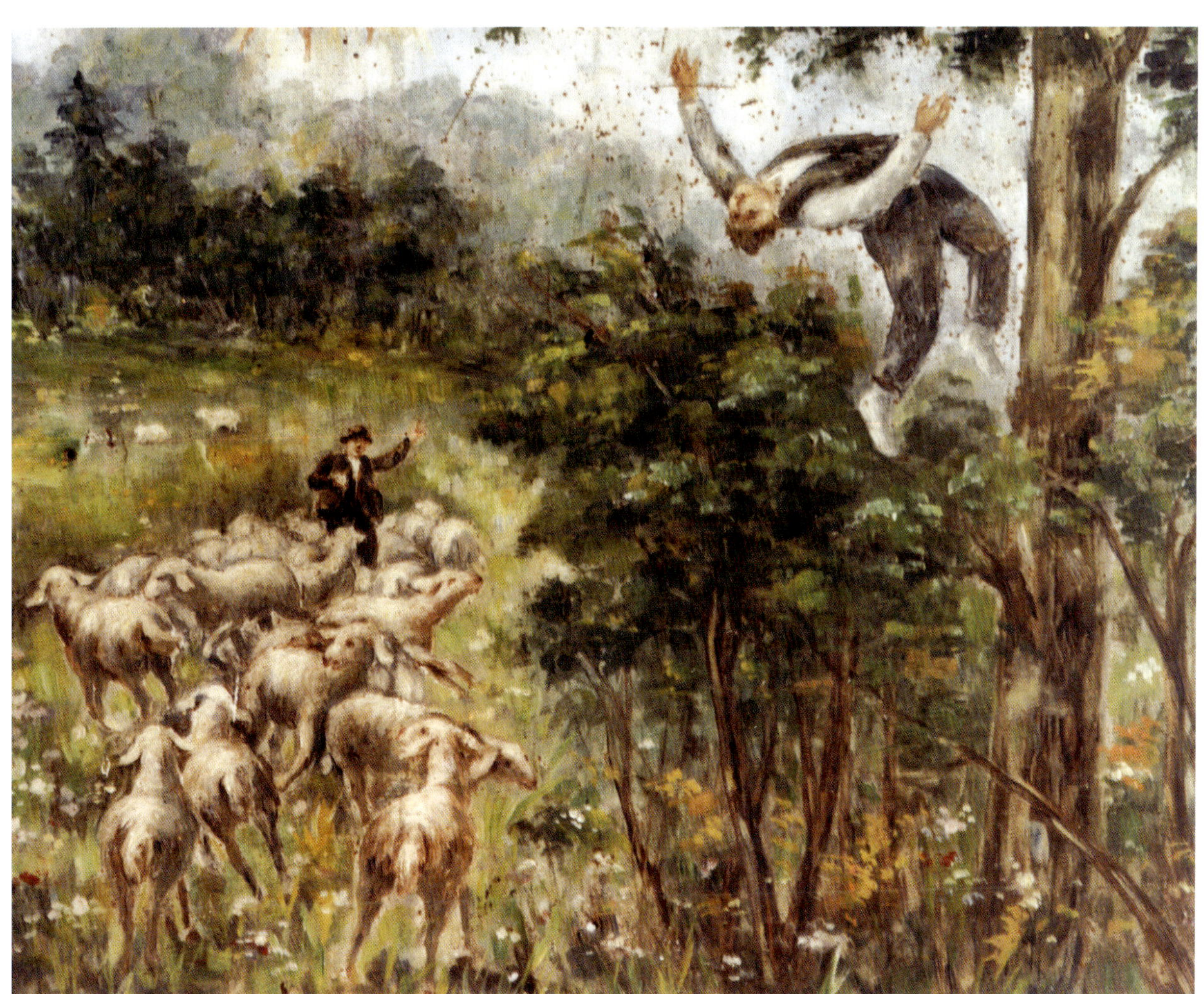

SMOKE
IMPLICASPHERE

Cabinet is pleased to present the fifth and, alas, final installment of our two-year collaboration with the London-based *Implicasphere*, the unique theme-based periodical created by Cathy Haynes and Sally O'Reilly. Past projects in *Cabinet* have focused on the Nose (issue 22), Salt and Pepper (issue 24), Stripes (issue 26) and the Onion (issue 28). This concluding edition looks for signals in Smoke, which is also the topic of *Implicasphere*'s exhibition at the Pump House Gallery in Battersea Park, London, on view from 8 October to 14 December 2008.

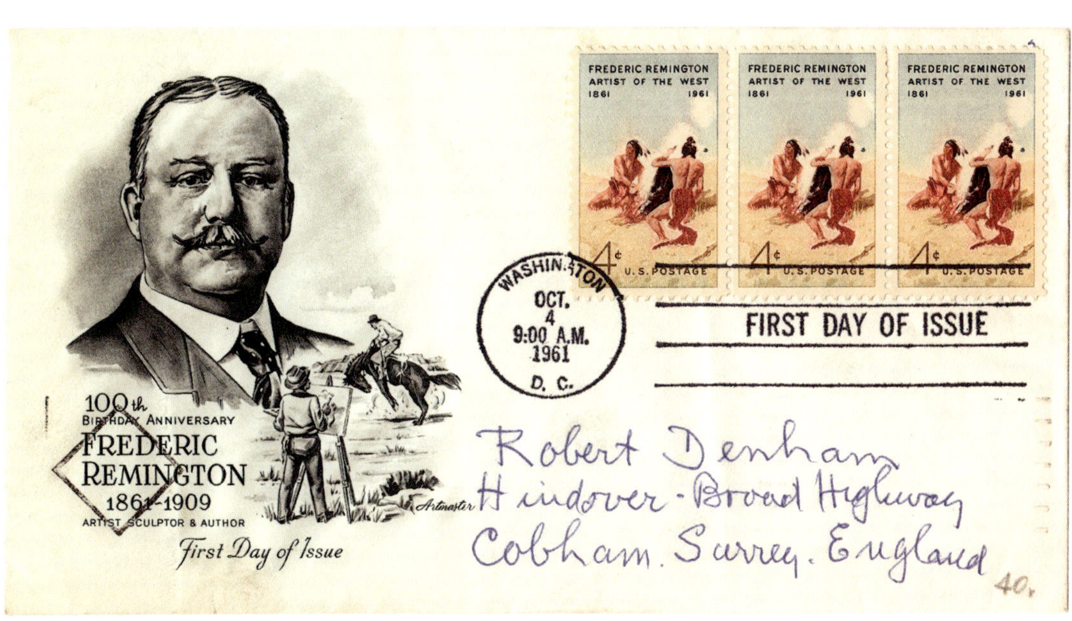

FREDERIC REMINGTON
ARTIST OF THE WEST
1861   1961
4¢ U.S. POSTAGE
FREDERIC REMINGTON
ARTIST OF THE WEST
1861   1961
4¢ U.S. POSTAGE
FREDERIC REMINGTON
ARTIST OF THE WEST
1861   1961
4¢ U.S. POSTAGE
WASHINGTON
OCT.
4
9:00 A.M.
1961
D. C.
FIRST DAY OF ISSUE
100th
BIRTHDAY ANNIVERSARY
FREDERIC
REMINGTON
1861-1909
ARTIST SCULPTOR & AUTHOR
Artmaster
First Day of Issue
Robert Denham
Hindover - Broad Highway
Cobham. Surrey. England
40.

"Naturall men have conceived a twofold use of *sleepe*;
That it is a *refreshing* of the body in this life; That it is
a preparing of the soule for the next." So writes John
Donne in his *Meditations*, neatly summarizing the biological and metaphorical significance of sleep. Nightly
repose is for the poet both a physical necessity and a
representation of the big sleep to come: it is brutish
and metaphysical at the same time. Not to be able to
sleep means to have lost touch with both one's animal
existence and with one's place in the universe. But at
the same time, the insomniac feels himself or herself
painfully reduced to bodily being and prey to a racing,
over-stimulated mind. Sleeplessness, it seems, is always
at least doubly freighted with meaning, as well as being
physically tormenting.

In her recent book *Insomnia: A Cultural History*
(Reaktion, 2008), Eluned Summers-Bremner, senior
lecturer in English at the University of Auckland, traces
the history of wakefulness from classical times onwards.
Medieval ascetics, she notes, relished a harsh bed and a
night of pious watchfulness. Lack of sleep, Summers-
Bremner argues, became a particularly pressing concern—rather than an impressive feat of alertness—in the
early modern period, when the secularization of time
and the uncertainty of financial speculation left many
unable to sleep at night. In the eighteenth century, stimulants available at the coffee house—caffeine, tobacco,
and enlivening conversation—were both distractions
for the sleepless and impediments to slumber. Today,
insomnia is seen as a besettingly modern malady:
popular medicine recommends that we regulate our
circadian rhythms and reduce our intake of stimulants.
But at the same time, not sleeping is a heroic indicator
of our work ethic and productivity: the corporate warrior
deliberately spurns slumber as a sort of weakness. Brian
Dillon interviewed her by email in July.

**You write that the inability to sleep is a double pri-
vation: the absence of oblivion, the negation of a
negative. Insomnia seems to confront us with empti-
ness—the vacant expanse of the hours to come—and
a troubling fullness: too much thought, too much
awareness of our own aching, twitching body. Can
you say something about this doubleness?**

This is very interesting: one's bed is a place of peaceful
promise and fulfillment on a night of good sleep, but a
place of torture and despair on a night of bad sleep. Yet
the one can turn into the other very quickly and at times
the two can overlap. One smoothes down the sheets,
gets back in, and it all begins again.

Descartes's credo "I think, therefore I am" can
be said to articulate a crucial gap in being, because,
although we can imagine ourselves able to think and be
at the same time, this trick is made possible by an act of
sleight of mind. There is something about attempting
to think being *and* yield to being in the same moment
that is difficult for us to manage. We can only do it by
momentarily leaping ahead of ourselves: we can't think
and be on the same topological plane. While we're
thinking, we're fully involved in that activity, which
requires us to ignore an equally significant range of
other activities. We can't go on being without sleeping,
but we can't sleep while we're thinking either, at least
not in the rational sense. Our material being operates
on mutually inaccessible yet continuous levels, and it's
intriguing to think that insomnia might be one of the
human events (to put it in Alain Badiou's terms) that
demonstrates the strangeness of our materiality most
clearly.

**Quite apart from the distractions that might keep us
awake, it seems that sleep is increasingly deprecated.
Do you have a sense of when this "I'll sleep when I'm
dead" attitude arose?**

The American version of the Protestant work ethic, in
which time became increasingly valued according to
its ability to produce money, is something we've clearly
inherited. We now also have a very strange thing hap-
pening whereby most of us know about the benefits of
good sleep and the health risks of not getting enough,
but at the same time our work practices and environments increasingly encourage us to, if not ignore this
knowledge, then certainly micro-manage it. So I think
we practice, or perhaps are forced to practice, a kind of
disavowal about our sleeping habits. I'm talking here
of people whose work is affected by globalizing work
environments, where the reigning logic is maximum
efficiency and if that means working to get something
done by a certain time on the other side of the world, we
do it. We increasingly fit our sleeping around the other
interactive components of our complex lives.

But having said that, I am not sure that the disavowal of knowledge of the benefits of sleep begins
with us. It's possible that the maximizers, if not the origi-
nators, of the Protestant work ethic—Dutch burghers
made wealthy by world trade and Calvinist reforms—felt

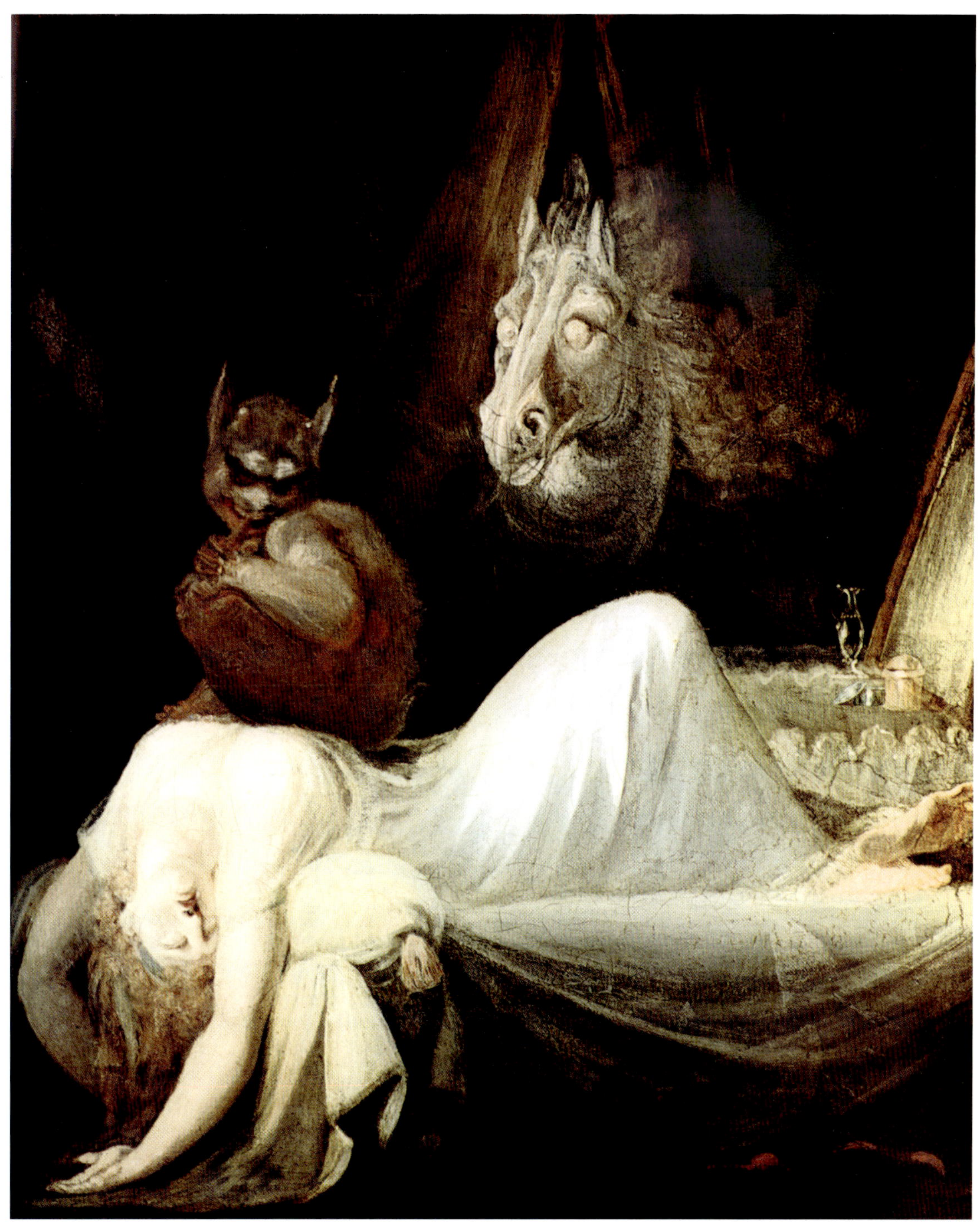

John Henry Fuseli, *The Nightmare*, ca. 1791.

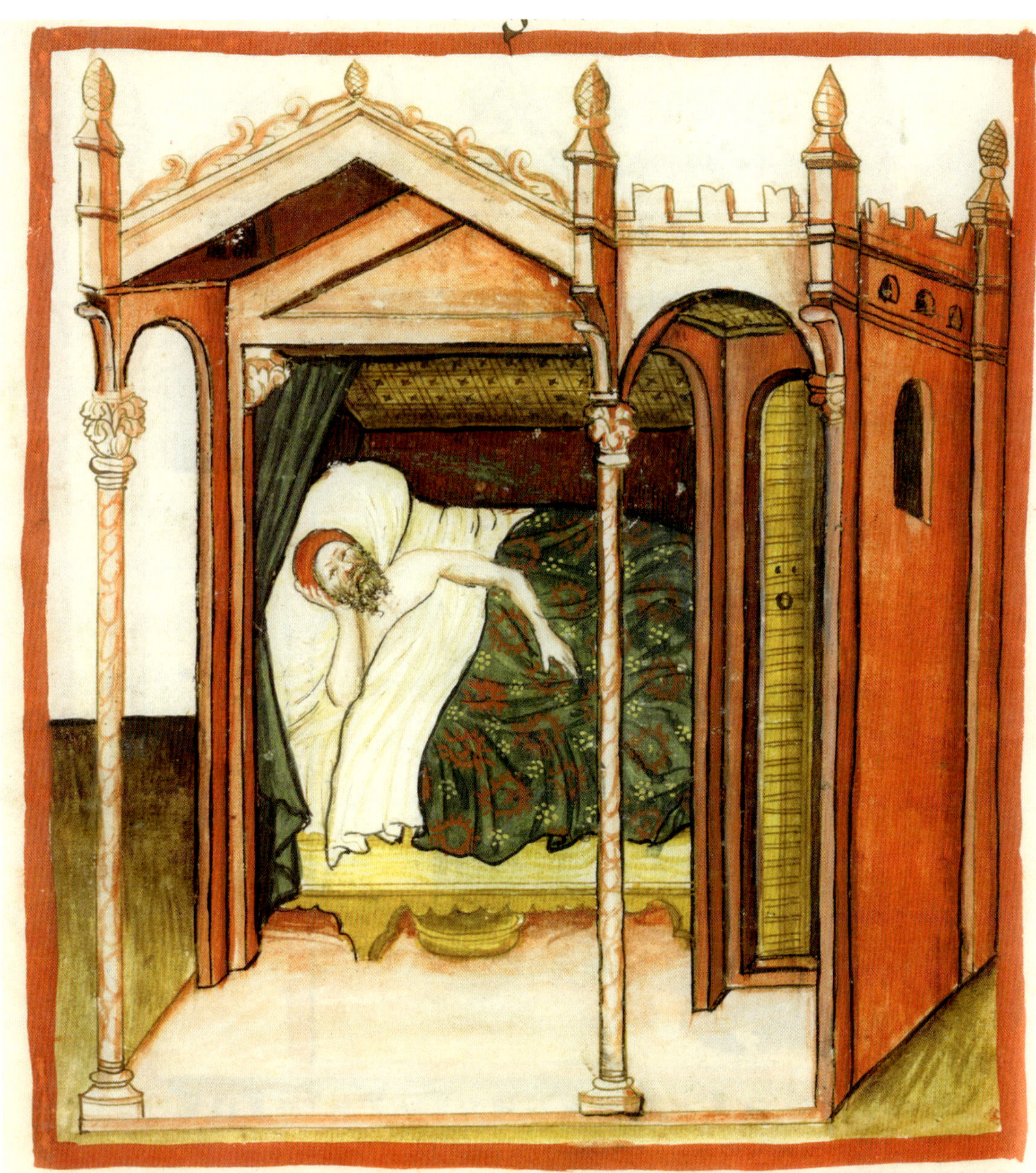

"The Insomniac," from *Codex Vindobonensis* (series nova 2644), a
late-fourteenth-century medical manuscript. Courtesy Österreichische
Nationalbibliothek.

something similar. They knew they ought not to spend time worrying about material wealth since all that was good was stored up in heaven, yet knowing that one ought not to worry about something is a recipe for self-consciousness, and so also for insomnia. Furthermore, as religious faith loses ground to secular concerns, people have even more to stay awake worrying about, because in addition to the lingering question of the fate of one's soul—which has not yet gone away—they become more involved in the activities of wealth: legal defense of one's goods, owing and pursuing debts, and so forth.

How far do you think the history of insomnia is linked to the increasing privacy of the bed and the bedroom among the middle classes? Is it possible that expectations of solitude and silence—as compared to those who shared their nights with extended family, livestock, and vermin—make sleeplessness less bearable?

Insomnia as a pathology or problem, rather than insomnia as the outcome of something else like demon possession, vigil, or all-night celebration, does seem to come into prominence as the bed and bedroom become more private, which of course has not necessarily ever been the case lower down the social scale, where people sleep where they must. Sleep seems to become a matter of private property and public concern in its own right in the early decades of the twentieth century, and an increased emphasis on psychologization—a sense of the privacy of the mind—is part of that. I do think privacy, solitude, and silence can create pressures in themselves: we often complain about noise stopping us from sleeping—the tick of a clock, the neighbors' stereo—but when viewed historically, sleep conditions can be terrifically varied, so what sends one to sleep most often is likely to be the environment one has become used to.

You argue for a link between modern insomnia and capitalist anxieties. What are the factors that interrupt the merchant's slumbers, roughly from the fourteenth century onwards? And how are those worries expressed by the sleepless?

In the thirteenth century, annual confession becomes obligatory for all Christians, and priests find themselves dealing with an increasing number of "cases of conscience." People want to know whether Church teaching, such as the requirement for Sunday rest, should always prevail over professional activities. Time becomes secularized in the sense that individuals become increasingly responsible for their use of it, while the answer to the question of how this use of time interacts with the final account of each person's life held in heaven is not knowable in advance. So there is an understandable increase in anxiety around labor and rest, and the accumulation and disposal of wealth. And as time is becoming the responsibility of the individual, it also becomes more liable to abuse. Wasting time becomes a sin from the early fourteenth century and labor becomes associated with working out one's salvation, a more active, but also potentially more conflictual process than simply performing penitential acts.

These increasingly individualized anxieties coexist, however, with a cosmology in which night is a time of temptation and danger, and in which the devil takes increasingly labile forms. The rise in importance of towns means more focused night-watching too: keeping the wrong people outside the city gates and guarding the wealth, or the wealth to be made, within. There seem to be new anxieties around the question of borders, of what the individual is and is not responsible for,

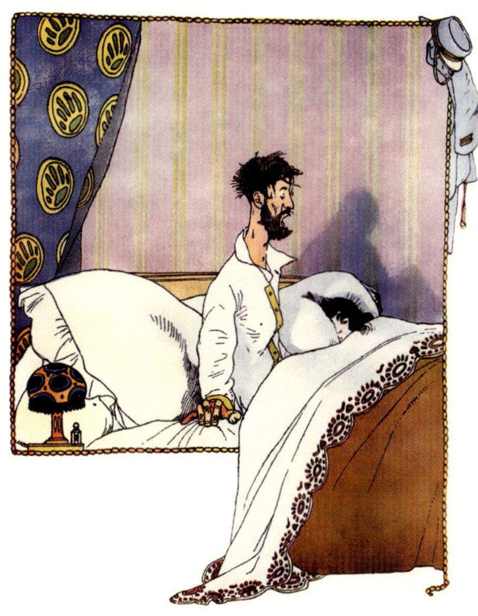

Marco de Gastyne, "The Anguish of the Infantryman: 'I can't sleep in this silence!'" Illustration for *La Baionnette*, December 1915.

anxieties that become more difficult to resolve in later centuries as trade networks make people more dependent upon each other.

When I was reacquainting myself with Chaucer's background, I was struck by the number and variety of jobs he did and how little actual time he had—time in which he could afford to burn light to read and write by, or use natural light—for his writing work. His insomnia can be seen to express anxiety not only about finding time to write, however, but also anxiety about finding time to sleep, since sleep and dreams were considered such rich sources for the creative imagination. So if wealth creates anxiety about eternal rest that seems to have disrupted people's sleeping, as there is some evidence that it did, so does the need to earn it. Add these two together, and we can see the beginnings of our own more frenetic calculations about the relative merits of sleep time versus work time, rest versus productivity, and so on.

You point out that until the eighteenth century it was usual for people to wake in the night after what they called their "first sleep," occupy themselves with work, prayer, and so forth, and go back to sleep later. Can you say something about this fractured sleep? Nowadays, such waking would be seen as one of the symptoms of clinical depression.

There is some evidence to suggest, as E. Roger Ekirch demonstrates in his book *At Day's Close*, that waking at least once in the night, and even getting up to do things, was more common in this period than in the eighteenth century and later. One has to bear in mind the practicalities of early modern sleeping: in town one might be routinely woken by church bells, night watchmen, revelers, and so forth, while in rural areas there would be livestock and domestic animals to tend to, and in winter a fire. And the expectation to sleep in one long, unbroken period can be problematic if it causes anxiety on waking that then affects one's chances of getting back to sleep.

The hiatus between the first and second sleep seems to point up a difference in expectations between the early modern period and the later industrialized era: the difference between trusting that one would be able to go back to sleep after one's first sleep, since we know this was something many people achieved, and our tendency to see sleeping in segments as a point of failure. The earlier emphasis on sleep as a communal activity—whereas for us, sleep is an individual achievement—may also have played a part in normalizing segmented sleep. The fact that the first and second

sleeps originated in the system of the canonical hours of the day and night developed by the Christian Church, marking points—three or four of them at night, known as *vigilae* or "watches"—at which monks and nuns pray for others seems as though it might have been of some comfort to people, not necessarily a comfort they were conscious of, but one that was built into their worldview. The thought that others were also awake or waking in the night might have helped to normalize the experience, and the thought of others' praying might have helped too, especially if one was vexed about the fate of one's soul.

The eighteenth century seems especially wakeful. Boswell and Johnson were extremely exercised by the problem of getting out of bed in the morning—to the extent of Boswell's imagining a mechanical device that would eject someone from bed—while Pope wrote in bed into the small hours. Is it in this period that we first encounter the notion that there is simply too much going on for people to sleep well or long enough?

Johnson felt oppressed by a need to keep inventing and thinking when he couldn't sleep—which of course wasn't always helpful—while simultaneously fearing the final judgment and being found in the more-animal-than-human act of sloth. He knew he had capacious gifts and worried—often, through the night—about whether he was using them in the right way and how that use would be computed at the end. I would say "his end," except that the concerns driving Johnson seem bigger than that. He was obsessed with the question of void, which he called "vacancy" but which seems to have been something more materially pressing than the term suggests, possibly having to do with his inability to stop thinking, and judging those thoughts as devoid of spiritual value, seemingly in the same moment—always filling up voids and emptying them. Matters of profit and loss also vexed him continuously; his housekeeper once found him in the act of attempting to calculate the national debt.

Educated eighteenth-century Londoners were certainly over-stimulated, but in ways they understood as well as in ways they didn't. People knew they were interested in newspapers and politics, of course, but didn't know about the biochemical effects of coffee, or that the food they were eating and the times at which they were eating it weren't conducive to good sleep. They didn't realize that if you go to sermons where the preacher rails at you for being slothful and you don't allow yourself to have a rest even there—where evidence suggests things were often dull and quiet, unless one happened to be in front of William Law—and then go home to focus on your inability to rise early, no matter when you've gone to bed, your sleeping is unlikely to improve.

In the nineteenth century, women's insomnia seems not only to arise from different causes from men's—often from sheer boredom and lack of daytime stimulation—but to be coded differently in terms of its social significance. Is there in such cases a closer identification of sleeplessness with hysteria or neurasthenia than in the case of the male insomniac?

A feminizing discourse of "nerves," "nervousness," and anxiety about the longer term effects of this new condition is part of the century's response to the ways people—men and women—themselves responded to industrial, urban work environments, in which they were being increasingly treated like components in a vast network of production and machinery. Insomnia was one of the symptoms of occupying such environments. As to women's and men's insomnia, the reinvention and reclassifying of hysteria by psychoanalysis and other medical or pseudo-medical fields may have meant that insomnia carried a lesser social stigma when exhibited by women than by men. A hysterical paralysis of the arm doesn't end where the arm physiologically ends in the nerves and muscles, but at the point at which the sufferer thinks of or visualises his or her arm ending. Insomnia is like the hysteric's physical symptom insofar as our thoughts can't get us out of it; they can only make it worse.

There were also, of course, a number of wars being waged in the period, in which only men fought, although women did war work of a non-combative kind such as nursing. And insomnia is both a nightly by-product and a long-term remainder of extended periods of combat, of waiting to go into combat, and so on. I think there's probably a closer identification of sleeplessness with hysteria in the female insomniac in the nineteenth century, if only because hysteria is considered a feminine malady at this time, but also perhaps a closer identification of sleeplessness with neurasthenia in the male, because neurasthenia—nerve damage—is the term used for male hysteria anyway, when it shows up again in full force after World War I.

I wonder to what extent insomnia has always been judged morally. Blanchot wrote that the insomniac "always appears more or less guilty" and there is certainly nowadays a popular notion that the sleep-

deprived are weakening their health. They're not exactly to be counted alongside the obese and the sedentary as potential drains on health services, but maybe that is coming....

Well, the devil is depicted, from medieval times, as an insomniac, and one can't go much lower morally than that. Even if insomnia hasn't always been judged morally, I think it has always been open to expressions of moral purpose or abuse. The rhetoric of the National Sleep Foundation in the US, which characterizes sleeplessness as an epidemic that threatens national health, comes very close, at times, to blaming the sufferer. People are said to be putting themselves at risk for injury, health and behavior problems, and so forth.

At the same time, there's a certain heroism to sleeplessness: E. M. Cioran—who was reputed not to have slept for fifty years—said that "insomnia is a form of heroism because it transforms each new day into a combat lost in advance" and that "insomnia is truly the moment when one is *totally* alone in the universe. *Totally.*" I wonder if insomnia is essentially solitary.

I think it is essentially solitary in one sense. That is, it feels so. When you can't sleep, you can imagine everyone else is happily sleeping and feel aggrieved and resentful. I think this mode of thinking can be a trap, however. The American poet Edward Hirsch says the sleepless form an unacknowledged community whose members recognize each other by their haunted looks, and while I admire Hirsch's writing enormously, I also feel there's something a little too self-congratulatory about that. In reality, insomnia is both an experience of solitude and an experience of community. Each of us must sleep each night or two or we go mad. And when we can't sleep, we are marked by our exclusion from humanity, or so we are apt to feel. It's strange to think that we might most truthfully enact our belonging to the human community by the act of falling into unconsciousness, the place in which we imagine others to be blissfully dwelling. Insomnia might not be unlike democracy in this respect: your only chance to get what you want—your vote choice, your sleep—means yielding up your material singularity, allowing yourself to (re)join the masses. It may be that we belong least to our conscious selves, and most to our communities, when we sleep.

SLEEP LIKE NAPOLEON: AN INTERVIEW WITH DAVID DINGES

AARON LEVY

"It is a matter of common sense that a human has to recover," a 1918 United States congressional statute reads, attesting to the societal importance of limiting the hours one can work each week and insuring proper time for leisure and recovery. Since 1918, however, the United States worker has seen the workday continually expand and leisure time consistently erode. We live today in a twenty-four hour, seven-days-a-week global economy that has pilots, NASA scientists, truckers, and editors all falling asleep at the wheel.

How does sleep today compare to ten years ago or a thousand years ago? In January 2008, Aaron Levy sat down with David Dinges, Chief of the Division of Sleep and Chronobiology at the University of Pennsylvania School of Medicine, hoping to explore this question and to learn how to sleep less and work more. Instead, he learned about the importance of being asleep at nine o'clock and about the physiological and cognitive changes that result from sleep deprivation.

Is there a way to quantify the benefits of sleep? "Sleeping in" has such negative connotations, as if it were embarrassing. How did sleep get such a bad reputation?

There's been six or seven million years of evolution, but it's only in the last 150,000-250,000 years that *homo sapiens* appears, distinguished primarily by a bigger prefrontal cortex. Those areas of the brain are particularly good at multi-tasking, and at imagining or anticipating time and space. It's at that point in hominid evolution when you suddenly see developments such as shift work, missions to the moon, artificial lighting, and fraternities—all the things that make up our modern and bizarrely artificial human existence. This endless assault on time and space comes from the frontal lobe. All the activities that don't involve heavy use of the prefrontal cortex, including sleep, are de-valued. Things that are seen as merely behavioral requirements in humans—physiologic requirements—are denigrated as lower-grade activities, and many people talk about them in a pejorative way.

Sleeping signifies laziness.

It certainly equates to that. Even my hero, Ben Franklin, has plenty of sayings about it. People who tend to wake up earlier in the morning—the natural larks, as it were—historically feel righteous, and they're the ones typically admonishing others that they should not stay in bed. They don't feel any guilt about being in bed asleep at nine o'clock in the evening, however, when the owls are up.

What is the physiological impact of living a sleep-deprived life?

If you don't get adequate sleep time, the ability to use your prefrontal cortex can be eroded. And it can lead to serious errors and mistakes, and potentially exacerbate stress reactions and poor emotional states. We know that attention, memory, speed of cognition, creativity, and judgment are all impaired by sleep deprivation. The problem is accelerating in the sense that we have more people awake more of the time. But culture can also simultaneously take corrective action so that people oversleep on the weekend, or they take caffeine. Of concern to me and other sleep researchers is that you see an erosion today of oversleeping on the weekend as well as of the recovery periods. In my discussions with federal agencies and industries—whether it's airlines, railroads, highway trucking, power plants, or any twenty-four-hour industry—I've come to realize that economic factors are the driving force.

So what goes on inside your sleep laboratory?

Most recently, we have set up a series of experiments where 260 people will be studied for 4,000 days in the laboratory. Each individual sleeps for four hours a night for five nights in a row to build up sleep pressure. About 85% build up pretty high impairment, and then we give them varying amounts of "recovery" sleep for two nights to determine how quickly and thoroughly we can bring back their performance to baseline levels. This gives us information on what factors influence the rate of recovery from sleep debt.

But there's a more fundamental question, and that's the recycle question. For NASA, we're looking at the recycle question because they, like in many other areas of society, cannot afford two days off, for instance if you're in space flight. So the question became: if you go five nights at four hours, and then I give you one night of a varying amount of sleep for recovery, what happens if I then send you back into five more nights of four hours? Is your rate of deterioration the same as it was initially, worse, or in fact better? And how much does the dose of recovery sleep influence it? That is biologically

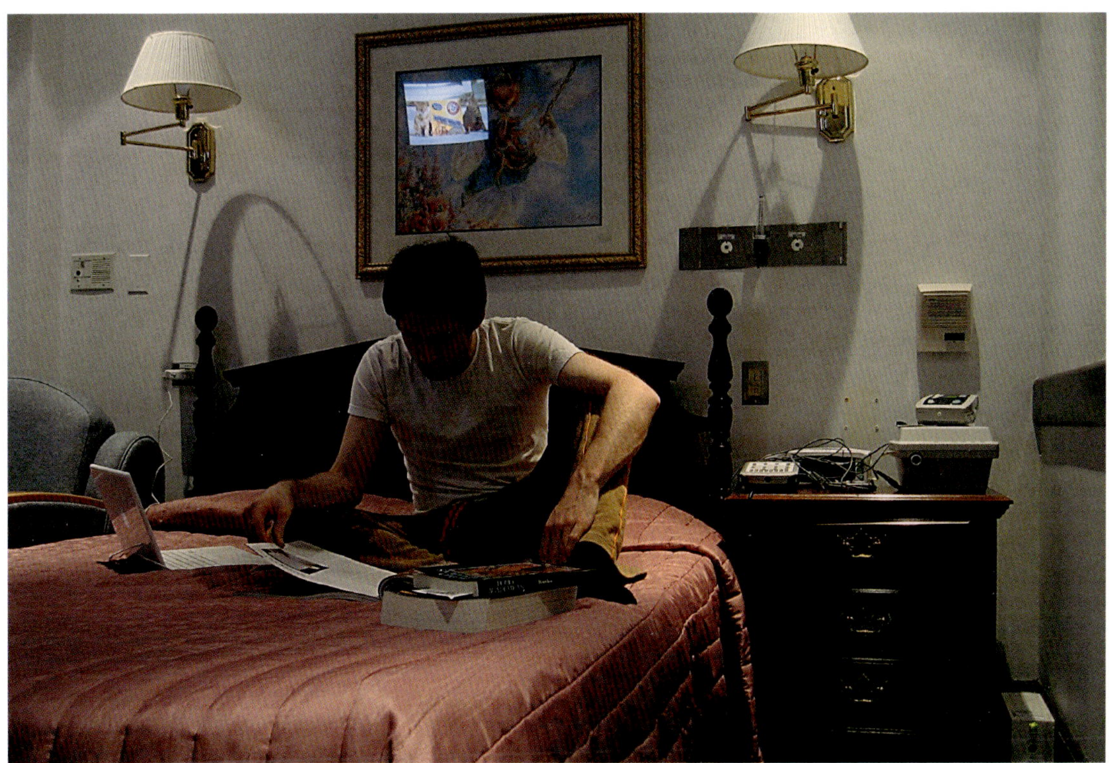

above and throughout: Aaron Levy, director of the non-profit Slought Foundation in Philadelphia, is in fact one of the more sleep-deprived Americans that we know. As background research for this interview, Levy arranged to be admitted for a one-night study at the Center for Sleep Medicine at Northern Westchester Hospital, New York. The photographs above and overleaf show Levy in his private monitoring suite at the hospital. Thanks to Doctor Nicholas Rummo, Northern Westchester Hospital.

and theoretically important in the sleep field, because if we find that it's worse the next go-round, then that suggests there are cumulative effects of sleep debt that go across weeks or months.

The real controversy in my mind, however, is this: are we working during sleep? This goes to the question of what sleep is for. Some of the current neurobiological theories suggest that it is for metabolic and synaptic downscaling, locking in memories of your experiences of the day, and cleaning out all the other stuff. By reducing the metabolic demand on the brain, you are both consolidating what was learned that day and preparing the brain to learn anew the next day. I find these theories very attractive because they fit with the paradigm that sleep is for making sure that the brain is maximally efficient so that behavior becomes maximally efficient.

To what extent can we control how we sleep?

The frontal lobe and other areas of our cerebrum can be thought of as attribution tissue; meaning these brain areas are continually making causal inferences about what we experience. This gives us the sense that we are willfully in charge of our lives, even though I would argue that biology doesn't wait for either our consciousness or our attributions. For example, we think our behavior before going to sleep is consciously controlled, but it may be more biologically programmed than we realize to ensure we can get to sleep quickly and stay asleep, without having to think about what must be done. We will all go home tonight and we will remove our clothing and we will go into a room that's kind of strange—its cool, it's a bathroom—and we will put water in our mouths, and if I ask you what you're doing, you'll tell me about oral hygiene and how you take care of your teeth. And then we'll lie supine in bed with our heads, hands, and maybe a foot out from under the covers. We may then fall asleep thinking about nothing in particular and confident that we elected to do all this willfully. However, these cooling down behaviors are what we must do to ensure we reduce body heat to facilitate sleep onset. A chemical released from our brain's pineal gland under the control of a biological clock in our hypothalamus further ensures that this genetically programmed behavioral repertoire occurs.

Now, I submit to you, despite all of your attribution arguments, that this is a biological response. You cannot avoid it, and in fact you are no different than a dog circling before it lies down. What the prefrontal cortex does, however, is to make up a story about it, and thinks that it willfully did that, and that's the illusion of conscious control of such a fundamental behavioral activity for a basic biological need.

That reminds me of Napoleon's remark that "different subjects and different affairs are arranged in my head as in a cupboard. When I wish to interrupt one train of thought, I shut that drawer and open another. Do I wish to sleep, I simply close all the drawers and then I am— asleep." It is as if sleep seems entirely volitional for Napoleon, rather than an involuntary biological and physiological need. He also claimed "I have never found the limit of my capacity for work."

Napoleon always talked about fatigue as the fundamental limitation. If you could keep your troops active for longer periods of time with less sleep, you had a greater tactical advantage, assuming they would remain behaviorally effective. You also just gave a perfect description of the way high-performing people with a great degree of prefrontal cortex control imagine they can extend that to sleep.

What is the prefrontal cortex doing while we sleep?

Neuro-imaging studies of the sleeping brain say that during REM dreaming sleep, with its rich and bizarre visual imagery, the pre-frontal cortex is offline, but not during slow-wave sleep, which is thought to be the synaptic down-regulation stage. There was a very careful study done many years ago, where they woke people from these stages of sleep and asked them about what was going on in their head. Surprisingly, when they woke them from dreaming sleep, with the prefrontal cortex offline, they all said, "I was asleep." But when they woke them from deep slow-wave sleep, they said, "I was thinking." This suggests that the brain may be processing information during certain stages of sleep. The neurobiological theories of Giulio Tononi and colleagues suggest it is removing some types of synapses and consolidating others, packing information in some neurobiologically efficient way to make the brain ready for another new day.

Is there an ideal period of time that one should sleep for, or does it in fact vary by individual?

In the large-scale experiments we have undertaken, involving thousands of days in the labs, we give different people eighteen different doses of sleep. Some people got six hours a night; other people got four plus a two-hour nap, five plus a one-hour nap, and so on. The idea was to see if we interrupted the buildup of the homeostatic drive for sleep with a nap, whether those people who received their daily sleep in two doses separated by twelve hours (i.e., a split-sleep schedule) end up functioning better. But the experiment revealed this not to be the case. It turned out that total sleep time per day— regardless of how it was acquired—was the dominant predictor of cognitive performance capability. And yet what everybody wants today is to get down to sleeping for four hours without consequences. Our studies reveal that sustained reductions of daily sleep duration result in reliable cumulative deficits in cognitive performance, especially in attention, cognitive speed, and memory.

I've read that people who work night shifts also have increased rates of heart attack. Why would this be?

This is a big scientific mystery. What are the precise effects of sleep displacement and circadian disruption in nightshift work? Why is it that nightshift workers may have higher rates of cancer? Why is sleep deprivation associated with mortality, obesity, diabetes, stroke, and heart attack? These scenarios aren't causal—we live in an age of epidemiology where we try to give meaning to our lives through correlation and causality. Sometimes we are very right, such as in coming to understand how smoking causes cancer, but sometimes we just don't know.

Many of the federal agencies that fund my laboratory's research do so to determine if we can find a way to reduce the need for sleep. Thus far, everything we have tried has had only modest effects. Despite all of our grandeur as a species, sleep is essential and binds us to our biological heritage on Earth.

One final question: what kind of coffee have you been drinking during this interview?

This is the breakfast blend—the biggest dose of caffeine.

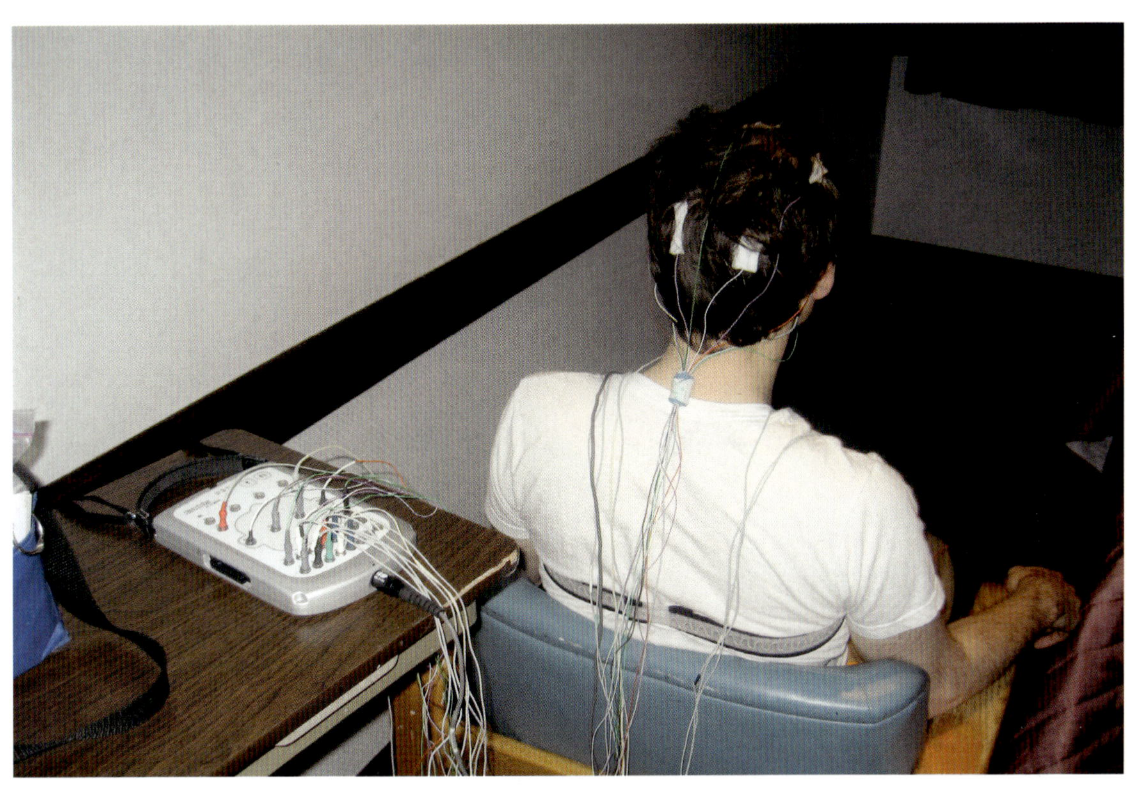

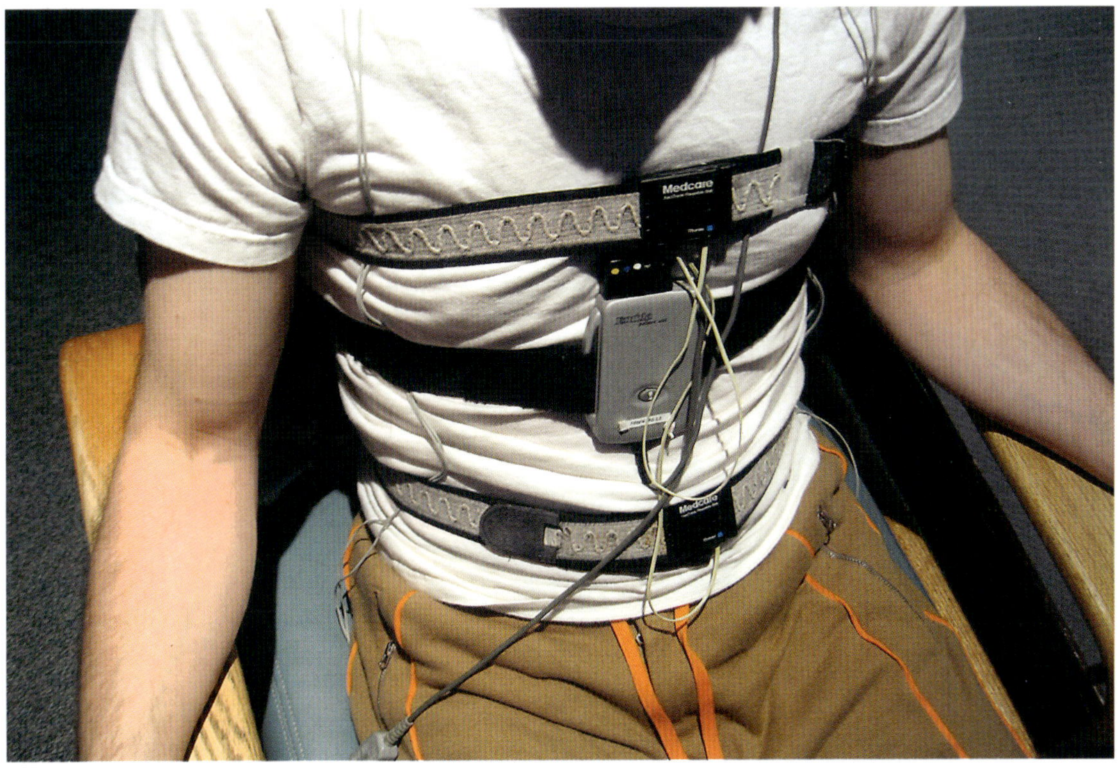

SHAME

For this issue's special theme section exploring shame, we have been fortunate to be able to rely on the rigorous yet imaginative scholarship of its guest editor Aleksandra Wagner. We first approached Aleksandra after learning of a course she was teaching on the subject at the New School—we were delighted that she agreed to work with us on the issue, and grateful for the intellectual energy and generosity that she brought to the collaboration.

THE WOMAN WHO KNEW TOO MUCH

ALEKSANDRA WAGNER

In the 1770s, the Paduan philosopher, natural historian, and Augustinian abbot Alberto Fortis (1741–1803) undertook several journeys to the other side of Adriatic, one of them to the lands of the *Morlacchi*. His travels were memorialized as *Viaggio in Dalmazia*, an epistolary travelogue printed in Venice in 1774 and translated into German two years later. It inspired Goethe to retranslate a folk poem collected by Fortis for his book and to recommend it for inclusion in Herder's collection of *Volkslieder*. Goethe's translation, initially published anonymously, made the "Xalostna pjesanca plemenite Asan-Aghinize" one of the most famous folkloric artifacts of the late eighteenth and nineteenth centuries in Europe.

The sorrowful poem about Hasanaginica, the noble wife of Hasan Aga, opens with the literary gesture known as "Slavic antithesis." This odd literary conceit refers to the following formula: a question is asked; an echoing suspense, in the negative, is offered first; and then we learn the answer.

What gleams white in the green forest?
Is it snow, or is it swans?
If it were snow, it would have melted by now;
And swans would have already taken to flight.
No, it is neither snow nor is it swans,
But the tent of Aga Hasan Aga.[1]

Hasan Aga has been badly wounded and is lying in his military tent. His mother and his sister come to visit; his wife does not. In various Slavic renditions of the poem, the diagnostic reason for her absence is given as *stid* (*"od stida ne mogla"*); it was *shame* that prevented her.

Once Aga begins to recover, he sends a message to his wife not to wait for his return. A few verses later, he will send her a written dissolution of their marriage. We learn quickly the consequences. She will have to return to her kin. Her brother will decide to remarry her. And the five children she had with her husband will have to be left behind.

There are two more pages of the ballad before it ends with the death of Hasanaginica. Yet, its emotional weight resides in events that occurred while the man and the woman were both still alive. Why didn't she go to her husband? Why did he dismiss her?

In Goethe's translation-*cum*-interpretation, which opened a path for many others, Hasanaginica could not go not because of shame, but because of modesty. This worked well. In those times, women were not supposed to enter male spaces. So, all too plausibly, Hasanaginica charts her destiny by resting her female case somewhere between modesty and obedience.

Interpretations that, while avoiding shame, turn our eye to its sanctioned derivative—modesty—suggest that Hasanaginica knew what is called "her place." This notion of "place" makes her into an obedient geographer who does the only thing imaginable: stay in. Viewed in this light, she merely acts out a convention. The sense of tragedy is then derived from the human failure intrinsic to the rule of patriarchy. In such a system, to know the rule and to play by the rule (a formula for success, or for passing as legitimate) can also be a formula for demise.

Yet, this interpretive gesture produces characters with no elasticity; women bound by custom, tragic heroines whose future salvation would be possible only if, and when, they acquired a tint of the "civilized." Such a reading can be inferred from the Slovenian ethnographer Matija Murko who wrote about his 1927 visit to the land of the famous ballad: "It is because she has been raised so strictly according to Moslem customs that Hasanaga's wife was not able, for modesty's sake, to go see her ill husband, even though he longed for her visit, having himself acquired more humanistic, more Western attitudes in the course of frequent travels to the cities of great civilization along the nearby Adriatic coast."[2]

Let us dispense with modesty. In the poem such

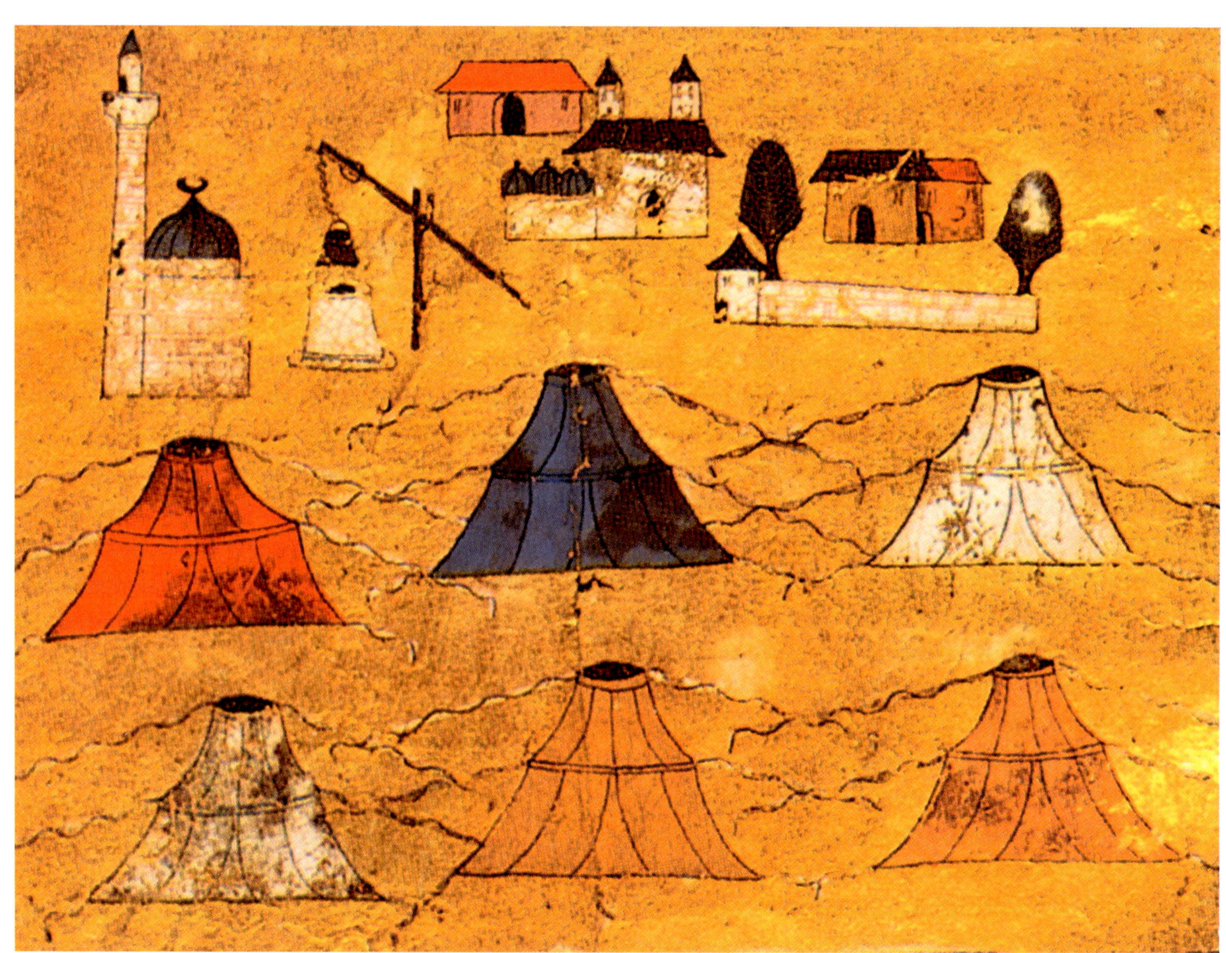

Ottoman military tents. Illustration from *Tarih-i Feth-i Siklos ve Estergon ve Ustunibelgirad*, mid-sixteenth century (detail).

a virtue is in fact not honored. Instead, let us ask what was Hasanaginica to see, had she gone? A set of crumbled ego-ideals: the diminished selfhood of a warrior; a weakened family protector; an incapable lover. She would have seen a man who would not want to be seen in such a state: an ashamed man. If there was a virtue to be found, it was in Hasanaginica's ability to identify with shame: her husband's, not her own. And, it is because of this sense of shame that she chose not to go and not to cast her eye. Instead, she opted for what she perceived as Aga's preservation. Or, should we say, the preservation of his manhood.

What did such an Aga get to know about his wife, by her not coming? After all, the mother and the sister came. They seem not to have been hindered by obedience and modesty. By her not coming, he knew not that the wife did too little, but that she knew too much. Viewed in this light, Hasanaginica was dismissed for her psychological acuity. She did not need to see the shame in order to know it. By not coming, she asserted herself not as an emotional extension of the wounded hero, but as an Other altogether. In place of the formula of obedience and modesty was now a far more dangerous thing: Aga's understanding that his wife knew him as weak and in need of protection, and that she had concluded, on her own, that this ought to remain a secret. And, indeed, this is the quintessence of the secret, if not of shame: once taken out of our possession, it is re-rendered as reality, as known to all. What Aga could not have known is the secret's future. In those times, it might have been assumed that the secret's knower might raise children even more unpredictable than herself. One thing assured by Hasanaginica's dismissal—by pronouncing her guilty—was that the secret would not be passed on. The knowing mother goes. The father's image remains intact.

But then, the sense of tragedy may be more importantly derived from the intensity of a male desire for the mixture of silence and secretiveness to be broken. Had he delivered a straightforward plea for her to come, what new type of family—and with it a whole human condition—might have arisen there and then? Had Aga revealed himself as an enlightened transgressor—liberating Hasanaginica from her upbringing, as well as from the solitude of her knowledge—would she have come then? Would she be willing to forego the pleasures of modernity that suggested she think on her own? Had she been another 'kind' of a woman, she might have successfully performed the "female principle" of a transgressive emotional life. One cannot fail to see its redeeming qualities: a healing power organized through the mutual recognition and acceptance of vulnerability. But, could she bear what she knew to be his shame?

Indeed, the proto-modernity of this couple might well be the core of the tragedy of the double-bind. Viewed in this light, the sorrowful poem is not to be understood as a measure of an orientalized difference, but as the West's emotional contemporary. Reflecting on the work of Norbert Elias,[3] Thomas J. Scheff writes that "in the late 17th and early 18th century, a change began occurring in advice on manners. What was said openly and directly earlier, begins only to be hinted at, or left unsaid entirely. ... The change ... is gradual but relentless; by a continuing succession of small decrements, etiquette books fall silent about the reliance of manners, style and identity on respect, honor, and pride, and avoidance of shame and embarrassment. By the end of the 18th century, the social basis of decorum and decency had become virtually unspeakable."[4]

Thus it should come as no surprise that the suspected female creator of the poem, as well as its listener, and later the reader, to whom its wisdom was addressed, knew that the patriarch who desires female transgression as an ultimate proof that his own rule can unravel—when convenient for him—can only be a silent one. His is the speechless kingdom, but one that assumes that the Other will undertake the proper reading of what remains unsaid.

It is exactly in such a kingdom—or is it a tent?—that most of us still live, now.

1 Translated by Thomas Butler as "Hasanaga's Wife," in *Spirit of Bosnia*, vol. 2, no. 3, July 2007. Available at <www.spiritofbosnia.org/?lang=eng&x=63&y=69>.
2 Matija Murko, "The Singers and Their Epic Songs," in *Oral Tradition*, vol. 5, no. 1 (1990), p. 112.
3 Norbert Elias, *The Civilizing Process: The History of Manners and State Formation and Civilization*, trans. Edmund Jephcott (Oxford and Cambridge, Mass: Blackwell, 1994).
4 Thomas J. Scheff, "Shame and Social Bond: A Sociological Theory," in *Sociological Theory*, vol. 18, no. 1 (2002), pp. 84–99.

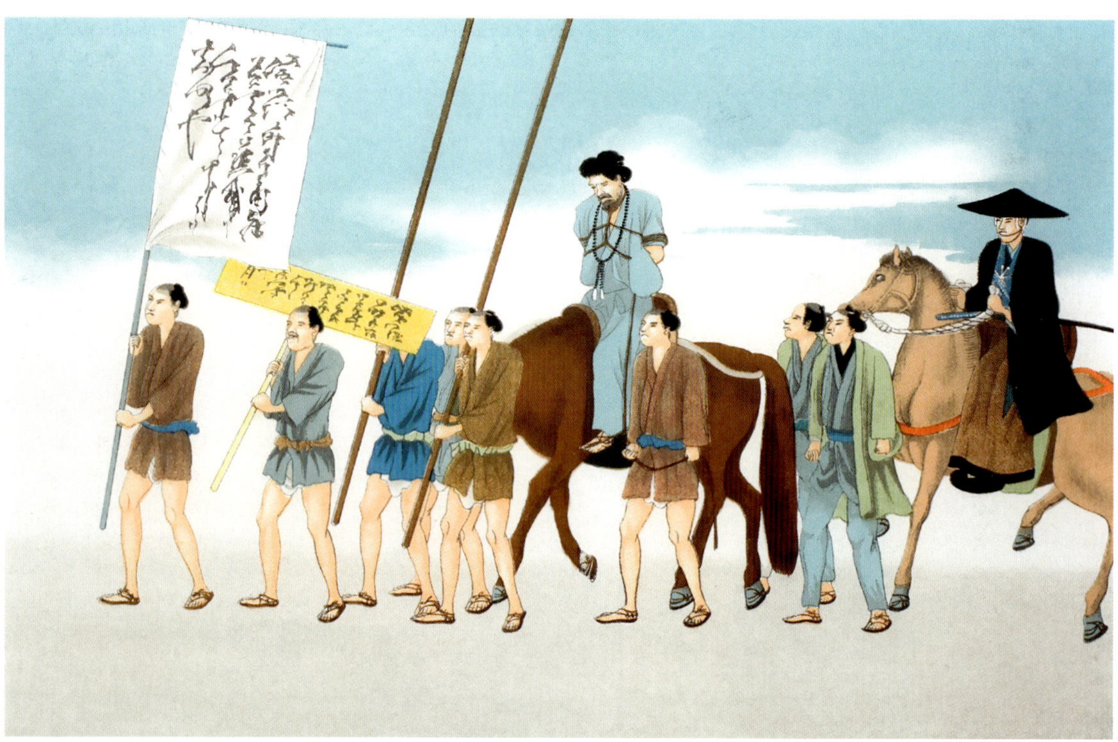

"Mode of Conducting a Criminal to Execution," from *Sketches of Japanese Manners and Customs* by J. M. W. Silver, 1867. The culprit is paraded through town preceded by a placard describing his crime. Silver, a lieutenant in Britain's Royal Marines, collected "native drawings" for his book during military service in Japan in 1864–1865.

BENEDICT'S SHAME

MARILYN IVY

"Shame is the Cinderella of the unpleasant emotions," wrote psychoanalyst Charles Rycroft in 1968, "having received much less attention than anxiety, guilt and depression."[1] Certainly Freud and his European descendants, including Lacan, thought little of shame. Laplanche and Pontalis, for example, included no entry for "shame" in their inestimable *Language of Psychoanalysis*. Although this orphan child found a certain place in American psychoanalysis (think of Heinz Kohut and self psychology) and has experienced a resurgence in recent years, it still remains strangely unmoored there. Unlike psychoanalysis, however, anthropology has long provided a home for shame.

Social structure, kinship, material culture, aesthetics, political formations: all these are enduring objects of anthropology, but none seemed to shape the golden age of American cultural anthropology as much as the role of emotion in the formation of personality, writ

both small and large, individual and cultural. Personality was imagined as an individual field of affects and emotions, structured by culture; culture was fantasized as a bloated expansion of a modal mini-personality. When personality and culture approach each other, two anthropologists inevitably come to mind: the redoubtable Margaret Mead (1901–1978) and the equally, if differently, formidable Ruth Benedict (1887–1948).[2]

Following Mead and Benedict, anthropologists imagined cultures as holistic unities, as aesthetic totalities, and as meta-personalities. Since culture operated as an inherited and transmissible template of prefab possibilities for subjects, individuals and their emotions would of course reflect the emotional repertoire of this elusively transcendental substance of "culture" in its myriad instantiations. From this viewpoint, cultural transmission occurred through child rearing—surprise!—and by studying this transmission in its psychological dimensions, key insights into the articulation of individual personality and cultural personality would emerge. This so-called "culture and personality" school of anthropology was thus profoundly psychological, if only fitfully psychoanalytic.

In 1934, Ruth Benedict's *Patterns of Culture* emerged as an elegant and exotic explication of cultural difference.[3] The very *notion* of culture, as developed by German theorists from the eighteenth century on, already implied an aesthetic totality, a unity, a whole, even a personality, which could then be described by regularities and patterns. It was this dimension of German cultural theory that Franz Boas inherited and transmitted to the founding generation of American anthropologists. As an heir to this legacy, Benedict made entire worlds of difference conform to aesthetic comprehension by presenting cultures as patterned wholes. She found that the most powerful way to convey these patterned wholes was to portray poetically—mythically?—the dominant emotional regularities, affective values, and feeling tones of a people. Her explications were memorable. How many undergraduates still remember the grand distinction between Dionysian and Apollonian cultures (epitomized, for Benedict, by Kwakiutl Indian vs. Pueblo Indian societies) long after they have forgotten any of the other details purveyed in Anthropology 101? Indeed, *Patterns of Culture* is probably the most famous work of American anthropology, the one which both your grandmother and your nephew might have heard of, and might even have read.

But back to shame. Shame is one of those emotions (affects? feelings?) that American cultural anthropology took on, even when psychoanalysis proper had not found it central. And here comes Benedict again: not only is *Patterns of Culture* arguably the most famous work in American anthropology, her later *The Chrysanthemum and the Sword: Patterns of Japanese Culture* (note the subtitle!) is probably the most famous work, in any genre, ever written about Japan. It might also be the most famous anthropological work on shame, even though the pages devoted to shame are disappointingly few.

This book produced Japan as a "shame culture" for American delectation. Written during World War II by contract with the United States Office of War Information and published in 1946 after Japan's atomic defeat, the book was formed through interviews with Japanese prisoners of war and Japanese-Americans (Benedict knew no Japanese and never went to Japan). *The Chrysanthemum and the Sword*'s mission was to explain to uncomprehending Americans the bizarreries of Japanese behavior, behavior that had led to such inexplicable extremities as *kamikaze* suicide bombings. Tacking back and forth from the antinomies of Japanese social life—the seeming incommensurable differences of "the most alien enemy the United States had ever fought in an all-out struggle"—to their rough American parallels, Benedict aimed to explicate the entire cultural personality of Japan.[4] In the process, Japan became America's evil twin, yet one now open to Americanized rehabilitation in the midst of its ruined cities and nuclear ashes. Likewise, the United States became Japan's good twin. *The Chrysanthemum and the Sword* is as much about the United States in its triumphal moment after the war as it is about Japan.

In this story of Japan (and the United States), shame plays a central role. Shame has a twin, too, in Benedict's story: guilt. In her para-Freudian anthropology, Japan is a shame culture, America a guilt culture: "A society that inculcates absolute standards of morality and relies on men's developing a conscience is a guilt culture by definition. ... In a culture where shame is a major sanction ... a man does not experience relief when he makes his fault public even to a confessor. So long as his bad behavior does not 'get out into the world' he need not be troubled. ... True shame cultures rely on external sanctions for good behavior, not, as true guilt cultures do, on an internalized conviction of sin. ... [Shame] requires an audience or at least a man's fantasy of an audience. Guilt does not."[5]

Ashamed, shame appears as less developed, less autonomous, less evolved than guilt. Shame is felt always in relation to the Other, unlike guilt with its sturdy, consistent standards of morality (guilt is confessable). Shame is more primitive. Shame allows the most heinous deeds, and all is well, as long as these crimes are not exposed to the gaze of the world. Guilt does not depend on crime's revelation. Guilt is internalized, autonomous; shame is externalized, heteronomous. Guilt is fixed; shame is mutable. Guilt is American; shame is Japanese.

These twinned affects are not that easily disengaged from each other, psychoanalytically speaking. But no matter for Benedict. It was crucial to open up a split between shame and guilt in order to maintain a hierarchical difference between Japan and the United States, and indeed between the non-West and the West (guilt is a Judeo-Christian thing; non-Westerners wouldn't understand). In understanding Japanese shame, Americans would understand as well the superiority of their guilt culture; through the immense labor of reconstruction demanded by the postwar Occupation, the occupiers would help Japan comprehend the shame of its shame culture, ensuring its future sublation as an Americanized ally with imported democratic values, mass cultural pleasures, and the proprieties of guilt.

What was unanticipated was the tremendous impact *The Chrysanthemum and the Sword* would have in Japan itself. Translated into Japanese almost immediately after its American publication, the book has been one of the most important influences on Japanese social psychology and native ethnology in the postwar period: millions of copies have been sold and high school textbooks quote from it.[6] It seems that many Japanese found the aesthetico-cultural totalities served up by Benedict as comforting as Americans did: this is who (we) Japanese are! Indeed, Benedict's book was indispensable to homegrown cultural theorists who keenly felt the shame of Japan's defeat, its postwar international isolation and dependence on American largesse. Benedict's orientalist tract was recuperated not only as actually descriptive of the truth of Japanese culture (itself a notion overdetermined by Japanese prewar fascism and its philosophers of empire—Benedict got many of her ideas about Japan from prisoners of war who had been thoroughly inculcated with the social rules of the wartime emperor system), but also as empowering in its rendering of social life by a series of easily grasped dichotomies. *The Chrysanthemum and the Sword* provided a persuasive explanation of *why* the West couldn't understand Japan, and Japan's shame— here transformed into a point of national pride—was at its base. A culturalist explanation, as proffered by Benedict, allowed the Japanese to claim something ineffable and essential about their "national character," as the term went. That ineffable something called "shame" became a fetishized point of identification, a mark of dramatic difference from the conquering Americans. Even if a shame culture was clearly not as advanced as a guilt culture in Benedict's cultural calculus, shame could nevertheless be claimed, stubbornly and defiantly, as a crucial part of the "national thing," that ineluctable "thing" which, by definition, cannot be understood by outsiders. The "Japanese thing," as developed by mass media, education, cultural critics, and the state alike, bears witness to the peculiar force of Benedict's shame and its continuing afterlife.[7]

Not all Japanese were taken by Benedict's book, though, and the critical response over the years has been fierce. Benedict had no notion of class; she mistook the ruling ideology for the everyday beliefs of the people; she didn't know what capitalism was; her drive to conceive of a modern nation-state as a timeless culture led her to ignore processes and possibilities of historical change; her incessant tabulation and dichotomization of values led to an impoverished, simplistic view of Japan;

her investment in aesthetic totalization caused her to ignore plurality and difference; her belief in the superiority of Western values led her to categorize, however slyly, non-Western ones as lesser; she imagined Japan as the dyad of the United States, while ignoring Japan's imperialism in the rest of Asia; she didn't know from shame; she was simply orientalist: these are some of the innumerable lapses that Japanese critics—folklorists, political theorists, philosophers, literary scholars, anthropologists—have detected over the years. Benedict's book still flourishes in Japan, however, somehow impervious to these irrefutable criticisms. Shame and its accompaniments are not that easily relinquished, it seems, and to hold on to the specificity of a culture of shame is to retain a negative difference from that guilt-ridden Americanism, that now, more than ever, would dominate the world with its imperial ambitions.

Yet the Japanese state, too—despite the so-called culture of shame—shows no shame in its unwillingness to acknowledge the atrocities of the war (the "previous war"—*saki no sensō*, as it is called in Japanese), through apology to its victims (apology is an admission of wrong-doing) or otherwise. In the kindly, conquering language of anthropological toleration, *The Chrysanthemum and the Sword* allowed the Japanese to forget their own colonizing and militaristic endeavors through the locked duality of the American embrace. With a logic that borders on the perverse, Benedict's tract provided a strange culturalist alibi for the forgetting of wartime atrocity. By arguing that the notion of "shame" could describe an entire culture, and that culture itself could account for the ethico-political actions of a modern nation-state, Benedict let the Japanese off the historical hook. In short, in Benedict's world, the Japanese aren't ethically responsible for wartime atrocities or their colonization of Asia because they belong to a shame culture, in which one feels no responsibility towards those outside one's social world: national-cultural Others don't count (a Japanese proverb states that "The traveler knows no shame"). One feels no shame towards those who don't belong to one's social world, and if the Japanese feel no shame for wartime atrocities committed outside of Japan, it's because of their culture. Who can argue against that? Benedict's notion of a culture of shame, and more fundamentally her notion of culture itself, is an essentialist explanation for Japanese behavior: the analytical buck stops there.

Haji is the Japanese term that Benedict rendered as "shame." Benedict's shame, and anthropology's, was to think that producing patterns of culture could take the place of political analysis, that "shame" could

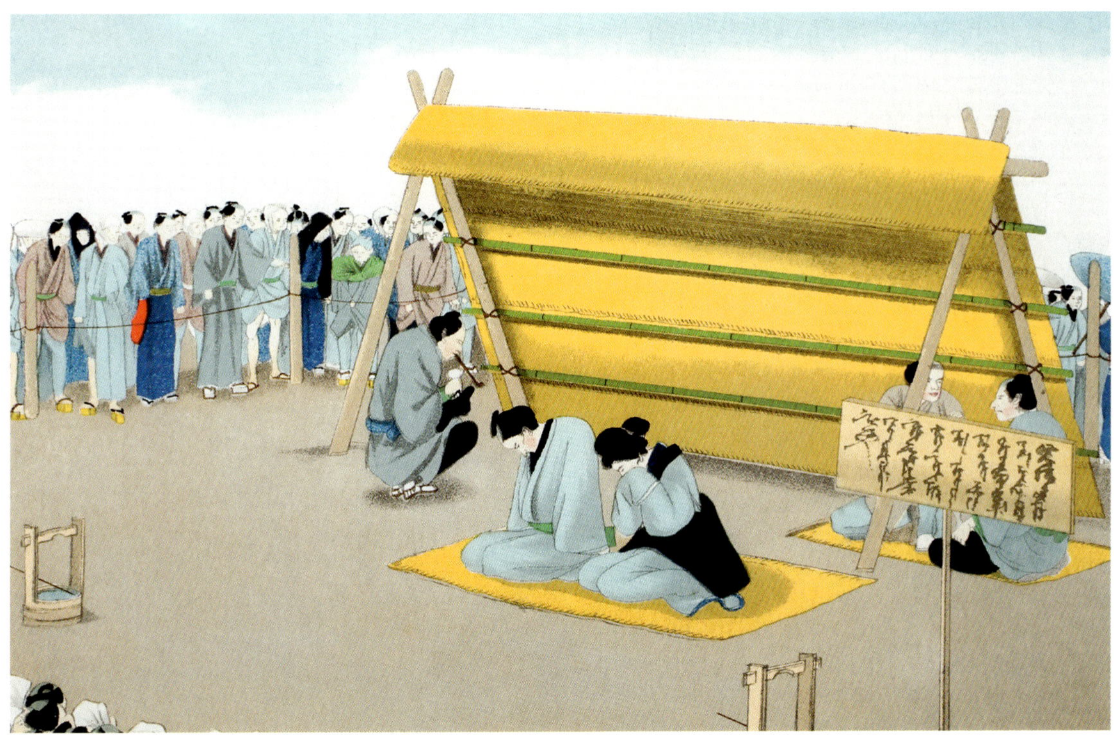

"Exposure for Infidelity," from *Sketches of Japanese Manners and Customs*.

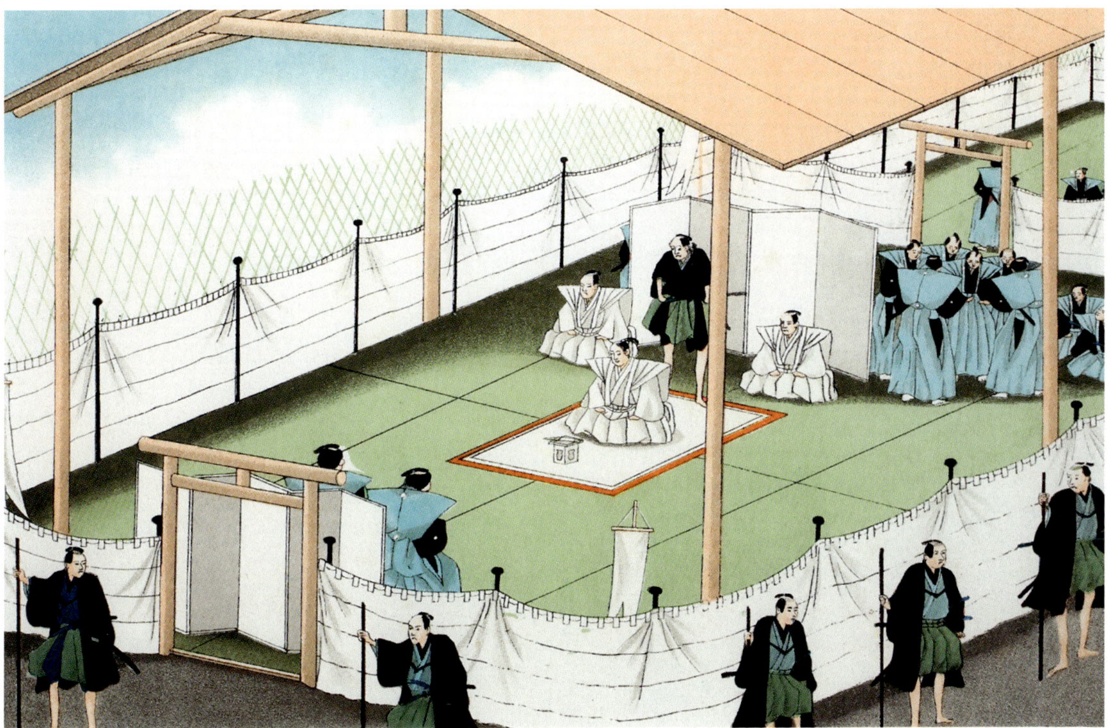

"The Sacrifice," from *Sketches of Japanese Manners and Customs*. This illustration represents the practice of *seppuku*, a form of ritual suicide originally reserved for samurai. *Seppuku* allowed a high-ranking person accused of a crime to free himself and his family from shame.

translate *haji* transparently, without remainders, and
that there was a "proper place" (a translated expression
used throughout *The Chrysanthemum and the Sword*)
for shame, a place called Japan. But shame can't be kept
apart from its guilty twin, and the improprieties of their
commingling (like those of the chrysanthemum and the
sword) disclose that shame can't be the special property
of a place called Japan, a "shame culture." Japanese
shame existed only in translated relation to American
guilt, emerging in the midst of Japan's failed empire and
war defeat. But shame has no proper place as it moves
between the United States and Japan, as it crosses
into guilt and back again, and as it circulates globally
(Benedict's notion of shame and guilt cultures spawned
endless anthropological attempts to categorize world
cultures in a similar fashion; not surprisingly, most non-
Western cultures came to be placed at the shame end
of the spectrum). If today, shame-in-general remains an
affective orphan, a psychoanalytic Cinderella, Benedict's
shame, itself a wartime child of the ashes, found its
(im)proper place in the twinnings of Japan and America,
of psychology and anthropology, of war crimes and
postwar amnesia. *The Chrysanthemum and the Sword*
discloses that shame has an uncanny home, not in
Japan itself (as Benedict claimed) or any other place
as such, but furtively, in between: in between social
subjects (Benedict's shame is always relational and situ-
ational, unlike guilt), between languages, and between
nations. Anthropology today—unlike Benedict's anthropology of 1946—must take on shame in that furtive
place of the in-between; to do so would release shame
from its confinement to any particular location, Japan
or otherwise. Benedict's shame might then come to its
long-anticipated end.

1 Charles Rycroft, *Critical Dictionary of Psychoanalysis* (London: Penguin,
1968), p. 152.
2 Mead and Benedict were both students of Franz Boas (1858–1942), the
so-called founder of American anthropology and, in 1897, the founder of the
Department of Anthropology at Columbia University, the discipline's first Ph.D.-
granting department in the United States.
3 Ruth Benedict, *Patterns of Culture* (Boston: Houghton Mifflin Company,
1934).
4 Ruth Benedict, *The Chrysanthemum and the Sword: Patterns of Japanese
Culture* (Boston: Houghton Mifflin Company, 1946), p. 1.
5 *The Chrysanthemum and the Sword*, op. cit., pp. 222–223.
6 See C. Douglas Lummis, "Ruth Benedict's Obituary for Japanese Culture,"
Japan Focus, available at <www.japanfocus.org/products/topdf/2474: 1-25>,
and Sonia Ryang, "*Chrysanthemum*'s Strange Life: Ruth Benedict in Postwar
Japan," *Asian Anthropology*, no. 1 (2002), pp. 87–116.
7 See Slavoj Zizek, "Eastern Europe's Republics of Gilead," *New Left Review*, no.
183 (September-October 1990), pp. 50–62.

ALAN JACOBS

It was not guilt they felt, not at first. That would come later, after instruction. Guilt must be learned; shame, it appears, comes naturally.

The story is so brief that even a mere summary of it amounts to commentary. The man and the woman were placed in the garden and allowed to eat the fruit of every tree there save one, "the tree of knowledge, good and evil"— I am using Robert Alter's translation—"for on the day you eat from it, you are doomed to die." But the serpent told the woman they would not die: instead, "your eyes will be opened and you will become as gods knowing good and evil."

And the woman saw that the tree was good for eating and that it was lust to the eyes and the tree was lovely to look at, and she took of its fruit and ate, and she also gave to her man, and he ate. And the eyes of the two were opened, and they knew they were naked, and they sewed fig leaves and made themselves loincloths.

Did they repent of their disobedience? Did they sense that the doom of death had fallen on them? Did they think, "The serpent was right—we are indeed as gods in our new knowledge"? Any of the above is possible; in reading this strange text we should never infer too much from silence, of which there is a great deal. Our author merely tells us: they were ashamed. We know that this concept is important to him because he had concluded his account of the Creation by writing, "And the two of them were naked, the human and his woman, and they were not ashamed." The tale of the world's making ends with the thought that the first couple had no shame; but it is a précis of their fall, and the breaking of all things, to say that shame came upon them.

Since the 1940s, anthropologists have distinguished between shame-cultures and guilt-cultures. People who belong to the latter suffer from an inner sense that they have transgressed some immutable law, and the hiddenness of that transgression can intensify the pain: thus the feeling of relief that can accompany confession in such cultures. But in shame-cultures, exposure is the great evil: not to transgress, but to have one's transgressions revealed. Thus in the *Iliad*, when Andromache begs her beloved Hector to stay in the city rather than return to the fighting, he replies that he cannot, for the shame of doing so would be too terrible.

What the man and the woman feel, in their garden, is not the pricking of guilt but the panicky flush of expo-sure. So before all else—even before they hide themselves in the woods for fear—they sew coverings for themselves from *fig* leaves. (Why fig leaves? Perhaps merely because of the leaves' size.) Even fear of God's wrath must be set aside so that the shame of nakedness can be removed.

But they are morally naked too—their deeds exposed as fully as their genitals—and help for this expo-sure must come from words, not leaves:

And the Lord God called to the human and said to him, "Where are you?" And he said, "I heard Your sound in the garden and I was afraid, for I was naked, and I hid." And He said, "Who told you that you were naked? From the tree I commanded you not to eat have you eaten?" And the human said, "The woman whom you gave by me, she gave me from the tree, and I ate." And the Lord God said to the woman, "What is this you have done?" And the woman said, "The serpent beguiled me and I ate."

The words both cover and deflect: the man seeks to turn God's eye towards the woman, the woman towards the

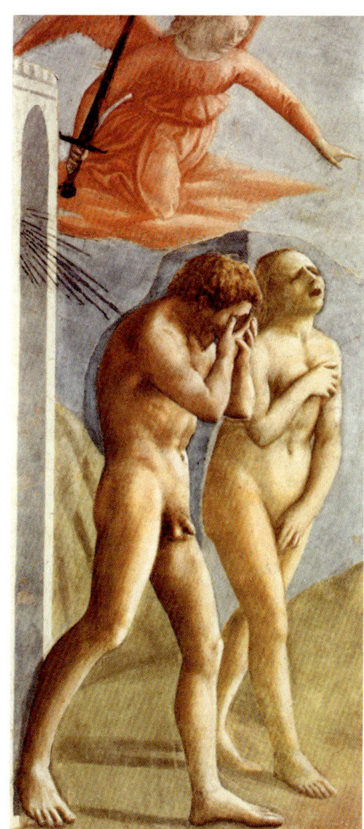

Tommaso Masaccio, *The Expulsion*, ca. 1426.

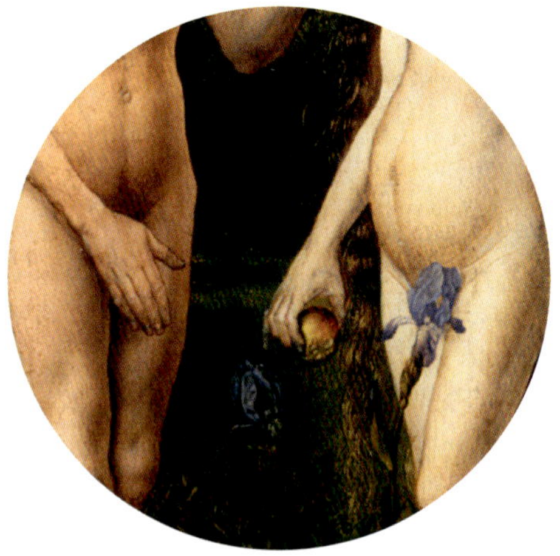

Hugo van der Goes, *The Fall of Man*, ca. 1470.

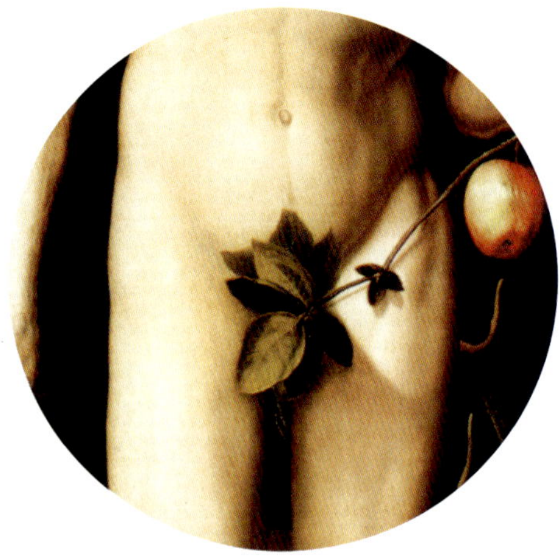

Hans Baldung Grien, *Adam and Eve*, 1507.

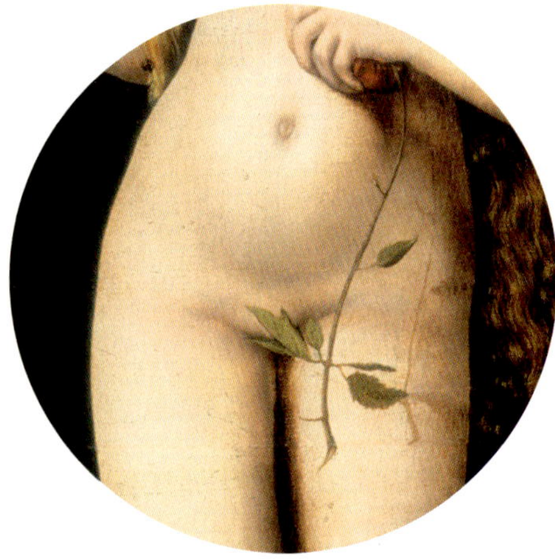

Lucas Cranach the Elder, *Adam and Eve*, ca. 1510.

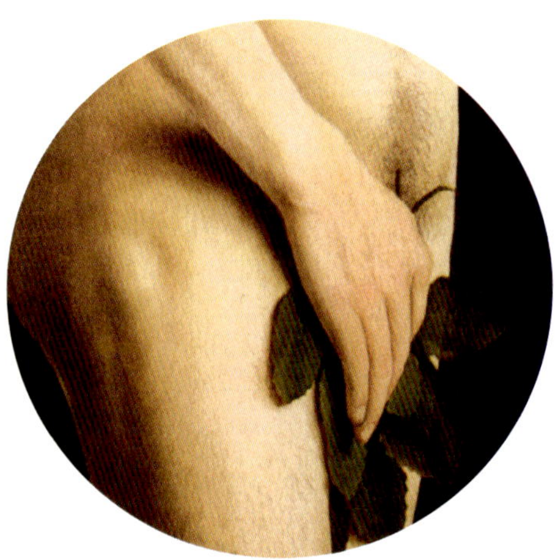

Hubert and Jan van Eyck, The Ghent Altarpiece, ca. 1432.

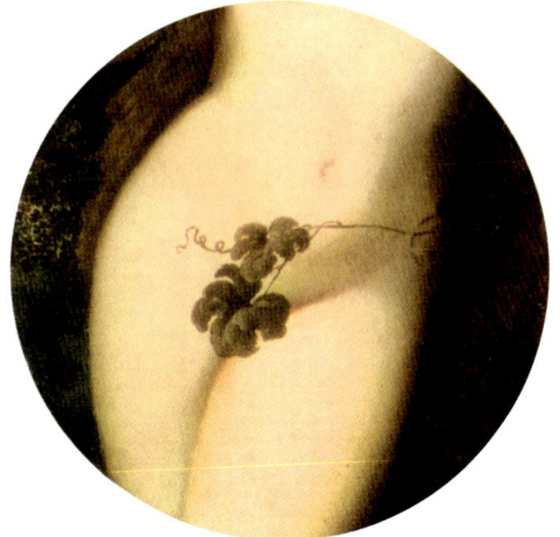

Peter Paul Rubens, *Adam and Eve*, 1599.

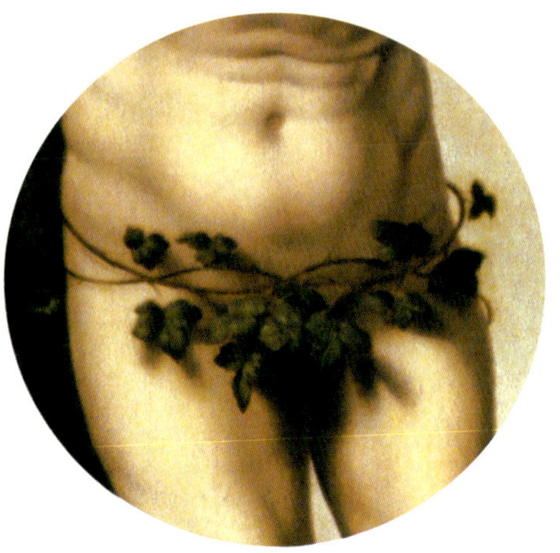

Jan Gossaert, *Adam and Eve*, ca. 1520.

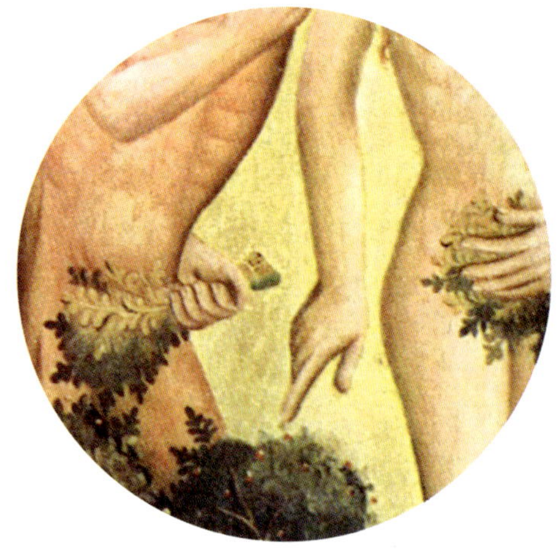

Meister Bertram von Minden, The Grabow Altarpiece, ca. 1383.

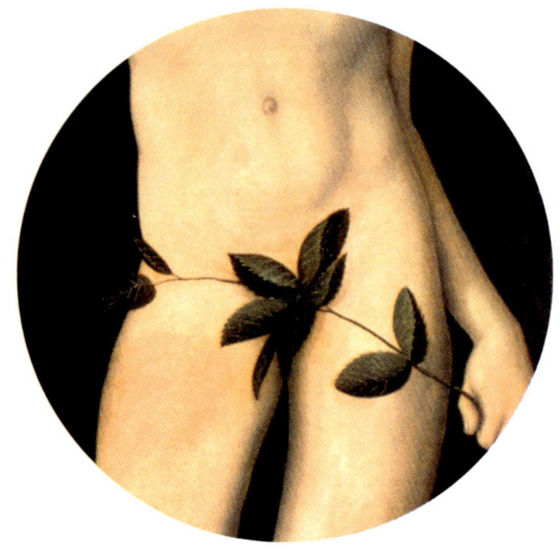

Lucas Cranach the Elder, *Adam and Eve*, 1528.

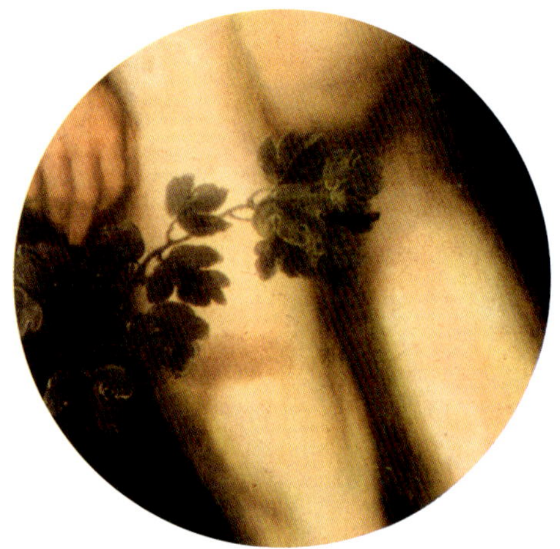

Peter Paul Rubens, *Adam and Eve*, 1599.

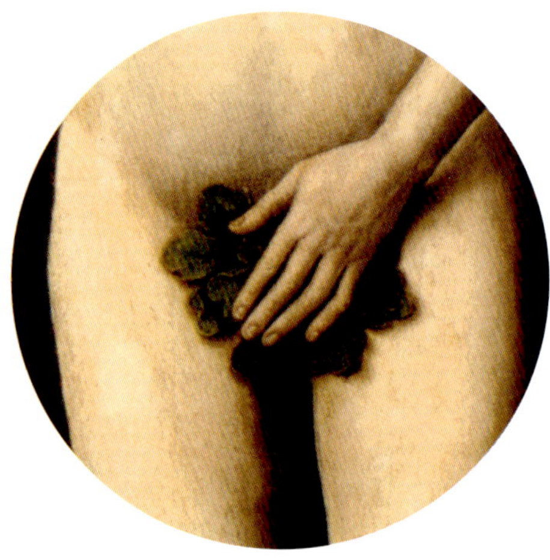

Hans Memling, *Adam and Eve*, ca. 1485.

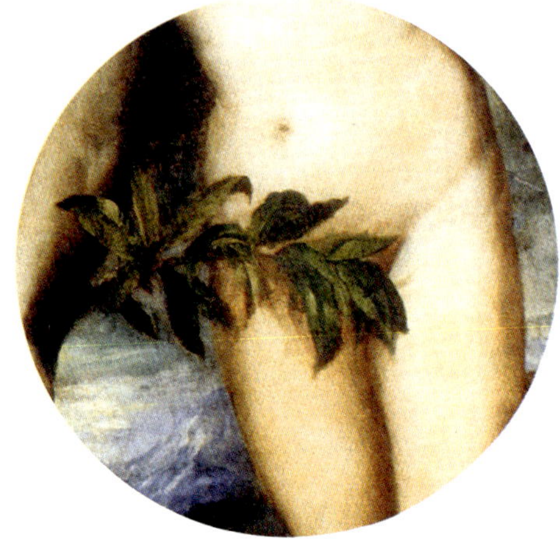

Titian, *Adam and Eve*, ca. 1550.

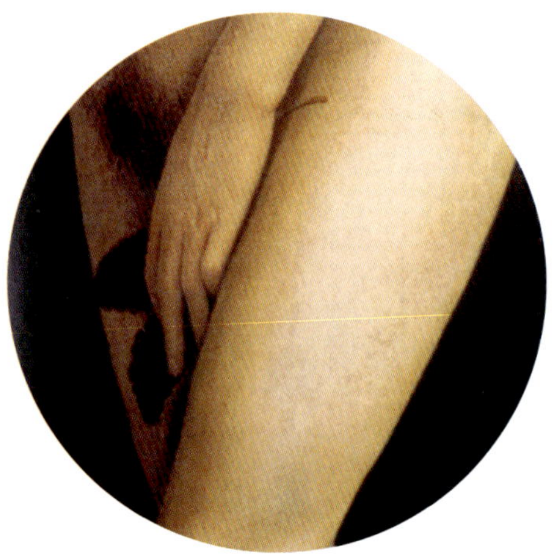

Hubert and Jan van Eyck, The Ghent Altarpiece, ca. 1432.

serpent. The man even suggests that their misery arose from a poor decision on the Lord God's own part: "The woman whom *you* gave."

But exposure cannot really be undone; what is revealed remains, in memory and image, even after it has been re-hidden. The words of the man and woman are transparently evasive. Likewise, the fig leaves merely call attention to what they are meant to hide, and in fact are another kind of evasion, another way of passing the blame, this time not to a creature or Being but to a part of the body, as though the sexual organs acted of their own accord—even though sexuality clearly plays no part in the story, in either its prohibitions or its rebellions. St. Augustine would be fooled by the leaves, and would preach to his congregation: If you want to know where your rebellion comes from, *Ecce unde! Behold the place!*

So shame, which rightly belongs to the rebellious human will, gets deflected to the genitals, and every fig leaf so strategically placed reinforces the deflection. Our sexual organs become *pudenda*, literally "the shameful parts." It's curious that this term is more often used to describe women's anatomy. Consider, for instance, Masaccio's great *Expulsion from the Garden of Eden*: Adam bends forward in grief, his hands covering his eyes—but the eyes of the two, once opened, can't truly be closed—and his penis clearly visible. This is intentional: we see him from the right, with his left foot forward. Had Masaccio placed the right foot forward, our view would have been blocked. But we see Eve's wailing face clearly, because her right hand covers her breasts, her left her vulva, which is partly obscured anyway by her right leg. She and Adam are out of step. Adam's posture suggests that he does not want to see, Eve's that she does not want to be seen, though no one could be looking, as the angel with the flaming sword hovers behind them. Everything in their portrayal suggests that they feel two different shames. Adam's is closer to the Biblical account, Eve's to the Augustinian shifting of responsibility to the genitals, the *pudenda*. If Adam's shame comports with the Genesis narrative, Masaccio's overall depiction seems not to, since we are told that God clothed them in "skin coats" before he dismissed them from their Garden. But Masaccio restores them to the moment they discovered their nakedness, thus telescoping the story, emphasizing the connection between exposure and expulsion.

Some centuries later, one of the Medicis ordered fig leaves painted onto the bodies of Masaccio's Adam and Eve, though presumably not out of a concern for Biblical fidelity. It became common to correct the artists of the Renaissance in this way: some of the classical statuary at the Vatican was similarly covered, and when the Duke of Tuscany presented Queen Victoria with a plaster replica of Michaelangelo's *David* in 1857 (cast from the original), she immediately gave the thing to the South Kensington Museum—now the Victoria & Albert—whose authorities in turn commissioned a fig leaf to give the Biblical hero proper coverage. As V&A documents tell the story, the plaster leaf "was then kept in readiness for any royal visits, when it was hung on the figure using two strategically placed hooks." Today, David has regained his original nudity, but the leaf has been preserved: it sits in its own case just behind the statue, which is a good thing, for the leaf is a fine piece of work, elegantly formed.

We all know, or think we know, about "Victorian prudishness," but even as we smile we should remember to distinguish the link between sex and sin from the link between nudity and shame. The former was not created by Augustine, but he is our primary source for it, and he forged that link so strongly that for many centuries it has been hard to see the nude Adam and Eve without thinking Augustinian thoughts. It might never occur to us that the miserable pair could be ashamed not of their organs' connection with sex but rather with the elimination of waste. (In some cultures this is a far more private matter than sex.) But if we *could* purge all such Augustinian assumptions from our minds, we would still be left, I think, with some discomfort—or, the story suggests, that's what we should feel. How do we experience the nakedness of our First Parents? To take an oddly echoing episode from later in Genesis that clearly has no sexual context: Are we like Ham, the son of Noah, who not only looked upon his father's nakedness as the old man lay drunk in his tent but also told his brothers about it? Do we, like Ham, experience no sense that Noah's nakedness was shameful, no desire to cover him and restore him to decency? Or would we be like Ham's brothers, who turned their heads away as they covered Noah and thereby saved him from further shame? The text says that when Noah awoke he "knew what his youngest son had done to him." We think, *done to him?* What have we done to Adam and Eve by looking upon their nakedness? Yet for his impudence Ham was cursed.

W. H. Auden, thinking of statues and saints, wrote that "The blessed will not care what angle they are regarded from, / Having nothing to hide." But we are not among the blessed; like Adam and Eve and Noah, we have much to hide, much that we would not have exposed. And nudity, while it can stand for many other human conditions—innocence, blessedness, desire—remains our strongest image of that exposure, that shame.

CARA PHILLIPS

I am a naturally small girl, with a very nice, curvy figure (I'm about a size 2 with naturally nice D-cup breasts). However, I have a little fat in my neck and a little in my tummy. I work out, and would like to get that little fat removed. I'm small, so it would look natural.
—Posting from the online plastic surgery forum, beautysurg.com.

In 1907, Charles Miller wrote the first medical text on "beauty surgery." The book provided instructions to combat the signs of aging, including a procedure to prevent expression lines by severing specific facial nerves. The pioneering volume was largely dismissed by the mainstream medical community, which at the time believed that plastic surgery should only be used to correct injuries or deformities. But a review of it appearing in the 1908 issue of the *California State Journal of Medicine* contained a prediction for the future of cosmetic surgery: "This small volume deals with an aspect of surgery remote from the interest of surgeons, but sooner or later featural surgery is destined to take its place as a recognized specialty." Charles Miller's one time "quackery" has evolved into a fifteen-billion-dollar-a-year business in the United States. America's beauty culture is a complex and pervasive phenomenon. Its scope and power can be found in the many cyberspace forums devoted to the subject. On these anonymous message boards, patients share their results, questions, and feelings. The easy access to information has triggered the rapid growth of the industry. In 2006, nearly twelve million Americans had a cosmetic procedure.

When Miller wrote his medical guidebook, modern technology was just beginning to enable us to correct or enhance our bodies. Today, there is a never-ending array of tools and machines to make us beautiful. Patients look in the offices of cosmetic surgeons for the promise of happiness. Instead, they often discover their own fears, self-loathing, and anxieties. In his essay on the purpose and nature of art, Ralph Waldo Emerson wrote: "The best of beauty is a finer charm than skill in surfaces, in outlines, or rules of art can ever teach, namely, a radiation from the work of art of human character." The American Society of Plastic Surgeons' website disagrees: "Even a small change on the outside can create an extraordinary change on the inside, allowing an individual's self-confidence to flourish."

The images on the following pages are taken from a larger body of my work that coincides with a long and personal struggle with body and self-esteem issues. In photographing these doctor's offices, I have been able to conquer many of my inner demons and, in the words of Susan Sontag, make "familiar things small, abstract, strange and much farther away."

page 74: *Beige Consultation Chair*, Beverly Hills, 2008.

page 75: *The Playboy Consultation Chair*, Newport Beach, 2008.

page 76–77: *White Consultation Chair*, New York, 2006.

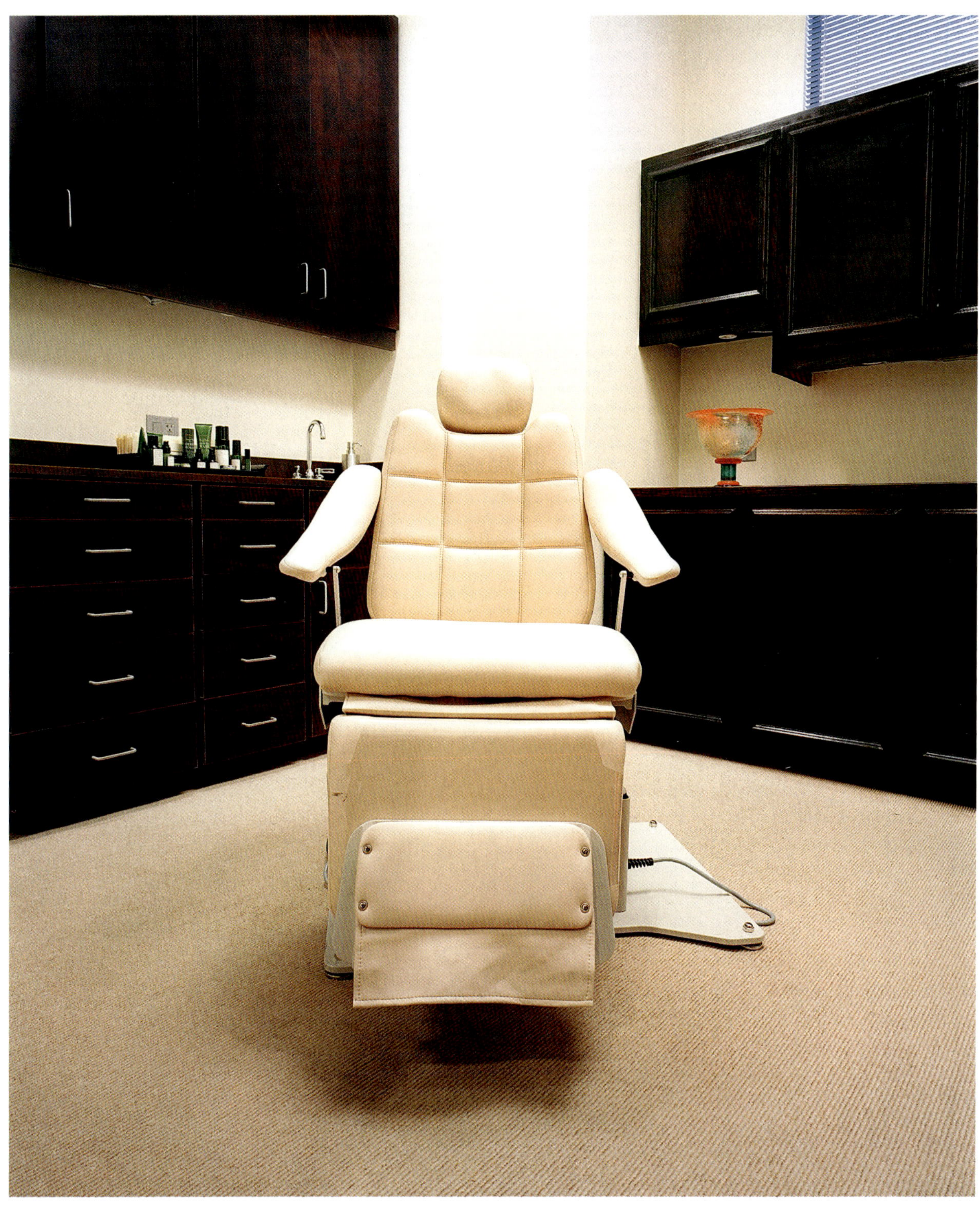

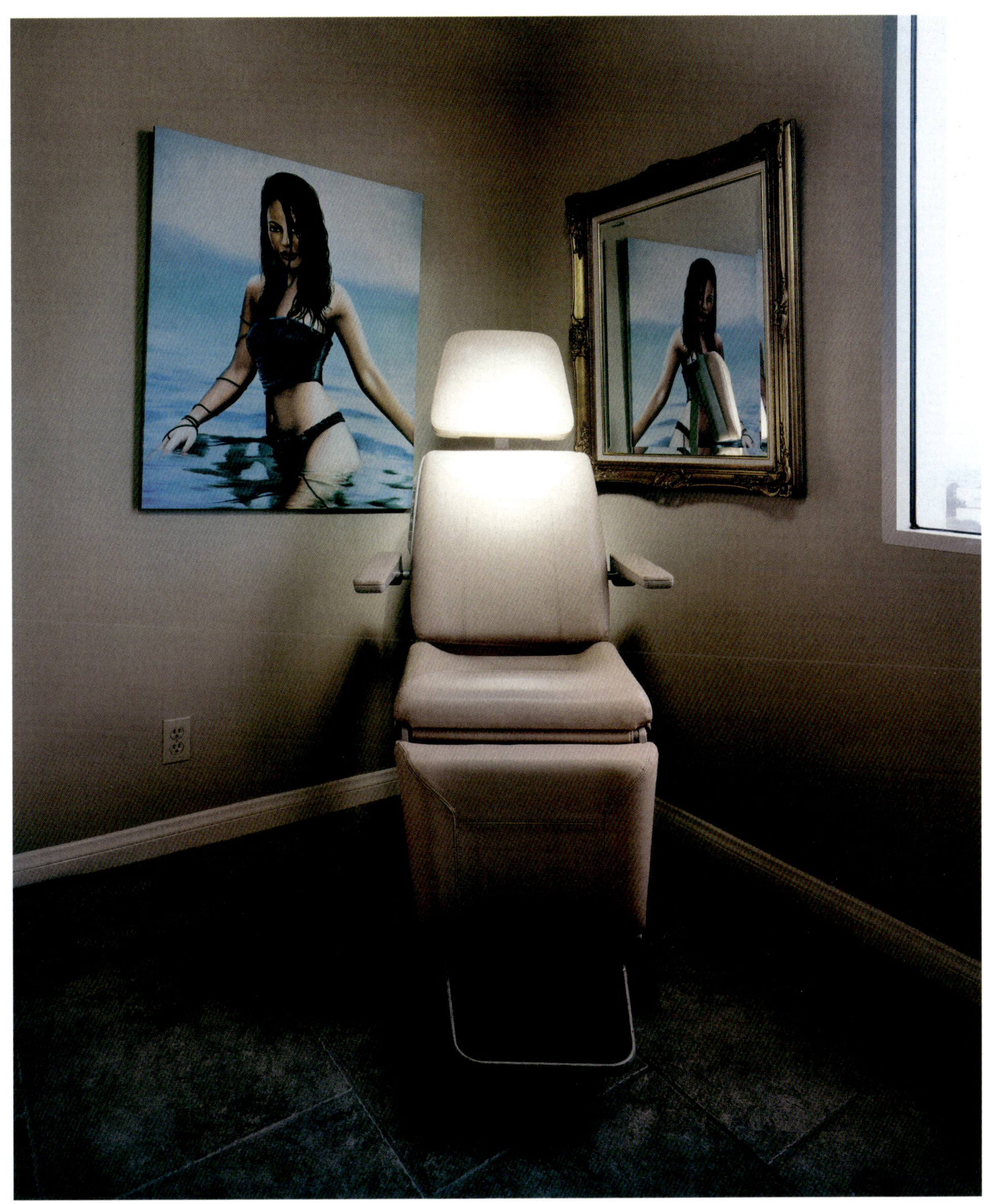

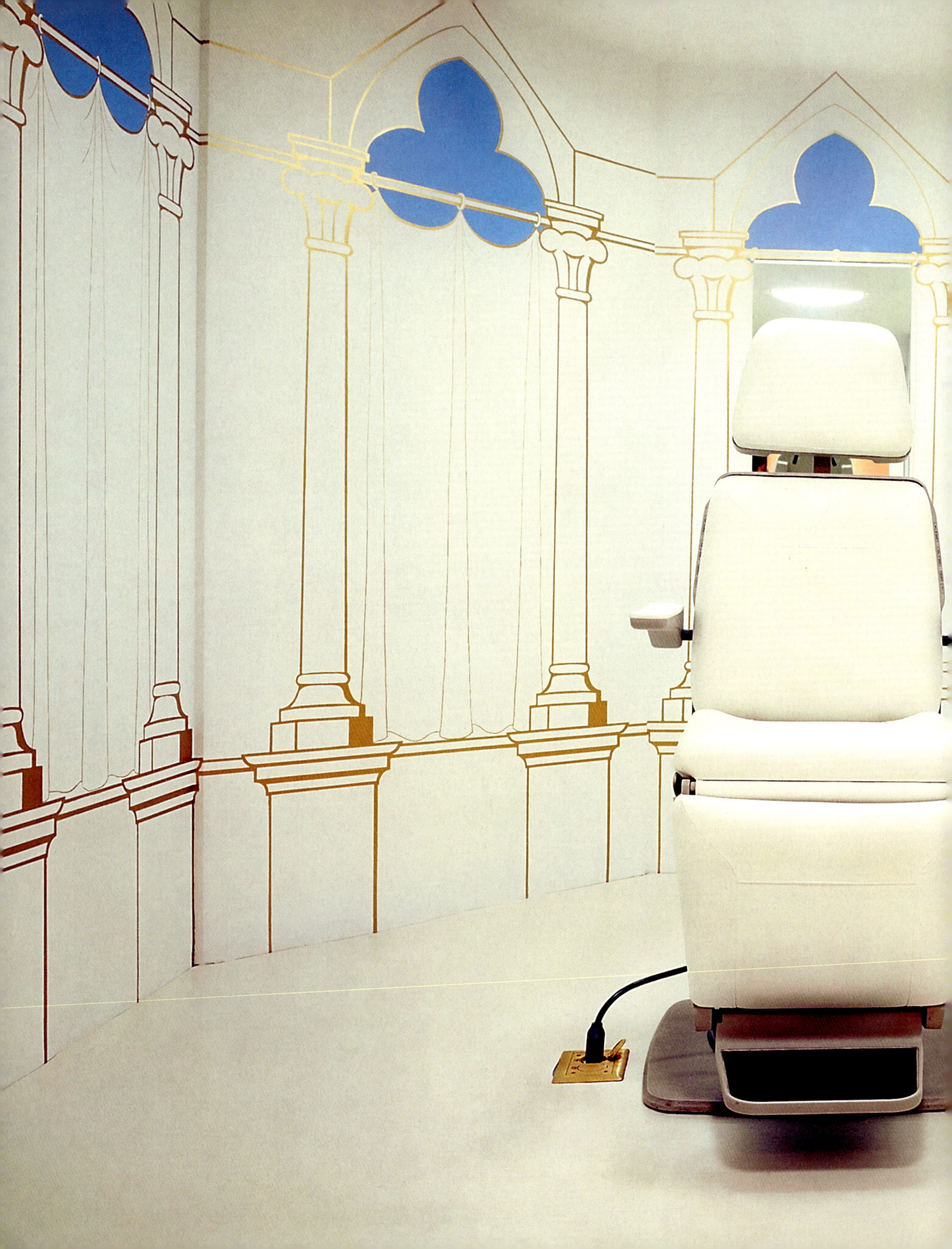

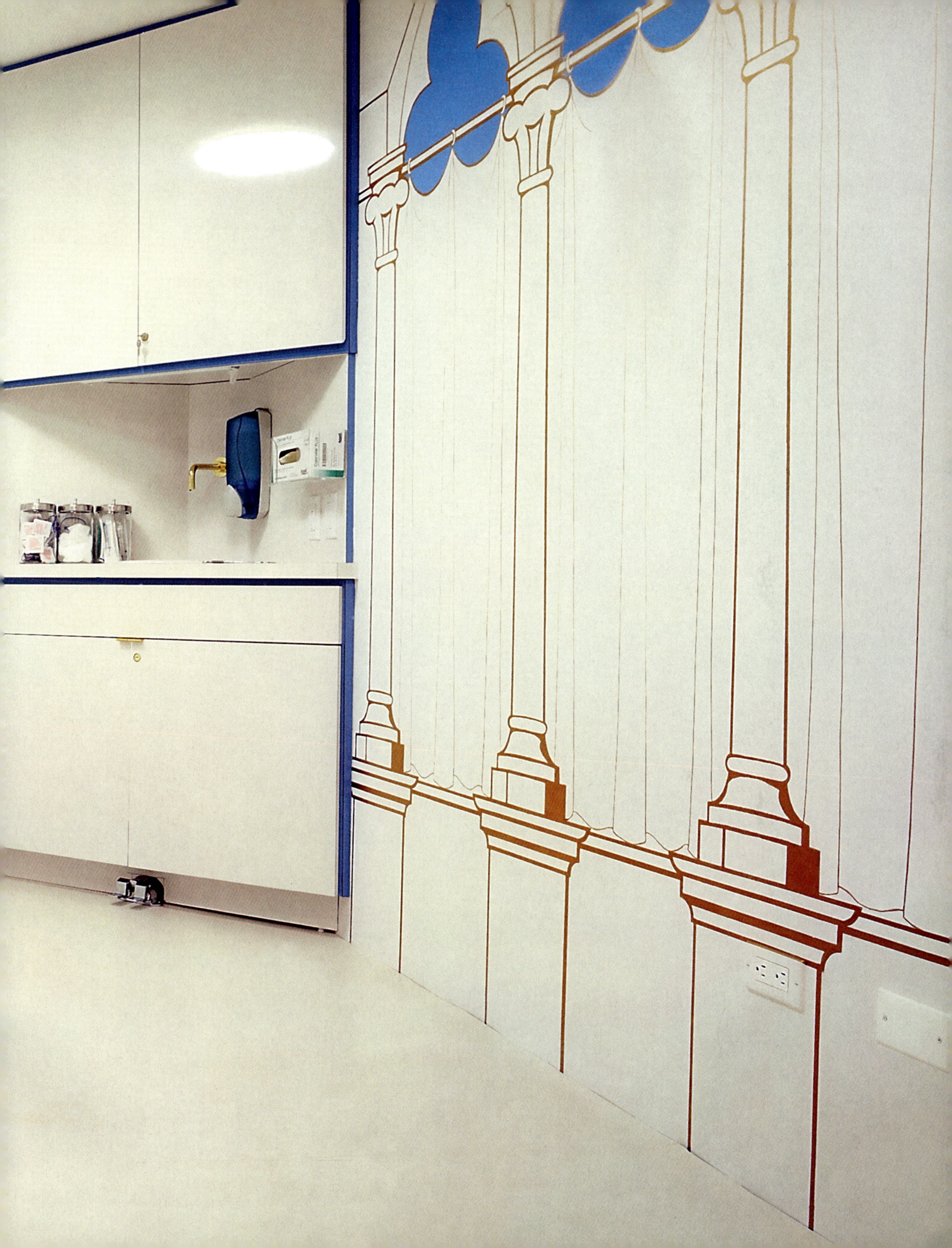

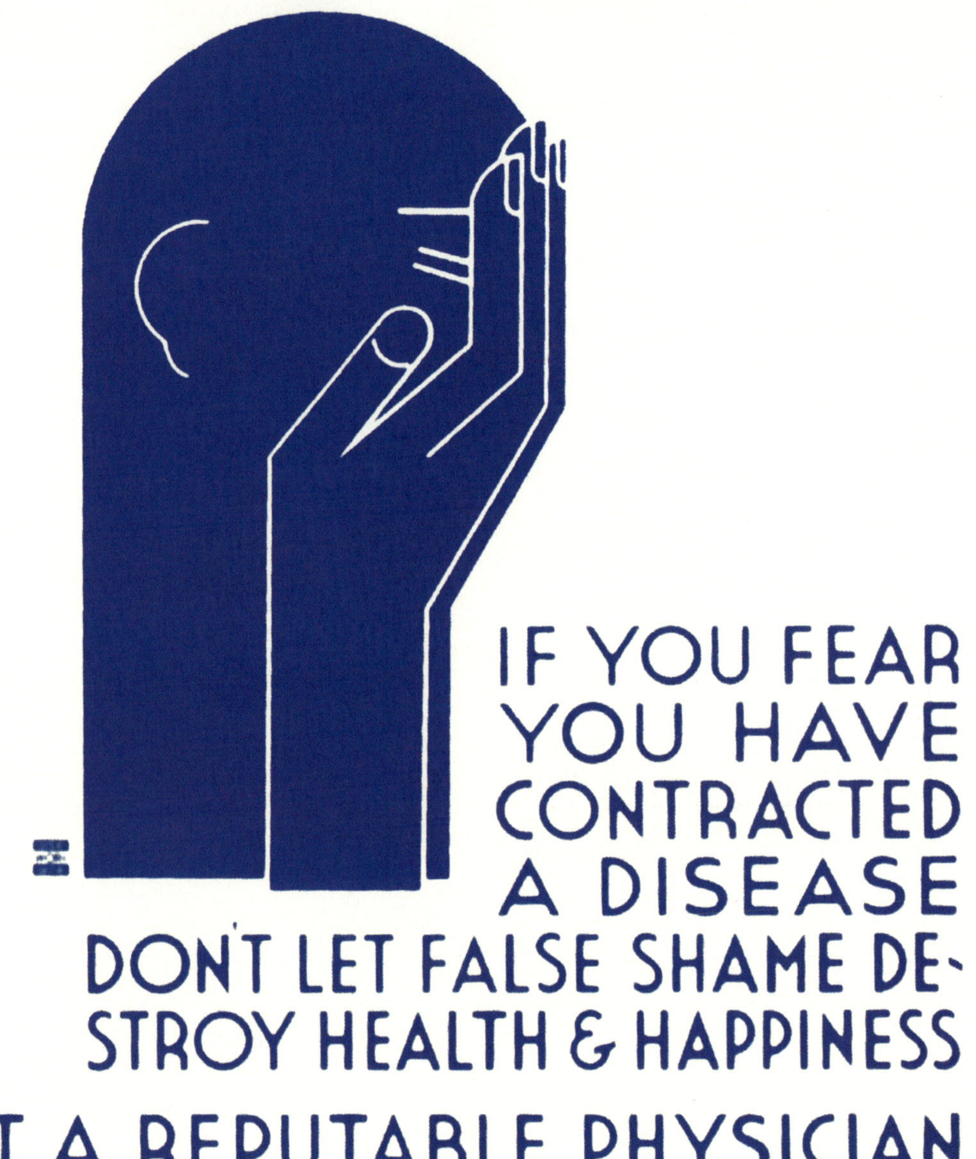

SHAME
MAY BE FATAL
IF YOU FEAR
YOU HAVE
CONTRACTED
A DISEASE
DON'T LET FALSE SHAME DE-
STROY HEALTH & HAPPINESS
CONSULT A REPUTABLE PHYSICIAN

While researching my history of psychoanalysis,[1] I stumbled onto this: the FBI was spying on an European émigré, a socialist, who had resettled in this country. As the Cold War built to a crescendo, the word went out to the local mailman and the neighborhood informants to report any suspicious activity at the foreigner's residence. They did. Every fifty minutes of so, the undercover agents noted, a car would pull up and a stranger would enter the house. Often these visitors looked nervous, as if they did not want to be seen. With bizarre, machine-like regularity, fifty minutes later, the first person would exit from a side door, while another would enter from the front. If the two guests ever crossed paths, they ignored each other and acted like there was something to hide. Again and again, all day long, this dance repeated itself. What furtive messages were being passed on in that home?

Like that exile, I traffic in secrets. We are both doctors, in our cases psychiatrists, who have sworn ourselves to a code laid down in the fourth century BCE. While forgoing any allegiance to "Apollo the Physician and Asclepius and Hygieia and Panaceia and all the gods and goddesses" as was initially demanded, my graduating medical school class agreed to abide by a central tenet laid down in the Hippocratic oath. "What I may see or hear in the course of treatment or even outside of the treatment in regard to the life of men, which on no account one must spread abroad, I will keep to myself holding such things shameful to be spoken of."[2] While this oath changed over time, its ethic of discretion persisted. In 1100, Constantine the African wrote that a doctor should "keep to himself confidential information containing the ailment, for at times the patient makes known to the physician things that he would blush to tell his parents."[3] Others went so far as to suggest that physicians should not employ assistants, for fear these helpers might break this sacred vow.

And so, for over two millennia, doctors have been receptacles for matters of body and soul that their own society found obscene.[4] Doctors hear of silent plagues, strange growths, acts of self-destruction and abjection, terrifying family legacies, sex of all sorts, crushing poverty and neglect, betrayals and violence, addictions, madness, bodily decay, and news of impending death itself. They are our everyday concerns.

The moment of revelation is familiar to me: a sudden pause or a faint blush, and a patient's face closes in thought. After some effort, he forces his way outward to disclose perhaps no more than the existence of some unspeakable subject, a private matter that might bring humiliation or a hail of stones if told in the village square. All doctors confront these critical junctures where public shame and medical necessity collide. And as Hippocrates understood, in these moments, propriety can be deadly. Old, mysterious Hippocrates, whose works are mostly a collated mish-mash of murky origin, this mythic father of medicine, established an ethic that overrode gossip, law, religious belief, and social morality, so that a physician might more fully enter into the lives of his patients. Physicians were obliged to keep their mouths shut, so their patients might not die of shame.

But what happens to the medical journeymen as they pass back and forth between the private and the public, and absorb so much their own community deems disgusting or reprehensible? What did old Hippocrates' simple commandment do to his own people?

Some can not bear the brute contradictions they have been forced to witness and reach the conclusion that it is not their patients but their society that is sick. Consider the French physician, novelist, and Fascist sympathizer, Louis-Ferdinand Céline, whose jaundiced eye focused on one brutal social sham after another, or the German doctor and writer, Alfred Döblin, whose brilliant *Berlin Alexanderplatz* exposes his society's rituals as insane, perverse, and hateful. Over the last century, revolutionary movements have often attracted disillusioned medical students and doctors, from Che Guevara to Ayman al-Zawahiri.

Of course, the overwhelming majority of Hippocrates' heirs simply become masters of forgetting. A kind of double-consciousness emerges during medical training, a mental lock-box for the working day in which social codes are replaced by the ideals of cool objectivity and scientific knowledge. This other room begins to be built in the first semester of medical school, when students undergo their shocking initiation in anatomy lab—cutting open faces, penises, and breasts. By the time young doctors treat their first patients, they have developed a different frequency on which to hear "symptoms."

In this register, the secrets themselves no longer even surprise. As patients step gingerly into my office, they are often convinced that they have a hidden mark that if discovered would make them outcasts. What they can't quite imagine is that in offices around the world, at the very same moment, similar confessions are being heard. When I was a novice, a psychiatry professor once stunned me by saying there really were only a

---

dozen or so "secrets." When a patient told him there was something he had never told a soul, it wasn't too hard to guess its nature.

However, even if people in the same culture hide the same things, I am interested in the fate of those untold stories, which involves not just their content, but the way these pieces of intense interiority crystallize so much else. In its earliest incarnation, psychoanalysis sought to liberate pathogenic secrets, but it soon became clear that confession alone was not enough. Secrets were not just sick-making; they were woven into the fabric of our being and helped color and construct our subjective worlds. Our interiority itself was a parade of concealed thoughts. I vividly recall my first recognition of this simple fact. I was perhaps five, and kidding around with my parents in their bedroom, when to avoid some perceived reproach, I blurted out a lie. I was confident my mother would, as always, gaze into my glass head and see that these words were untrue. She said nothing. Stunned, I locked myself in the bathroom and stared at the cold porcelain tiles on the walls. Ashamed and confused, I now faced a totally unforeseen dilemma. And for the first time in my life, I felt the loneliness, the weight, and the power of having a mind that was constantly humming and hidden.

In our era of massive health databases and managed care, patient confidentiality is at risk. What, we have been forced to ask, is this ethic worth? As our societies shift toward a global inter-connectedness, perhaps we will have no need to remain so hidden. A friend who was going through a divorce dreamed of such a utopia. As she worried that her doctor's notes would be requisitioned by the court and made available to the press, she wondered what it would be like if everyone gave up this game, and loosed their private lives into the public arena. Perhaps we would all be more charitable, and no longer act so dismayed by the clandestine things humans think and experience. Or maybe we would need to create new secrets to symbolize all that remains unspeakable in our subjective worlds, that private inner realm that must be anti-social by its very nature, and yet thanks to Hippocrates, can be safely shared with a select few, so that our shame does not kill us.

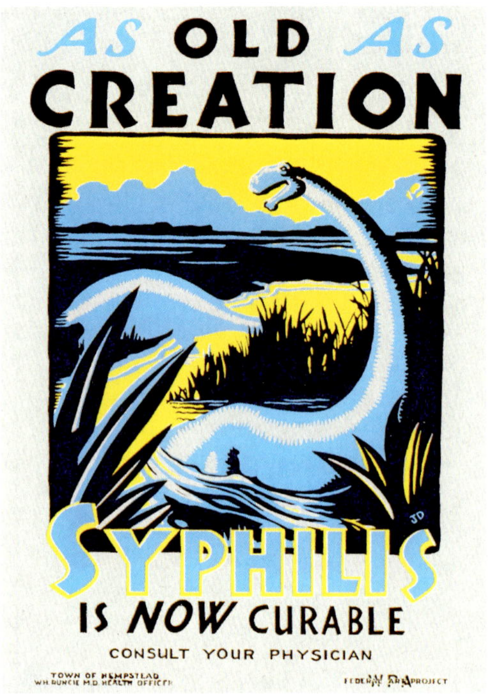

Poster designed for the WPA Federal Art Project, artist unknown, 1937.

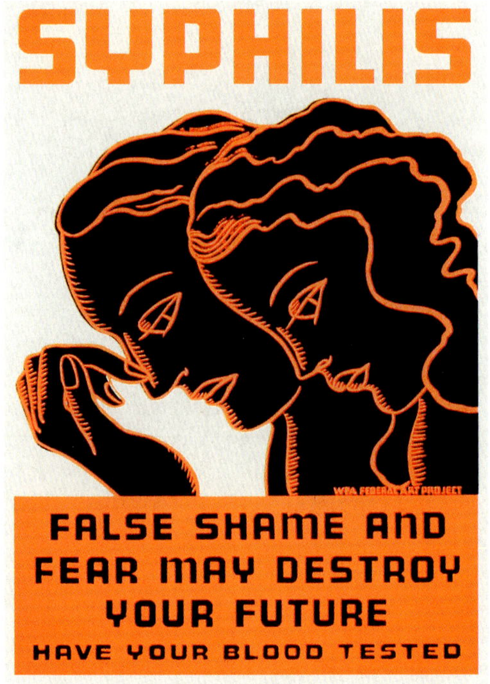

Poster designed by Erik Hans Krause for the WPA Federal Art Project, 1938.

1 George Makari, *Revolution in Mind: The Creation of Psychoanalysis* (New York: HarperCollins, 2008).

2 I have cited the 1943 translation of the Hippocratic Oath by Ludwig Edelstein, as reprinted in Loren C. MacKinney, "Medical Ethics and Etiquette in the Early Middle Ages: The Persistence of Hippocratic Ideals," in *Bulletin of the History of Medicine*, vol. 26, no. 1 (1952), p. 31.

3 Ibid., p. 27.

4 See Steven H. Miles, *The Hippocratic Oath and the Ethics of Medicine* (Oxford: Oxford University Press, 2004).

According to psychologist Silvan Tomkins, the child experiences shame when the object of desire, for example the mother, does not reciprocate and breaks the circuit of attachment. This leads to an emotional disorientation in which the child internalizes disconnection, thus creating the conditions for embarrassment and self-loathing. Many cultural theorists have adopted the notion of the "broken circuit" as a way of examining how specific social relations could shame members of marginalized groups and determine their experience as shamed subjects. But does the breaking of the circuit—some form of emotional disconnection—necessarily lead to self-loathing?

Lauren Berlant, the George M. Pullman Professor of English at the University of Chicago, has written extensively about the relationship between affective investments, practices of sociability, and questions of citizenship and community. For her, the self-loathing that we typically associate with the concept of shame is only one of many possible outcomes of the "broken circuit." Sina Najafi and David Serlin spoke with Berlant by phone in July 2008.

When did contemporary cultural criticism begin grappling with the category of shame?

In terms of charting a *contemporary* genealogy (i.e., one that doesn't look to Erving Goffman's *Stigma* (1963) or the modernist ethnographic convention of nominating shame and guilt cultures), we might begin with Eve Kosofsky Sedgwick's *Epistemology of the Closet*, published in 1990, which asked questions about the relationship between socially marginalized identity categories and modes of psychological or affective subjectivity. In Sedgwick's rephrasing of margin-center relations, populations that were associated with non-normative modes of life—in this case, queer and non-normative sexualities—were deemed to be shamed populations. I want to say something precise about what her revisionary operation entailed. What Sedgwick was saying was that a structural social relation—enacted by stipulated and administrative laws and norms—was *shaming*. She was adapting an affective language to a political analysis. At the same time, the shame of being deemed a member of that population was said to produce a shamed *subjectivity*, which meant a subjectivity that felt a lot of shame.

This particular arc of thinking about shame is probably related to St. Augustine's claim that sexuality is at the center of the subject, that sexuality is definitively shameful, and that shamed sexualities produce shamed subjects who then have to negotiate life from a perspective of already being fallen and unworthy. Foucault criticized the model of sexuality that posits it as the subject's truth, of course. As for Sedgwick, I think that this spreading mimeticism around shame (oppression works through shaming, and produces subjects organized by shame) is a very controversial claim about persons. At the time her ideas were first circulating, it was not deemed controversial but incredibly emancipatory, because they proposed an affective structure for a political relation. It explained how it would be possible to think of the structural subordination of a population in terms of an emotional map of the very identities of the people who were being named by it.

I wouldn't want to misrecognize the interest in shame as only coming from *Epistemology of the Closet*, however. There was also a lot of feminist work on interrupting sexuality as the site for the reproduction of gendered shame that is never acknowledged enough. Angela Davis, Gloria Anzaldúa, Shulamith Firestone, and Pat Califia, for example, had long been busy trying to invent ways of thinking about how sexual shame is actually a powerful register for trying to understand what it means to be identified, or not identified, with the normativity of a nation. Yet it was also incredibly dramatic for Sedgwick—and Judith Butler, too, but Sedgwick especially—to make a claim that what looks like a political structure is fundamentally an affective structure that forms our subjectivity. I don't think it can be overestimated how big that shift was, but it was also a shift that came out of a long discussion.

How does Sedgwick's work fit within explorations of shame by psychology?

In the mid-1990s, Sedgwick and Adam Frank recovered the work of psychologist Silvan Tomkins (1911–1991) and reintroduced it for scholars interested in the concept of shame. Following Tomkins's work, Sedgwick and Frank describe the experience of shame structurally as the experience of a "broken circuit" of attachment and desire that ought to circulate between the subject and its treasured object. (Their presumption, I think, is that one can make demands for reciprocity on both persons and worlds.) So if somebody has a form of longing that gets attached to a person or world, the moment of shame is when the person/world breaks its relation of reciprocity with the subject. For Tomkins, shame occurs when a child experiences the refusal of their attachment. When the child looks away because it feels that it's been refused or rejected by its mother, that is the exemplary moment of shame.

In my own work, I argue that the feeling of the world withdrawing from you and therefore throwing you back on yourself *could* be described as shame, but that says nothing about the *experience* of it. The broken circuit could also involve anger, numbness, hunger, a desire to self-stimulate, a compulsion to repeat, the pleasure of a recognition, grief, and/or curiosity, and these wouldn't merely be defenses against the impact of the pure feeling of shame, but actually different responses to being affectively cut off.

Although the *structure* of shame for Sedgwick and for Tomkins isn't necessarily aligned with the *experience* of shame, much work by scholars using shame as an analytical category assumes that the structure and the experience of shame are always aligned, that the broken circuit would be *felt* as shame, a shame we would recognize as the conventional emotion. But this is a mistake, and I think it occurs because the language of emotion often produces a sense of generality and transparency that enables things that aren't very like each other to seem as if they are. So, let's ask again: what does it mean to shame X? Is de-shaming X the same thing as de-repressing it? If I used to be ashamed of my queerness and had to produce defenses around that shame, does delaminating shame from my queerness also emancipate my sexuality? Is that emancipation the same thing as being shameless? Is de-shaming queerness the same thing as having pride? (This is what the Gay Shame movement is always asking.) My point is that I want our discussions of affect and emotion not to presume their clarity, coherence, or intensity of drama, nor to see them as *grounding* the subject for better or worse in an identity or a social population. The leveling effect of biopower (everyone in the shamed population is alike defined by the shaming quality) is not lived *a priori* coherently or homogeneously. But that's an empirical question.

For you, is this incoherence productive or counterproductive?

What's not productive is when people aspire to an explanation of a social relation through the fantasy that the emotional event tells a simple, clear, visceral truth about something. One way my claims revise Foucault's is that I think emotions, and not sexuality, are what took up the place as the "truth" of the modern subject. What we understand as sexuality was one among many scenes of installing conventionality in the people who were defined according to projections about their capacity to manage appetites and affects. So if I say I'm a "shamed subject," that represents me as someone who is grounded by my own emotional self-understanding. On the other hand, this concept of myself as affectively simple makes me seem more open to change. If only! Also, if my shame is to represent injustice, then my lack of shame should represent justice—and you know that's not true, because shamelessness can be a bullying mechanism or a defense too.

Negative political feelings provide important openings for measuring injustice but their presence or absence isn't really evidence of anything. I might be a bourgeois who thinks that the world owes people like me who work hard an unprecarious life that will add up to something, too, but then my sense of injury isn't objectively a measure of injustice. It's a measure of wounded privilege. This is why I work against the idea that emotions actually ground you somewhere in true justiceland. Emotion doesn't produce clarity but destabilizes you, messes you up, and makes you epistemologically incoherent—you don't know what you think, you think a lot of different kinds of things, you feel a lot of different kinds of things, and you make the sense of it all that you can. The pressure on emotion to reveal truth produces all sorts of misrecognition of what one's own motives are, and the world's. People feel relations of identification and revenge that they don't admire, and attachments and aversions to things that they wouldn't necessarily want people to *know* that they have.

It's part of my queer optimism to say that people are affectively and emotionally incoherent. This suggests that we can produce new ways of imagining what it means to be attached and to build lives and worlds from what there already is—a heap of conventionally prioritized but incoherent affective concepts of the world that we carry around. We are just at the beginning of understanding emotion politically.

In your article "Unfeeling Kerry," you discuss how John Kerry lost the 2004 election in part because of his shame over and subsequent disavowal of a certain part of his own life, namely his post-Vietnam protests against the war, which he imagined rejected his previous patriotic behavior as a soldier in Vietnam. You argue that the electorate was not comfortable with the lack of unity in Kerry evidenced by this shameful disavowal.

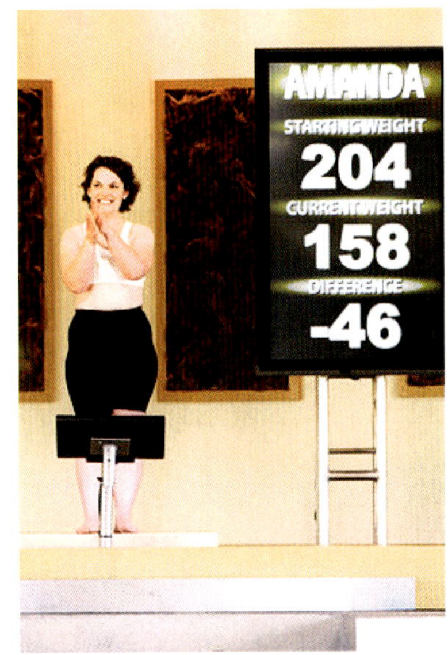

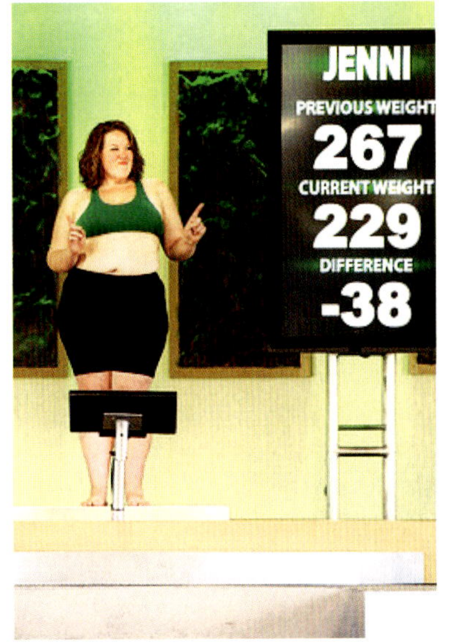

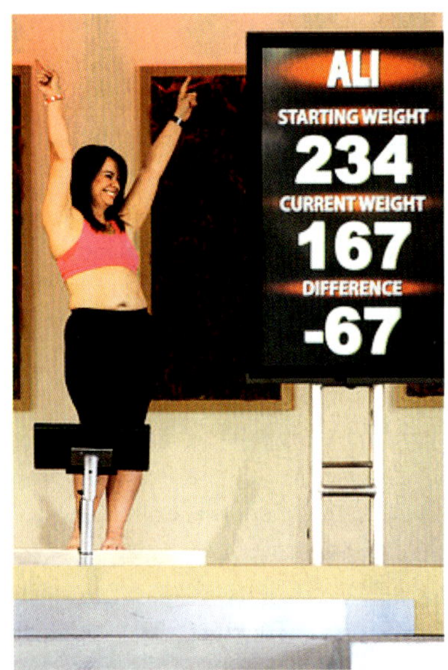

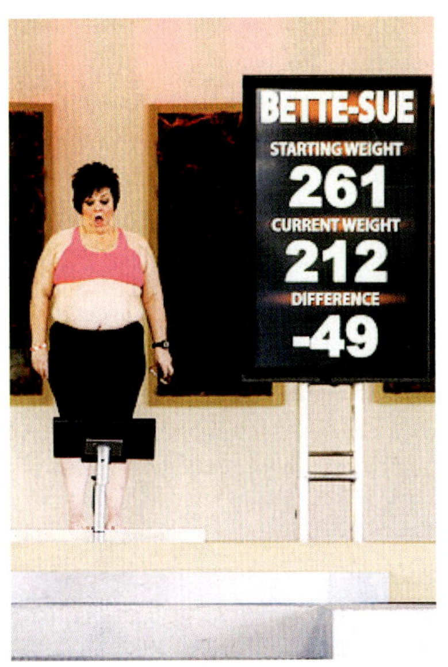

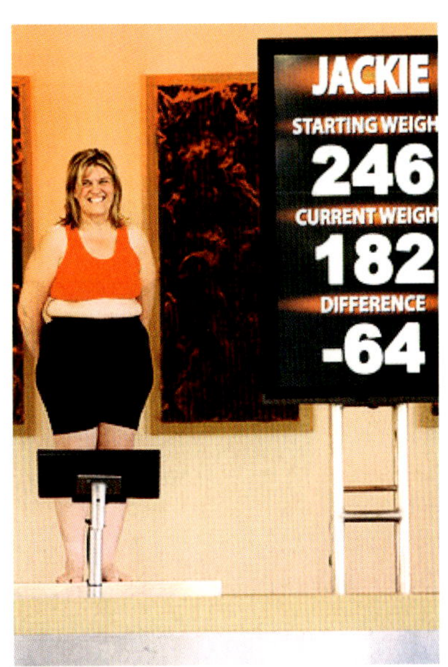

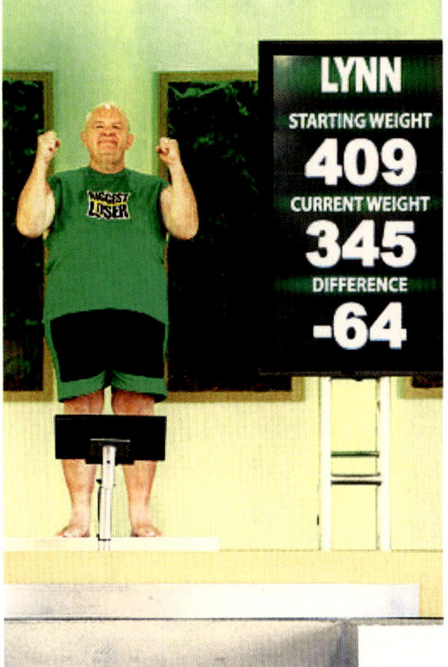

Stills from NBC's reality television series *The Biggest Loser*.

That essay argues that one of the things that people are purchasing when they decide to go with their "gut feelings" about a candidate—a phrase about affective discernment that has wide currency now from Malcom Gladwell and Stephen Colbert to Gerd Gigerenzer and George Lakoff—is some sense of whether the candidate is affectively intelligible to them at all. So what Bush represented—it was totally fictive, but he's a good actor—was a coherent masculinity at ease with itself, whereas Kerry represented an incredible disavowal of the magnificent performance of sovereignty and freedom from the need to be respected that he manifested at the end of the Vietnam War. As a candidate he had to pretend that he had just been a good soldier all along. Maybe he was a good soldier all along, but that wasn't the point. The reason that he was worthy of respect wasn't that he was a good soldier; it was that he used the knowledge that he gained in Vietnam actually to break with the system.

He was what Foucault might call a specific intellectual.

Exactly. And when the system tells you it doesn't respect you, you owe nothing to it and can make yourself free. That sounds kind of hokey, but it's an important lesson about possible responses to the broken circuit other than trying to reason with it, convince it, be a good teacher of it, re-seduce it, or be pragmatic in a depressive collaboration. Anyway, Kerry was proud of his freedom after the war, and then during his presidential run he had to pretend that all along he was conventionally patriotic, when actually he had been interfering with the terms of the reproduction of patriotism itself.

We are interested in pursuing shamelessness. Are you?

Not so much, because I am in the middle of working through an almost antithetical theoretical problem about sensing the historical present. It's a kind of proprioceptive history about the present as a relatively affectively formless space: this project articulates models of affect management (anxious attachment disorder and the like) with Lacanian conceptions of fantasy that see life as a comedy of misrecognition and the Deleuzian project of fomenting potentiality as the subject's undoing. In contrast, shamelessness is structured as a moment of clarity within normative frames. But for you, I'm game!

You may be asking about shamelessness as a political end and as a political tactic. These are two different things. As a political end, I want the end of erotophobia, the fear of sexuality as such that produces so much shaming pedagogy around it. As a political tactic, shamelessness is the performative act of refusing the foreclosure on action that a shamer tries to induce. Stop masturbating, you idiot! But if I act shamelessly, I also might be daring you to shame me again, and come to love the encounter with shame. This shapes the hyperbolic spaces of outraged shamelessness in the right-wing media. Bring shame on, they say, we're shameless; so give us your best shot!

Shamelessness as political tactic might also perform freedom in the way I described before, the freedom to give up getting legitimacy in normal terms. This may be what people respond to in Barack Obama: there are things that he feels strongly about that he's not interested in justifying to anyone. Obama's claim is a pretty sentimental, practically contentless formal claim about "America" as the name for the possibility of a social world, not one made of individuals but one that's fundamentally collective, interdependent, and politically self-organized. He uses civil society language to say that people should understand themselves and act fundamentally as members of a public. He's claiming that to commit to the process of an active debate within a field of solidarity is what's best about politics, and that the idiom of policy is practically another scene altogether. So he doesn't care so much when people don't like his particular political decisions. He's more invested in the process of fomenting publics that desire the political. It's a pretty shameless strategy, in the sense that he is refusing the normative ideological contracts that have shaped mainstream politics over the last 40 years.

Could one identify shamelessness, then, as an affect of neo-liberalism?

No, I wouldn't go there at all. I mean, think about civil rights actions. Look at, for example, the class/biopolitics of the distribution of composure. Whose forms of self-regulation get legitimated, whose forms of self-regulation are ways of going under the radar, and whose forms of self-regulation are in-your-face messages? For example, you go and sit at a lunch counter where you're not allowed and you refuse to act as though you shouldn't be there. And it freaks everybody out because you're not having the affect that they need you to have in order for them to be outraged by it. So I think that shamelessness doesn't always have to be exuberant or confrontational. It can be a form of the performance of composure in places where people don't expect it.

We often think of shamelessness in its most outrageous manifestation.

That's the problem in working on emotion—people always imagine it hyperbolically and melodramatically. The structure of shamelessness doesn't necessarily involve in-your-faceness. It can involve any frank refusal to produce the affect for you that you need someone to have in order for you to feel in control of the situation of exchange. It is to take control over the making and breaking of the terms in which reciprocity will proceed, if at all. But it doesn't have to be *big*. What often happens when you refuse to provide affective security for people is that they fall apart, get anxious, and start acting out, often not knowing why. The affective event of performative shamelessness initiates, therefore, the potential for unraveling normative defenses. On the other hand, people often thrash around like monsters in that situation, not having skills for maintaining composure amidst the deflation of their fantasy about how their world is organized. Take the whole question of academic gentility, for example. How does the fear of being shamed, exposed, or losing face foreclose potentiality (resistance, creativity) in any kind of workplace, and what is the relation between public and cloaked forms of control? Collaborative institutions are like big reality shows, theatres of emotional performance in the guise of something else.

Speaking of which, what role do you think reality TV programs play in making visible the culture of shame?

In my work, sentimentality operates when emotions communicate authenticity that enables identification and solidarity among strangers. It doesn't only mean that if I cry on screen you feel sad; it also means that if I'm exuberant on screen, you feel exuberant, too, or if someone humiliates me on screen, you might not only feel *schadenfreude*, but you might also take pleasure in my survival. When I talk in general about sentimental culture, it's a scene of emotional transmission that reveals the affective intensities of the everyday by showing what's overwhelming and providing a gratifyingly simplified distillation of experience. So in that regard, reality TV is an extension of sentimental culture rather than its opposite. We're used to thinking that sentimentality is about the risk of sociality and the need to survive suffering, but narratives about this can take place in many idioms—comedy, irony, romance, satire, and other genres of intensity with a pedagogical edge.

I don't watch a lot of reality TV, but I have seen something recently that interested me—*The Biggest Loser*, which I had a student working on so I had to watch, and I wept while watching it, because people are so shockingly naked on it. This show is the only place in America where you get to be a loser and it's a good thing. In a larger sense, it's about managing people's feelings of loss everywhere. But this show is also about a culture of shamed appetites, and in that sense it's also about contemporary sexuality.

With shows like *Survivor*, you have the other problem of getting voted off if you're too good at the game, so it's also about strategies of mediocrity, about staying below the radar. That's also really interesting. On *The Biggest Loser*, people actually cry when they vote a friend off because he or she was too good at the game. Therefore reality TV is not only about dramas of humiliation and victory, but about other forms of networking and collegiality in which you don't try to be extra great—you just try to be competent so you're perceived as reliable.

Being normal is a nervous place, because you can never finish performing your relation to it; on the other hand, being comfortable is also another way of thinking about what normativity provides, because if you can pass as normal then you can scoot under the radar. The whole question of how you lubricate the social never stops being difficult, and it never stops being a matter of shame, because when one confronts one's ambivalence and incoherence one feels in a bad faith relation to the model of ethical solidity we expect from ourselves. But what if we just trained ourselves to accept that all of us are incoherent, subject to a variety of aversive and connective impulses that we are always managing? The social then would be a totally different space of intimacy and anxiety.

ARTIST PROJECT / UNTITLED

AMY CUTLER

The characters depicted in Amy Cutler's meticulous drawings inhabit a world where internal emotional states are physicalized—where anxieties and obsessions are expressed in uncanny physiological mutations, improbable costumes, austerely mysterious settings, and often indecipherable individual and communal behaviors. The flat, affectless expressions worn by Cutler's women (and they are almost exclusively women) are strategically inscrutable: they can be read to suggest either a disregard for the gaze of those who view their compulsive ritual activities or a pervasive sense of shame related to this exposure, a shame whose effect has deadened their countenances as it has eroded their spirits.

page 87: Amy Cutler, *Rations*, 2002.

page 88: Amy Cutler, *Safe Keeping*, 2005.

page 89: Amy Cutler, *Elephant Ferries*, 2006.

Photos by Jeffrey Sturges. Courtesy Leslie Tonkonow Artworks + Project.

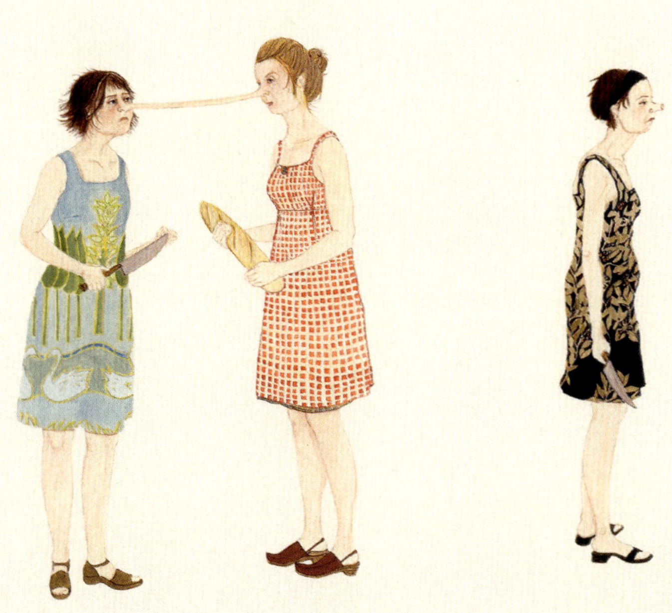

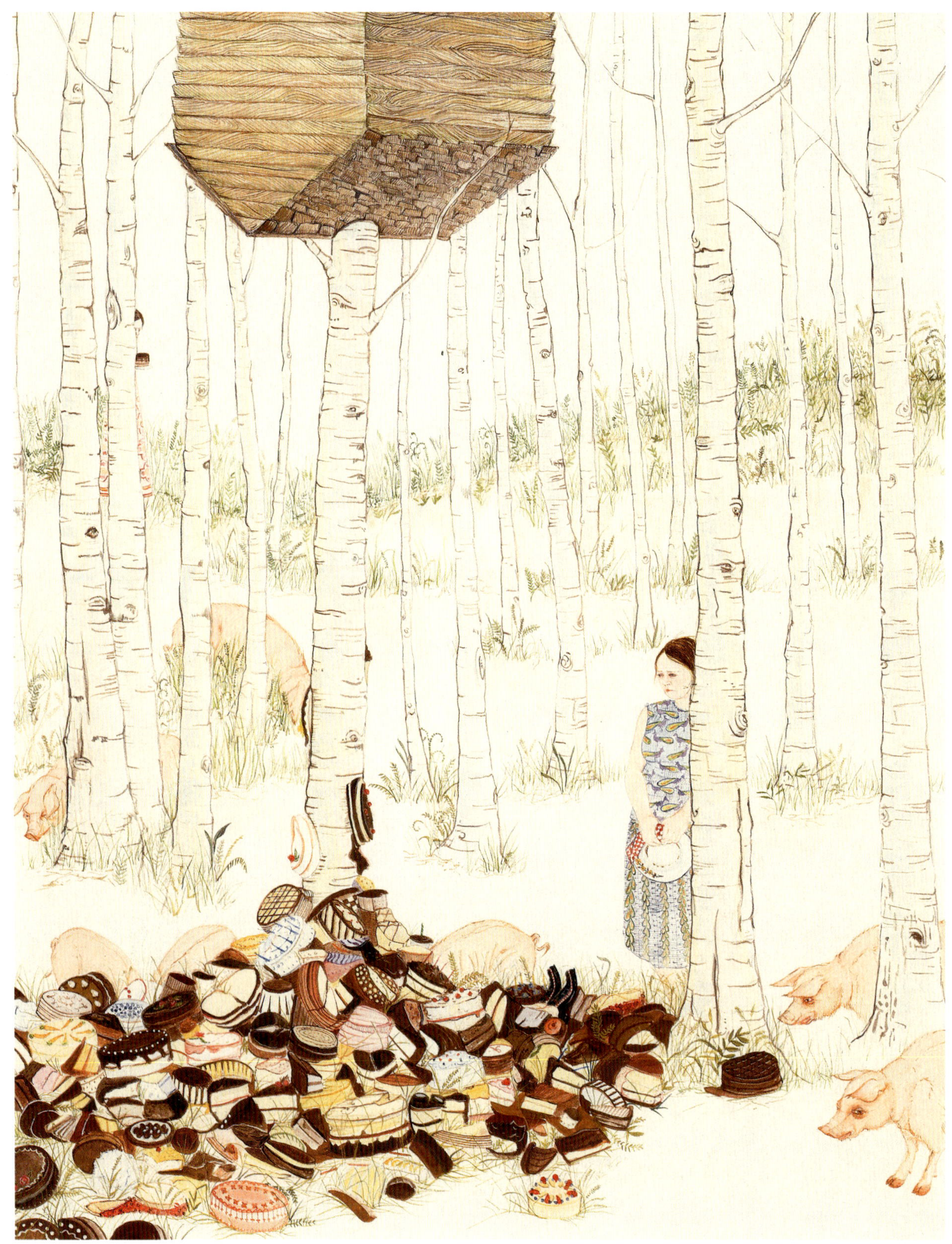

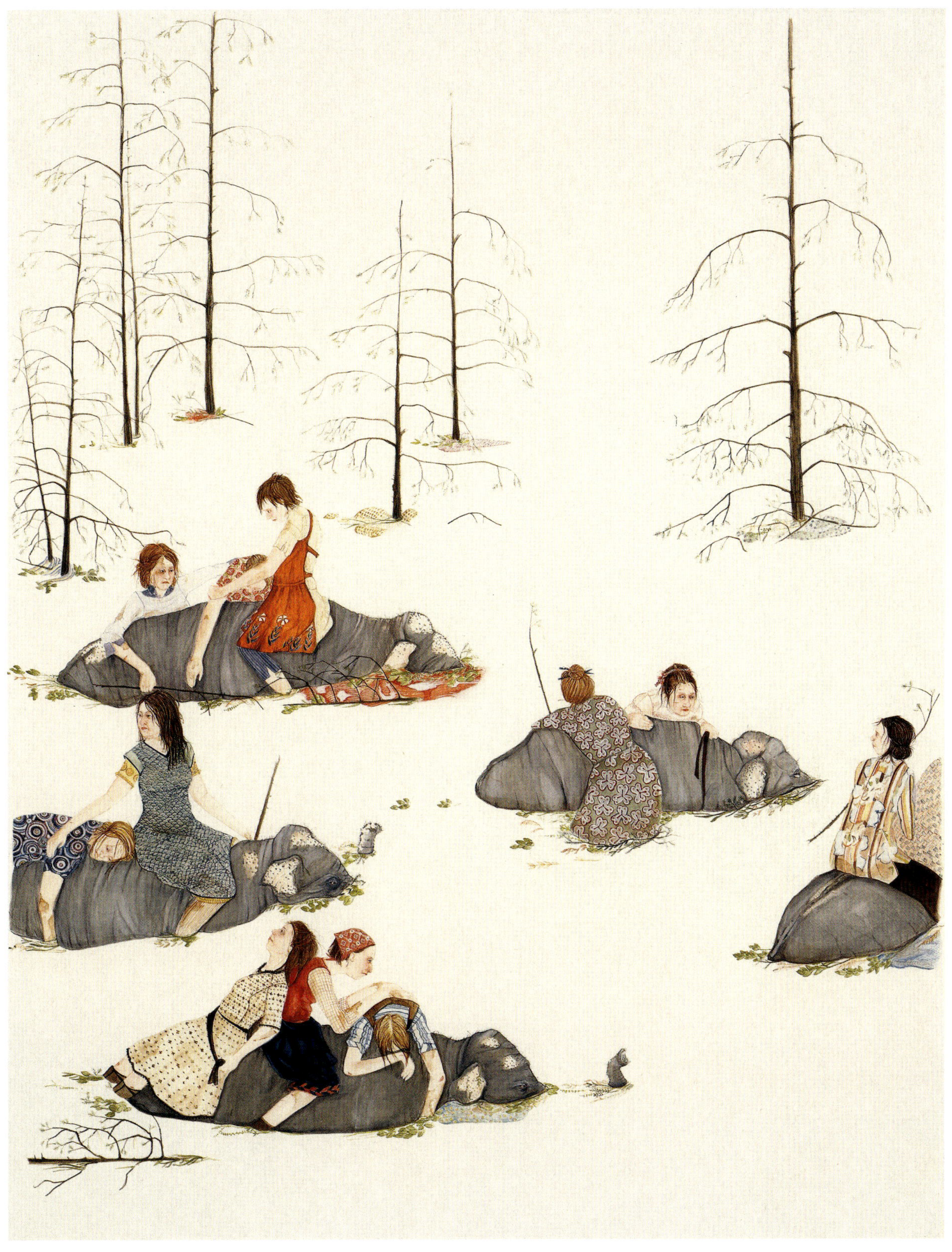

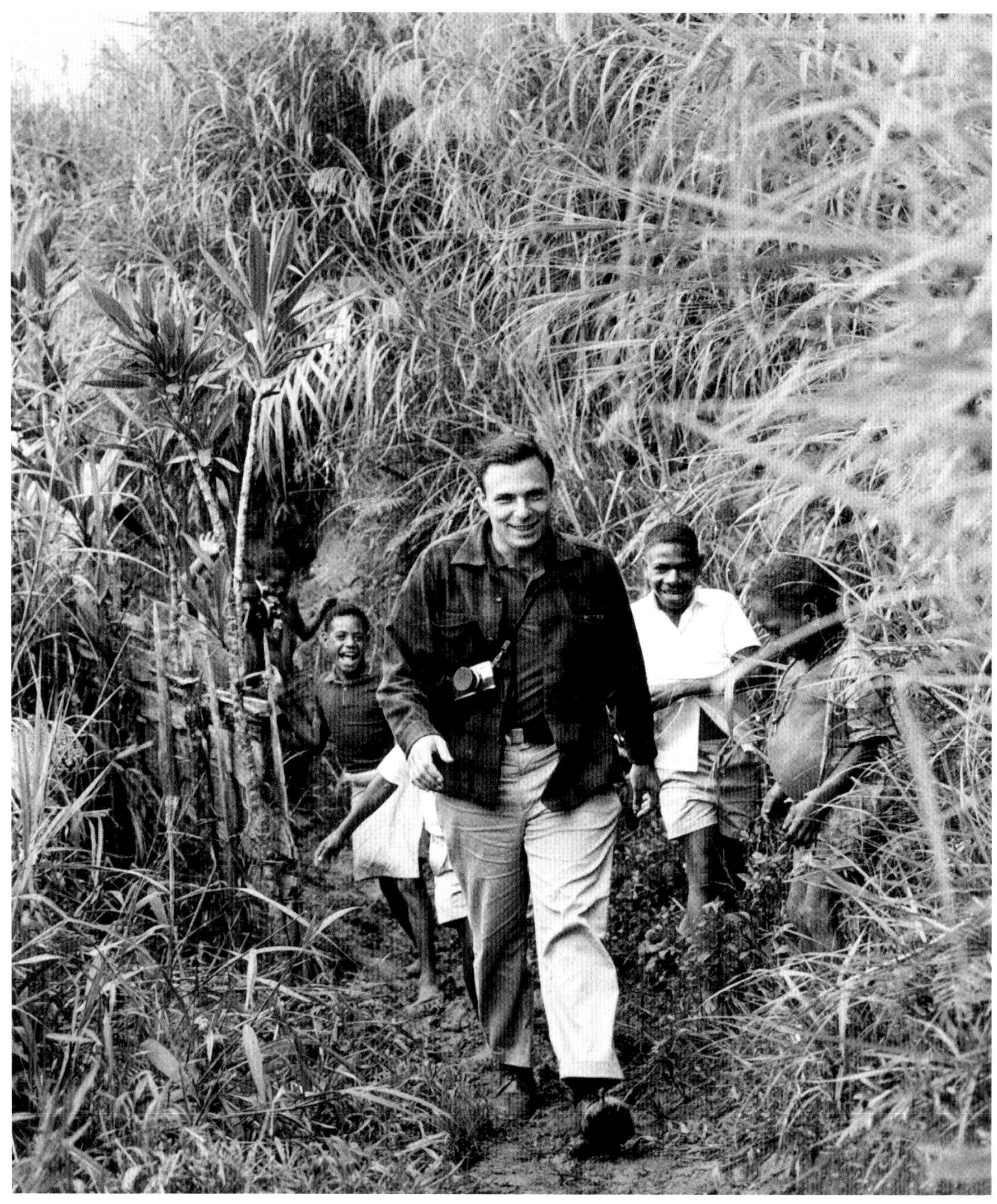
Paul Ekman in Papua New Guinea, late 1960s. Courtesy Paul Ekman.

SHAMEFACED: AN INTERVIEW WITH PAUL EKMAN

CHRISTOPHER TURNER

Thirty years ago, Paul Ekman, who runs the Human Interaction Lab at the University of California, San Francisco, co-published the Facial Action Coding System (1978), a 500-page catalogue of 3,000 "meaningful" facial expressions that is used by organizations as varied as Pixar and the CIA. Ekman is the world authority on facial expression, about which he has since written numerous books, including The Nature of Emotion (1994), What the Face Reveals (1997), Face of Man (1980), Telling Lies (1985), and Emotions Revealed (2003). He is currently working to help the Department of Homeland Security identify "expressions of immediate deadly intent" with CCTV systems, and, before he met with Cabinet in New York, he had just spent a week in Washington DC coaching government employees in the subtleties of the human face. The seventy-four-year-old psychologist sat down to talk with Christopher Turner about shame, blushing, lie-detection, his research in the jungles of Papua New Guinea, and his work as a counter-terrorist consultant.

How and when did you come to study facial expression?

In the mid-1960s, the Defense Department, of all things, got caught doing research that it shouldn't have been doing, and it had to get rid of a lot of money quickly. By accident, I bumped into the guy with the job of distributing it, and he awarded me a grant. He was married to a woman from Thailand and thought that the problems in their marriage had to do with her misunderstanding his expression and gestures.

At the time, there were two schools of thought concerning expression. The psychologist Silvan Tomkins followed Charles Darwin in thinking that expressions are innate and universal. Darwin had written in *The Voyage of the Beagle* that when he met the Fuegeans, a wild people, he couldn't understand what they said but he thought he could understand their emotions. The anthropologist Margaret Mead, on the other hand, thought that a smile meant a totally different thing in another culture, that it's a symbolic, totally cultural product. She showed that in some cultures people smile at funerals, so clearly a smile represents grief in some places, whereas it means happiness in others, and she therefore concluded that expression is a purely cultural product. She thought that any agreement about what expressions mean was a result of cultural contamination, of people watching the same movies and TV shows.

It was clear to me that the way to settle the issue was to find a people who had had no contact with the outside world. In 1967 and '68, I went to Papua New Guinea, and spent time in the jungle there with one of the few surviving stone-age cultures. I would show them photographs—they'd obviously never seen photographs before—and ask them to make up a story, to tell me what happened before and after the picture was taken. They did it because I would give them a bar of soap or a cigarette, and they like both.

The next year I went back, and this time, to refine my results, I told them a story and asked them to choose a picture depicting the expression that best represented that story. I returned a hero; I had left a lot of audiotape that I'd not used and they had woven it into jewelry—it was all over, they loved the audiotape. And I was a respected man because they had said that if I died, they would eat me, and they only ate people they respected.

If expressions are universal and innate, what is the expression for shame?

As best as I can determine, shame doesn't have its own signal. And neither does guilt. They're very hard to reliably distinguish from the family of emotions: sadness, disappointment, grief, discouragement, and anguish. It's not that I think shame and guilt are the same; it's just that they are the same in signal. Now, if I was an evolutionary psychologist, I could make up a story as to why shame wouldn't have evolved its own signal. The last thing you want when you're ashamed is for others to know you're ashamed, because if they discover it, they will be disgusted with you. Guilt is about an action: I can undo guilt by confessing, by doing penance of various kinds. You can excuse guilt. But disgust is about the person. And you're never going to forgive me if you really are going to be disgusted—you're going to want to get away from me. Shame is a response to prevent the other person's disgust, and there is a lot of self-disgust intermingled with that shame.

Can you say what a sad expression, the expression you describe as most closely related to shame, would be in terms of the Facial Action Coding System, in which you assigned numbers to the forty-three muscles of the face, and itemized which are used to create a given expression?

Yes, it's a one-four-six-fifteen, sometimes with a slight seventeen. There are 10,000 combinations of facial muscles that can occur, of which about 3,000 I have identified as meaningful. And we've catalogued all of them. It's amazing that, before my study [co-authored with Wallace Friesen], people didn't know the answer to the question of how many different expressions a human being can make. It's as if nobody had climbed Mount Wilson; it's there, how could you not know it? The face is so interesting.

There are certain muscles that are much harder to activate than others, even for someone practiced like me. When we were codifying the expressions, I often had to ask a surgeon in the anatomy department to stimulate my facial muscles with a pin in order to verify that I was actually moving the muscle I thought I was moving, because the muscles lay one on top of each other. I'll show you one expression that's very difficult—Woody Allen does this all the time [Ekman contorts his eyebrows into an angst-ridden circumflex]. Most people can't do it.

Can I do it? [The interviewer attempts to make the same face.]

With a mirror, you'd be able to learn to do it. You're on the way. Now you have to learn to stop blushing! There is a great chapter on blushing in Darwin's book on expression [Ekman edited the third edition of Charles Darwin's *The Expression of the Emotions in Man and Animals*, 1872]. He doesn't use the word *embarrassment*. Embarrassment is very interesting. The seven core emotions—anger, disgust, fear, joy, sadness, surprise, and contempt—have a snapshot expression; cameras can capture them easily, but you can only pick up embarrassment if you can watch someone over a series of three to five seconds. It's not a snapshot. Of course there's blushing, and as Darwin pointed out, blushing is not shown in every race of mankind; blacks blush but you can't see it. There is no other emotion that you can't see on blacks but you can see on whites.

Darwin also wrote that blushing was a kind of veil of love. He connected it with piety, and with shame. He cited a Chinese expression, "to redden with shame." What role would blushing have in relation to shame?

One of my big arguments with a lot of psychologists, linguists, and anthropologists is that words are representations of emotion and it's very hard to represent the same emotion precisely with the same word in different cultures. There are emotions like *schadenfreude*, which

Germans have a word for, and we don't. Does that mean we don't enjoy the suffering of our enemies? No, we just don't have a word for it. Tahitians don't have a word for sadness or grief, but you'll see the same pattern of behavior occur in the same social context. So one has to be very careful not to be misled by words, particularly when they are translated from another cultural setting. That's why in the field I prefer to use stories than words. When I ask someone how they would respond to the death of a healthy male child, I know there isn't a culture I could go into where they wouldn't understand that idea, and they'll associate it with a particular expression.

Now, is shame related to embarrassment? Darwin said, and there's no reason to question it, that embarrassment is caused by undue attention to the self. It can be caused by flattery; you could say, "Oh, what a smart young fellow you are," and it gets you to blush. With a woman, if she's a blusher, just tell her how attractive and beautiful she is. But shame is really, in my thinking, something you ought to hide.

Darwin does say that a man who feels thoroughly ashamed at having lied can feel thoroughly ashamed without blushing. But if he's detected, if he's suspected of having lied by someone he respects, he will blush.

He's wrong. I have an article, "Darwin, Deception, and Facial Expression," in which I review the six sentences in Darwin's expression book where he talks about deception. Most of what he writes is wrong. It's interesting, but it's wrong. I've done a lot of original research on that question, and people who are ashamed don't blush.

He's almost trying to distinguish, I thought, between shame and guilt, because he connects blushing with shame. He says that if you feel guilty before God, if you're very religious, and you feel that God is omnipotent and watching you all the time, you won't blush. So blushing is a signal of shame and not guilt.

I don't think that's right, either. It's nice that Darwin was wrong about a few things—in the *Expression* book he was working with mainly anecdotal rather than observational data. If you look at his other major works, he relied upon an enormous amount of raw data, but in the expression book all he had were the responses to the photographs he sent to various correspondents around the world. And, regrettably, he fed them the answers he wanted to know, which is not the right way to proceed.

I've spent a lot of time studying serious liars, that is,

ones who could lose their freedom if they get caught, or certainly their reputation, or their job. One can lie about almost anything. If you take the example, which is the one I use most often with police, that you suspect someone of being a child rapist, there's a reasonable likelihood that most child rapists are ashamed, and they are concerned that you'll be totally disgusted with them if they admit it. So what you want to do is shift them from shame to guilt, because when you're guilty, you can expiate it, and if you confess and say how sorry you are, even go to jail, you can make up for it and get a clean bill of health.

How can someone steer a person from shame to guilt by observing facial cues?

You don't need the facial cues at all. You just need to understand shame and guilt. You say to the suspect, "You know, the way those mothers dress up those little girls in those sexy outfits, I mean, I've had those fantasies too, I haven't acted on them, but I could understand how, in a moment of weakness—I mean, they're just trying to get you to feel sexual about those little girls, they shouldn't do that. And if you tell me about it, you're going to feel a lot better." As long as there's shame there, let me tell you, you'll get a confession if you shift it to guilt.

That's interesting, because psychotherapists often talk about the shame/guilt cycle, and how to break it, how to stop shame turning into humiliated fury or whatever. For Freud, shame is a reaction-formation and a defense against excessive pleasure, against libidinous feelings. Silvan Tomkins talks about shame in that way in his book *The Faces of Shame*. He says that shame is deployed to diminish interest and excitement when it would be socially unacceptable. Do you think that's true?

I don't know. It seems to me unlikely that that's the only source of shame. Tomkins was a philosopher, but he was psychoanalyzed according to Freudian analysis. You can see a little Freud in there, which doesn't mean it's wrong, but is that a sufficient explanation of all the circumstances in which shame occurs?

Do you think the face never lies?

No, it lies all the time. It lies more often than it tells the truth. But micro-expressions, the very fast signs of concealed emotion that occur in 1/25th of a second, never lie. Most people miss them. But we are, much to my surprise, learning that we can teach people to recognize

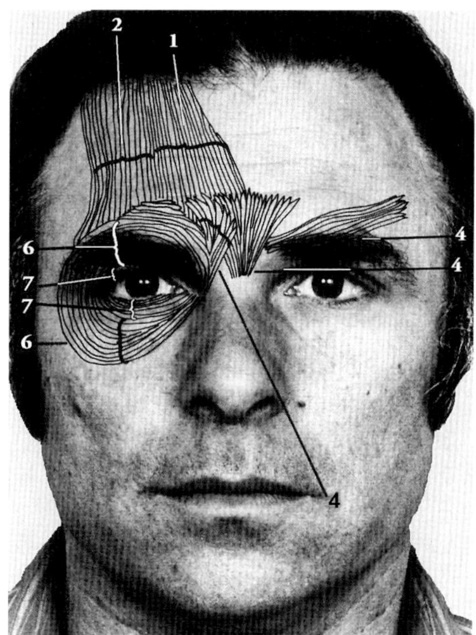

Charting the muscles underlying facial actions (AUs), here in the upper face. AUs 1 & 2—inner and outer parts of the *frontalis* pull the medial and lateral parts of the forehead skin up; AU 4—combination of *corrugator, procerus,* and *depressor supercilii* pull the brow down and together; AUs 6 & 7—outer and inner parts of *orbicularis oculi* raise the cheek around the eye and tighten the eyelid. Image from a revised CD-ROM version of *Facial Action Coding System* by Paul Ekman, Wallace Friesen, and Joseph Hager.

them very quickly, even after an hour of training. People find out what I do at a party or something and they say, "Oh, you can read my mind." I can't read your thoughts, I can't know what triggered your emotions, but I probably know what you're feeling even if you don't want me to know. Because the face reveals it in a number of ways, probably in a micro-expression that you can't prevent. Most people won't see it, but I will—I've learned how to see them.

How has having that skill changed your life?

Sometimes I know more than I would like to know, but you can't turn it off. It's like when you learn to read music, you hear music differently. You'll never hear it like you heard it before you could read music.

My methods are now being used by everybody from Procter & Gamble to the State and Defense Departments: the primary thing people want to be able to understand using my techniques is what another person is feeling. I teach non-coercive methods of interviewing and surveillance of public places. Whether the person you're talking to is a witness, an informant, or a perpetrator of something that's already happened or is about to, you're never going to get them to cooperate and open up to you unless you know how they're feeling.

For example, even second-generation Japanese rarely maintain eye contact with someone who's an authority. That doesn't mean that they're lying; it's just that they're being respectful, and we teach people to be aware of those sensitivities. There are also feelings that the other person is having that they might not even know they're having. One of the interesting things about a micro-expression is that it occurs not just with deliberate concealment, but it occurs with repression. And so you could see on someone's face an emotion they're not aware they're feeling. They may not ever become aware of it, but you may be able to take a counter-move and better guard how you talk with them.

And what are your boundaries? Do you worry that your teaching might ever be abused?

I get inquiries from the Chinese, the Iranians, and the Syrians on how to use my work, which I don't respond to. I can't know everything our government is doing, both because it's too vast and because I don't have a security classification, but, in the last three days, I've met people from secondary agencies who are using my work and they're telling me they want to use it more because they feel they're having such success with it in catching, as they put it, bad guys, people who are perpetrating crimes.

When you hear about interrogation techniques in Abu Ghraib and things like that, doesn't that make you worry about the possible abuse of your system?

I think that's the result of not teaching people effective non-coercive techniques— the chief ringleader of that business, where they were putting ropes around inmates' heads and photographing them, was fired from his old job as a prison guard for abusing prisoners. And then they sent him to Abu Ghraib. He's now in jail. The tragedy in my mind, the big tragedy, is that we're not preparing people for the job we're giving them. I can go on and on about that, but it's not my area. I do worry about the misuse, but I operate on the assumption that the more we understand about each other, no matter what our context is, the better off we are. And although there will be occasions where that might not be the case, the side of the sword that facilitates mutual understanding is a sharper side than the one that facilitates exploitation.

Why wouldn't you teach CIA officers to be better liars?

I don't run a school for liars. I run a school for lie-catchers. And there are multiple reasons for doing that. One is, I don't want more lying. I think it just makes the system noisier. I've been asked to train political candidates to make them more electable. I'm not going to do that, even if I like that candidate and want them to win. I don't want to further distort the system. I won't do jury selection for the same reason. Crooked lawyers do use my methods for jury selection; I'm opposed to such attempts to try and defeat the system by creating biased juries. There's a second reason for not running a school for liars and that is, it probably won't work. I know I can teach people to catch liars, but I have serious doubts if I can make people better liars unless they're already natural actors. If they want my help, it's probably because they're pretty bad to begin with.

Why do you think your job exists? Why are we so bad at decoding the expressions of others?

We don't always want to know the truth. Do you want to find out that you've hired someone who's embezzling from your company? Do you want to find out that your children are using hard drugs? Do you want to find out that your spouse is cheating on you? This is the Chamberlain phenomenon. Chamberlain wrote, on the night after his first meeting with Hitler, "I could tell from the look on his face that he'd be telling me the truth." And, of course, Hitler was lying as deliberately as he could—the order for the mobilization for the invasion of Poland had already been given. He just wanted to be sure that he caught everyone with their pants down, and it didn't take long for Chamberlain to find out the truth. Most of us want to put off bad news. Why? The truth can be painful and you often avoid it.

It must be hard for your family not to succumb to the panopticon effect and feel that you're permanently invading their privacy. Even if you don't see it, they'll think you have.

No, I think they really think I miss these things. I don't make much use of it, because that's not my job as a spouse or a parent, unless I see something that's really troubling. And with my daughter, I'll almost always say, what are you upset about? For years they think they've gotten away with things because I haven't said anything about it. I think they feel more relaxed than they should.

NOBODY HOME
RENATA SALECL

Capitalism brought dramatic changes to the character of funeral rituals in Slovenia. In the past, bereaved family members usually visited a state-run funeral home where they selected from among several basic funeral services and a couple of different coffins or, in the case of cremation, caskets for the ashes. Today, the ritual more often resembles a shopping experience and one that provokes feelings of shame. When the bereaved visit a funeral home, they now must make decisions about numerous details as to how the funeral ritual will be conducted.

Most of these decisions concern objects that will either never be visible or will be immediately ruined. If, for example, the deceased will be cremated, the family needs to decide how elaborate and expensive the coffin used for cremation will be. Then they need to decide how much to spend on the casket in which the ashes will be stored. This casket will later be buried underground. In addition to determining how extravagant the casket will be, other things to consider include flower arrangements at the funeral, musicians for the service, and even the size of the announcement to be placed in the daily newspaper.

Why it is that such a shopping experience provokes shame? When making choices in front of the salesperson in the funeral home, one has the feeling of

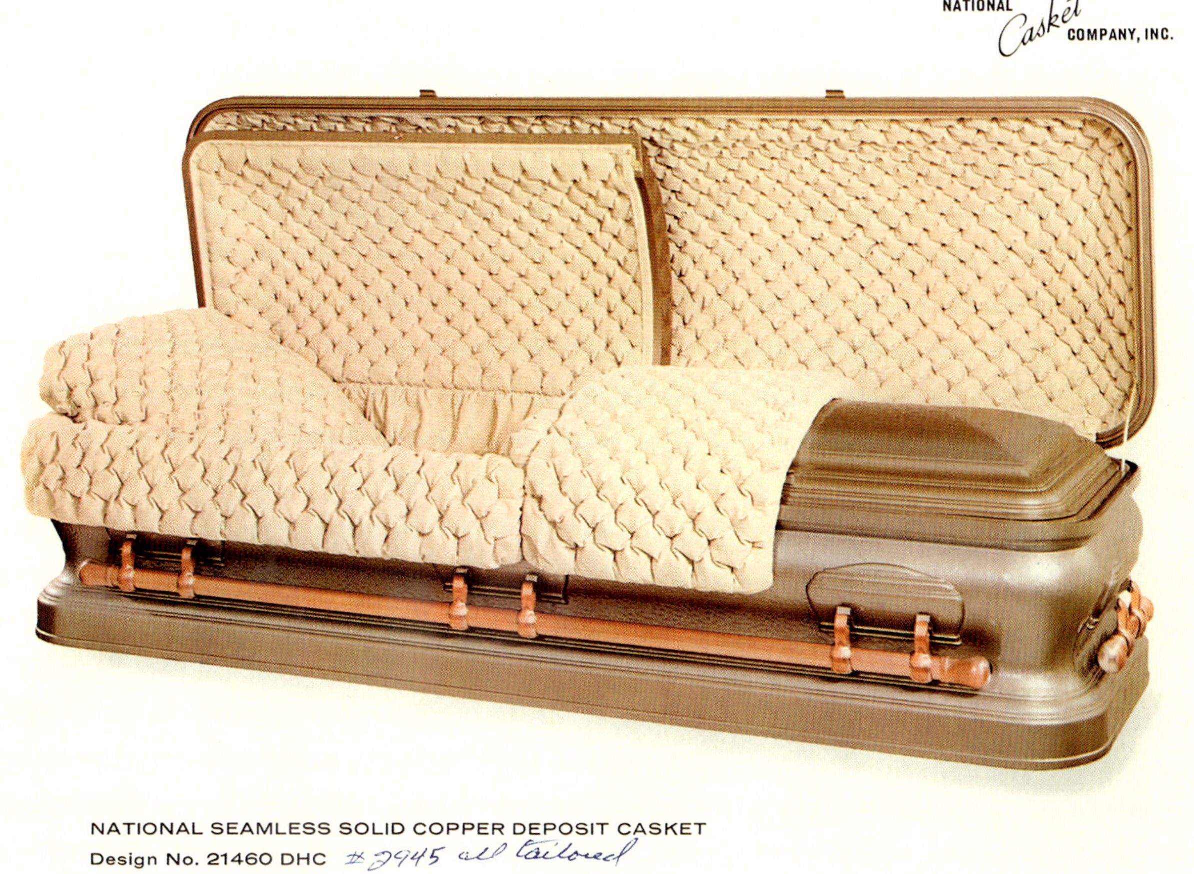

NATIONAL SEAMLESS SOLID COPPER DEPOSIT CASKET
Design No. 21460 DHC *#3945 all tailored*

Not a casket to be ashamed of. Courtesy Jon Austin, Museum of Funeral Customs.

ONE LARGE , ONE SMALL ROOM

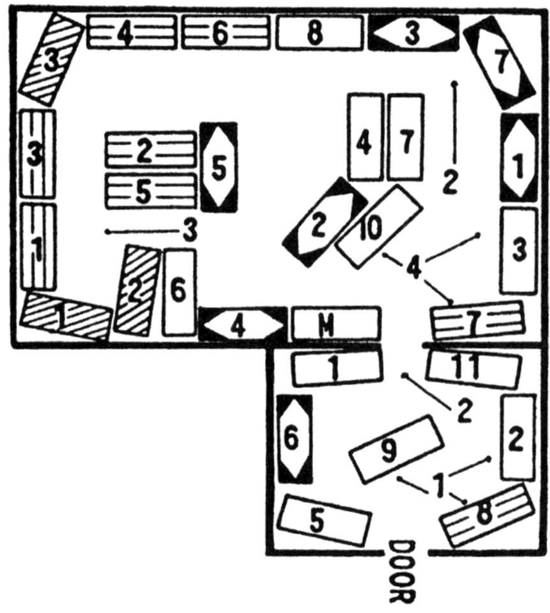

ONE LARGE ROOM

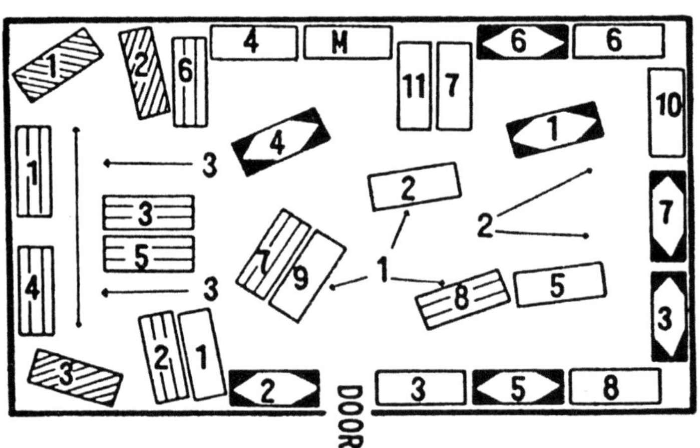

FOURTH QUARTILE	07 UNITS	23%	1. KEYSTONE APPROACH
THIRD QUARTILE	12 UNITS	40%	2. WIDE AISLES
MEDIAN			3. RESISTANCE LANE
SECOND QUARTILE	08 UNITS	27%	4. SECONDARY KEYSTONE
FIRST QUARTILE	03 UNITS	10%	

being exposed to two types of gazes. There is the gaze of the individual who is selling you the services, but one also feels the gaze of a non-substantial other who appears as an abstract agency looking at our choice from above. This abstract other is not the deceased but rather what Jacques Lacan called the Other—the social symbolic structure that governs our lives. The Other comprises society at large, from social institutions to cultural rituals and, especially, the language in which we live.

Lacan's assertion is that the Other does not exist, but it still functions. In other words, the social symbolic order in which we live is not coherent; marked by antagonisms, it is essentially inconsistent. People nevertheless create their own fiction of a coherent Other, this desire not to see its inconsistency being crucial for their self-perception. Since the subject is also marked with a constitutive lack—i.e. is also inconsistent—he or she tries to find some perception of him or herself as consistent by turning to a fantasy of a consistent Other.

The term *shame* is often used in conjunction with identity. Someone, for example, might feel ashamed for being poor, a member of a particular nation, and so on. One might also feel ashamed when not acting in accordance with a symbolic mandate with which the subject has identified. For example, a soldier might feel ashamed that he is not acting like a brave member of the army when he is anxiously trying to avoid active involvement in a battle, a father might feel ashamed for not acting like a paternal figure, a judge for not acting like an authority, etc.

The shame one experiences when arranging a funeral ritual triggers similar feelings of failure, of not acting properly. No matter what you do when presented with the choices in the funeral home, you fail. If you refuse to buy the extravagant casket, you will feel stingy, but if you choose the most expensive options, you will feel like you are showing off. Failure is inevitable.

Such feeling of failure can be explained by looking at how Freud linked the experience of shame with other feelings of self-reproach: "The affect of the self-reproach may be transformed by various psychical processes into other affects, which then enter consciousness more clearly than the affect itself: for instance, into anxiety (fear of the consequences of the action to which the self-reproach applies), hypochondria (fear of its bodily effects), delusions of persecutions (fear of its social effects), shame (fear of other people knowing about it), and so on."[1]

When we are ashamed, what is it that we are afraid that other people will know about? It is not simply that we feel like a failure since we did not in fact perform in accordance with some social expectation or did not fulfill some symbolic role. Shame also confronts us with the acknowledgment that we are *never*, by definition, able to fulfill these expectations or roles. What we do not want others to know about is that we are in essence always a fraud. We might temporarily take on some symbolic role and bask in the fantasy of its consistence, but sooner or latter we will be exposed in our nakedness, and our identity, marked by a constitutive lack, will be shown to be a sham.

The iconography of shamed individuals often shows them with their heads hanging and eyes downcast. On the one hand, they are avoiding the gaze emanating from others, but they are also trying not to look at the others. For example, in many cultures, one looks down when approaching a figure of authority. What is it that ought not to be seen when confronted with authority? Here we can say that shame also concerns the fact that we are not supposed to see others in their nakedness. To show respect to someone is to avert the gaze, to not look at what lies behind his or her symbolic insignia, and not see the lack that lies behind all authority.

Shame is, therefore, related to the inconsistency of the subject; to the inconsistency of the specific authorities that we deal with in our lives; and to the inconsistency of the Other. Here again we have the problem of visibility. When I feel ashamed, it is not simply that I am try to avoid the disapproving gaze of the Other in front of whom I feel humiliated. By averting my own gaze, I am also trying not to see the fact that the Other is itself also inconsistent, or, better, that the Other, in the final analysis, does not exist. As Joan Copjec points out: "Shame is awakened not when one looks at oneself,

---

opposite: Diagrams from Wilbur M. Krieger's 1951 *Successful Funeral Service Management*, illustrating how to arrange a showroom in order to maximize sales. Based on the author's "Keystone Approach" to effective, low-pressure merchandising, the arrangement of caskets is aimed to secure consistent sales in the upper, but not necessarily highest, price range. Krieger recommends that upon entering the selection room, the bereaved first encounter a casket in the third (i.e.; second most expensive) quartile of the funeral director's inventory—a unit approximately $150 more than the median in 1951. Should the buyer balk at the price, he is shown a cheaper unit that provides "strong contrast both in price and quality" and is positioned such that he must turn his back on the first casket. Recoiling from the unappealing second option, the buyer then turns to the third casket in the Keystone arrangement, a "rebound unit" priced at $50 over the median, and thus eases back into the third quartile, seemingly on his own terms. For the buyer who after being shown the first option wants to see something even better, Krieger advises turning right into a wide aisle that provides easy access to upper third and fourth quartile units. This technique is based on a conversation the author had with a "red-coated Royal Mounty" who told him that people lost in wide-open spaces "always turn in a great circle to their right." The customer whose budget prevents ambling through the selection room in this "natural" manner is taken, on the other hand, down a narrow "resistance lane" on the left to a corner where a few first and second quartile units are kept out of the way.

or those whom one cherishes, through another's eyes, but when one suddenly perceives a lack in the Other. At this moment the subject no longer experiences herself as a fulfillment of the Other's desire, as the center of the world, which now shifts away from her slightly, causing a distance to open within the subject herself. This distance is not that "superegoic" one which produces a feeling of guilt and burdens one with an uncancelable debt to the Other, but is, on the contrary, that which wipes out the debt. In shame, unlike guilt, one experiences one's visibility, but there is no external Other who sees, since shame is proof that the Other does not exist."[2]

When societies try to invent new rituals of shaming, it looks as if they are desperately trying to hold on to the fiction of a consistent Other, while in fact they are doing nothing else but exposing its inconsistency. This is often most visible in how shame is used in judicial systems. In China, for example, when a criminal is to be executed, his or her family is asked to pay for the bullet. This demand in part relies on the shame that the family feels to have a criminal in its midst. Paying for the bullet thus functions as symbolic compensation for the criminal's deeds. However, this act can also be understood to mean that the judicial system cannot act like a full authority and needs the family's "help" in meting out punishment.

Other societies are also trying to introduce more shame into their penal systems. The British government, for example, has commissioned research on how best to involve communities in the fight against crime and raise public confidence in the criminal justice system. The proposal written by Louise Casey, the former head of Tony Blair's Respect Task Force, suggests that offenders sentenced to community punishment be put to work wearing high-visibility bibs that identify them as criminals.[3] Here, we have a particular demand to make the criminals visible, to expose them to the public, and, of course, to make them experience shame in regard to their crime. The observing public is supposed to feel satisfaction in seeing that criminals are punished in a socially useful way instead of simply biding their time in a prison. But the judicial system does not simply make shamed criminals visible to the public; it also uses them to divert the public's gaze from itself—from its own utter failure as the authority that is supposed to deter crime.

1 Sigmund Freud, "Draft K – the neuroses of defence ," in "Extracts from the Fliss Papers," in *Standard Edition*, ed. James Strachey (London, The Hogarth Press and the Institute of Psychoanalysis, 1953–1974), vol. I, p. 224.
2 Joan Copjec, *Imagine There Is No Woman: Ethics and Sublimation* (Cambridge, Mass: MIT Press, 2004), p. 128.
3 *The Times*, London, 16 June 2008. Available at <www.timesonline.co.uk/tol/news/politics/article4144470.ece>

THE PEDAGOGIES OF SHAME

CHRISTINA TARNOPOLSKY

In recent debates about the place of emotions in liberal-democratic theory and practice, many have challenged their characterization as irrational bodily disturbances that disrupt rather than enhance our deliberative capacities. Yet there still seems to be a distrust of certain emotions, and connected to this, an unquestioned acceptance of a distinction between "positive" and "negative" emotions. Even theorists who argue forcefully that emotions can and ought to play a role in democratic deliberations and practices often find a place only for "positive" emotions such as love, trust, and compassion, while carefully excluding "negative" emotions like shame. For instance, political thinkers such as Jon Elster, Martha Nussbaum, and Toni Massaro have all argued that shame is problematic precisely because it is so painful to experience and because the primary reaction to it is one of hiding or covering the self.[1]

Distinguishing between negative and positive emotions is not new for theorists of liberalism. In fact, this strategy was first invoked by a number of early modern liberals, such as Adam Smith, Thomas Hobbes, John Locke and David Hume, concerned with designing political institutions that could overcome the wars that were plaguing their own polities. Their strategy was not, as it had been for many medieval philosophers, to condemn all of the passions as dangerous affects that are best repressed.[2] Rather, they chose to use greed, avarice, or the love of lucre to counter the passions for glory and honor that were allegedly at the heart of political and religious wars.[3] In a second move, the former passions, condemned by the ancients as some of the lowest forms of human motivation and by the medievals as cardinal sins, were reclassified as "interests."[4] Finally, these theorists accorded "interests" the status of rationality by arguing that they, unlike the "hot-blooded" passions, were calm, calculable, and communicable to others.[5]

According to this line of reasoning, shame was seen as one of the dangerous and warlike passions linked to glory and honor, all of which needed to be kept out of politics. As Stephen Holmes argues, "the principal aim of liberals who wrote favorably of self-interest was to bridle destructive and self-destructive passions ... [and] to induce people, so far as possible, to act rationally, instead of hot-bloodedly or deferentially."[6] Linked with this was a tendency to see people still moved by passions, rather than reason or interests, as "ignorant," "primitive," and part of the "lower orders."[7]

Three centuries later, political theorists are no longer convinced that greed is likely to lead to a *decline* in aggressive warfare. However, many have adopted a number of elements from this early liberal strategy, including the distinction between "positive" and "negative" emotions, the distrust of "primitive" emotions like shame or honor, and the belief that such emotions must be carefully excluded from the public sphere. The criteria they now use to distinguish between positive and negative emotions are different from the ones chosen by the early liberals, but they still target shame as characteristic of a more primitive stage of human development.

A classic text useful for correcting these simplistic views of shame is *Gorgias*, a dialogue written by Plato in 380 BCE. In it, Plato uses the figure of Socrates to demonstrate the various ways in which shame can disrupt or enhance deliberations within a democratic polity. Analysis of the dialogue demonstrates why it is that no emotion should simply be classified as "positive" or "negative" for democratic politics, given the complex roles played by emotions in both personal and political life.

PLATO AND THE POLITICS OF SHAME

Gorgias stages a conversation between Socrates, a teacher of rhetoric named Gorgias, his student Polus, and a potential Athenian statesman named Callicles. The dialogue is unique in the Platonic corpus because all of Socrates' refutations involve shame at a crucial step in the argument. Plato actually has two of Socrates' three interlocutors pointedly complain that shame (*aischunê*) has been used as the crucial element in Socrates' refutation (*elenchos*) of the other interlocutors: Polus asserts that Gorgias was "ashamed not to agree further with [Socrates] that the rhetorical man also knows the just, noble, and good things."[8] Callicles then reiterates this charge with regard to Gorgias, and adds that Socrates caught Polus "being ashamed to say what he thought" and so agreeing insincerely that doing injustice is more shameful than suffering injustice. Finally, Socrates twice states that shame has been involved in his refutations of Gorgias and Polus, and his lengthy encounter with Callicles involves repeated attempts to make Callicles feel ashamed of the consequences of his indiscriminate hedonism thesis.

The first thing that *Gorgias* teaches us about shame is that there are many different reactions to it. Under the critical gaze of Socrates, each of his interlocutors is eventually forced into the painful recognition that his definition of the best life is inconsistent with other things that he also believes. Hence, they all experience

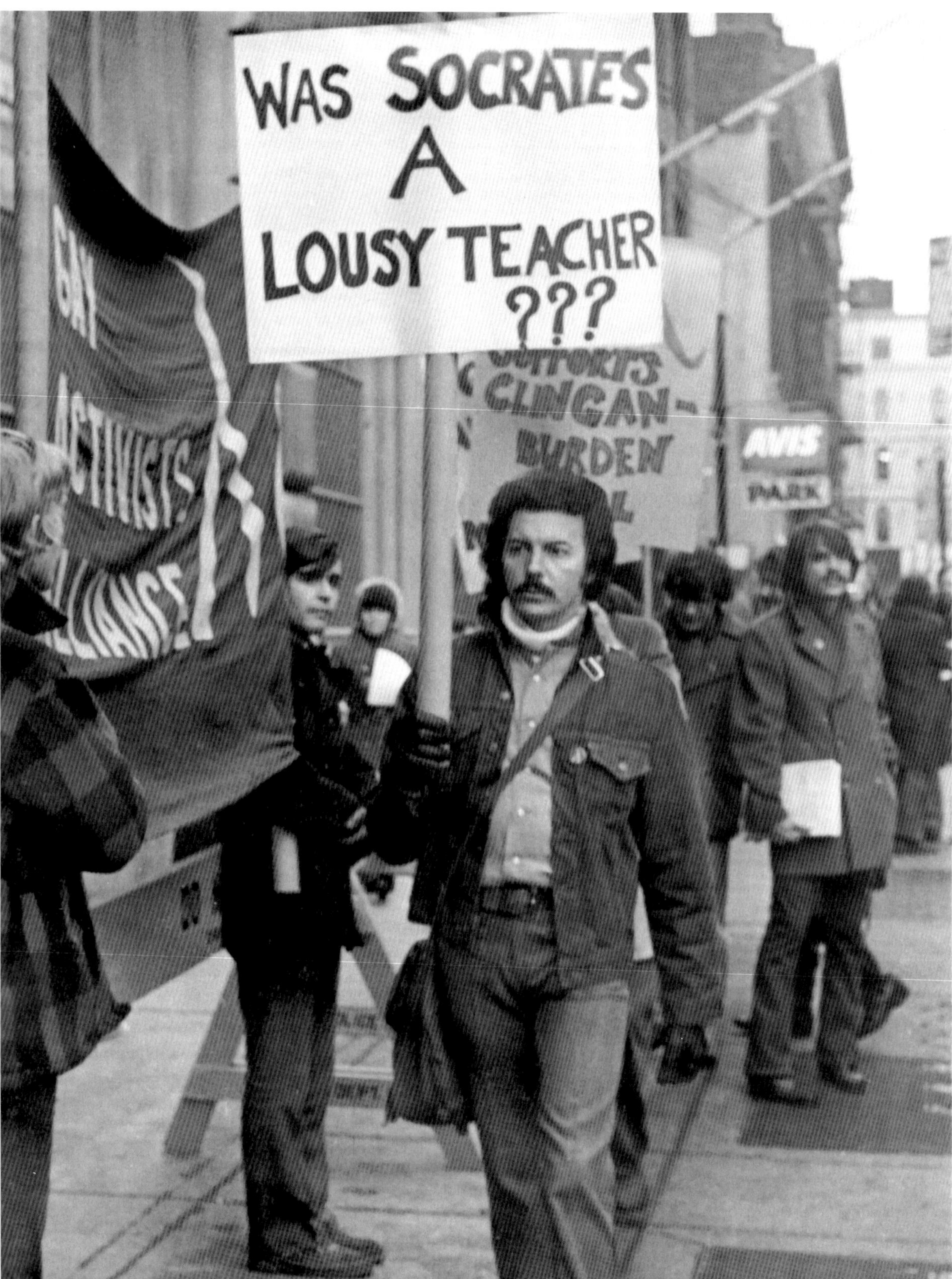

WAS SOCRATES
A
LOUSY TEACHER
???
GAY
ACTIVISTS
ALLIANCE
SUPPORTS
CLINGAN-
BURDEN
AVIS
PARK

the painful cognitive-affective recognition of the gaze of an "other" that reveals a certain inadequacy in the self, which is central to the experience of shame. They then react to this experience either by professing confusion (Polus), by trying to hide from this revelation about themselves (Callicles), or by altering their definitions and even their way of life in accordance with the insights gleaned from the conversation with Socrates (Gorgias). In the dialogue itself, Gorgias illustrates a positive reaction to shame by continually re-entering the discussion after he has been shamed by Socrates, either to push the discussion forward and learn something new about rhetoric or to contest the cowardly way in which Callicles is reacting to Socrates' shaming refutation.

Most contemporary political theorists who have criticized shame focus only on the reaction of hiding or covering the self in response to the pain that is inherent to shame. Such theorists overemphasize the painfulness of the experience and assume that it is necessarily linked to its perniciousness for the person suffering shame. Overemphasizing the pain of shame can lead to the kind of politics favored both by Polus and Callicles who, in describing to Socrates how one should address the Athenian Assembly, tell him that one should flatter the audience. In tailoring one's remarks to the audience's existing prejudices such that it never has to hear anything unpleasant about itself, this strategy seeks to avoid the painful feelings of shame on the part of both the speaker and the audience, who share a common political identity. Flattery aims at the pleasant without the best because it aims at the pleasures of mutual recognition without regard to whether we ought to be complacently pleased with the self-affirming image of the good citizen it offers us. As Socrates puts it, such orators are like pastry chefs who offer children the sweets they want without ever considering whether these are beneficial and whether, like doctors, they might have to administer painful procedures to achieve the health of the patient.

In contrast, the Socratic model of politics involves a kind of shaming as an integral part of deliberation and debate. Here, it is important to note that in Attic Greek the word *elenchos*, which is used to describe Socrates' incessant questioning of everyone he meets, means both a disgrace or dishonor and a cross-examination for purposes of disproof or refutation.[9] Socrates shames those he meets in an attempt to get them to think reflexively about their actions by recognizing the gap between their self-images and their specific actions, and his refutations are perplexing and painful because they always sunder the interlocutor's easy identification with his beloved ideals. But what can be positive about this painful experience is that it can disrupt one's unthinking identification with a problematic ideal, and it is this potential that underlies Socrates' shaming encounters with his interlocutors in *Gorgias*.

There are then important differences between the "flattering" shame that Polus and Callicles preach, and the "respectful" shame practiced and preached by Socrates. In the case of "flattering" shame, one fixates solely on the pain that is inherent to the recognition of losing one's ego-ideal under the shaming gaze of the other, and tries to avoid such pain altogether. The speaker's sense of shame thus attunes him to his listeners, but in such a way that neither he nor they ever need endure the pain of having their identity or ideals criticized by the other. A false consensus forms wherein "debate" becomes a reciprocal exchange of pleasantries.

"Flattering" shame thus endangers democracy in two ways. First, it aims at the pleasures of mutual recognition, thus foreclosing the possibility that the person we are addressing might show us something different and even unpleasant about ourselves. And it proposes a world of complete certainty and invulnerability inhabited by mythic "normal" citizens, omnipotent and free from all forms of pain, including that inherent to the emotion of shame. Those aspects of the self that do not fit this mythic image are then displaced onto other individuals or groups in the shaming practices of derision and stigmatization.

Socrates' sense of shame, on the other hand, offers a model of respect that is grounded in preserving our openness to judgment by the "other." This kind of "respectful" shame is oriented toward dissecting the mythical unity of the image of the "just" or "normal" citizen in an on-going project of mutual reflection. The morality grounded in this kind of "respectful" shame consists not in assimilating to a standard or norm, but rather in remaining open to the on-going possibility that who we are cannot be captured by any particular norm or self-image we currently possess. It also requires understanding that the demands of morality might well run counter to the false moralism of the established norms of society and its conceptions of citizenship.[10] These elements of Platonic "respectful" shame provide the basis for a critical examination of a widely held contemporary view of shame such as the one offered by Martha Nussbaum in her book *Hiding from Humanity: Disgust, Shame and The Law.*

Nussbaum's strategy, which harkens back to the early modern liberals in significant ways, is to differentiate the emotions that entail a denial of our vulnerability and humanity from those that serve as valuable reminders of it. According to Nussbaum, these latter emotions can help us enact reasonable laws that respond to the types of harm that befall vulnerable human beings.[11] She lists anger, fear, grief, compassion (and later, guilt) as emotions that are linked to our normative conceptions of what a "reasonable" person should do in response to such circumstances.[12] Alternately, she argues that the emotions of disgust and "primitive" shame are more likely than others to be linked to faulty values about our humanity and to a denial of our vulnerable natures. "Primitive shame" for Nussbaum arises out of the infantile omnipotence experienced in the womb that lingers in all of us to some extent, thus posing an "ongoing danger in the moral and social life."[13]

At other places in the book, however, she does suggest that when connected to valuable ideals and aspirations "constructive" shame may have a positive role to play in human development and political life.[14] The problem is that not everyone transcends primitive shame and even those who do still carry remnants of it around with them. Thus shame is "likely to be normatively unreliable in public life, despite its potential for good."[15] Beginning with a distinction between "primitive" and "constructive" shame, Nussbaum ends up reverting to a simple condemnation of shame and warns that we need to be more skeptical about "even the moralizing type of shaming."[16]

Nussbaum and Plato actually agree on a number of issues. The fact that Nussbaum finds "primitive" shame to be pernicious for liberal democratic institutions, which should produce and sustain a respect for liberty and equality, and for a norm of humanity as "a condition of shared incompleteness"[17] is consistent with Plato's criticisms of "flattering" shame. Moreover, the "respectful" shame that Plato advocates rejects rigid, static norms or idealized "others" in our political deliberations (especially when these take the form of an omnipotent and wholly autonomous "other"). Similarly, Nussbaum argues that shame can occur against an *antinarcissistic* background of respect, where both parties acknowledge their mutual responsibility and interdependence.[18]

However, one of their key differences lies in the fact that she argues that certain emotions are more reasonable and more attuned with a realistic notion of humanity than other emotions. Secondly, while Plato believes that "flattering" and "respectful" shame represent two distinct kinds of shame, Nussbaum thinks that "constructive" shame is always likely to revert to a more "primitive" form.

But her first argument, which relies on a rigid distinction between "positive" and "negative" emotions, is in tension with her own theory of the emotions more generally, which states that *all* emotions "are responses to those areas of vulnerability, responses in which we register the damage we have suffered, might suffer, or luckily have failed to suffer."[19] Shame and disgust, like grief, fear, anger, guilt and compassion, can all alert us to important problems in our physical, social, and political environment.

Even more problematically, Nussbaum's argument that shame is one of the emotions that inclines us to conform to the problematic standard of the "normal" seems to be in tension with her view of shame as the painful emotion that responds to our discovery that we are in some ways "abnormal."[20] Shame then would seem to be a very valuable emotion precisely because it shows us that we have fallen below the standards of the "normal" that our society sets for us and that we have internalized as a personal, though also deeply social, vision of "normality." Indeed, this is what I argued with respect to the painful moment of recognition within shame. In this moment the person recognizes that they are in some sense inadequate or weak in relation to an ideal they hold dear, and the experience can then serve as a valuable reminder that we are not the omnipotent, autonomous beings that tend to be valorized in our notions of the "normal" citizen. Indeed Nussbaum herself later admits that this type of recognition can underlie the more constructive shame that humans acquire as they become mature adults.[21]

The problem, for Nussbaum, is that even constructive, or what I would call "respectful," shame never fully overcomes the "primitive" shame that points backwards in time to an ever-present but deceptive longing for the infantile omnipotence of the womb, and inwards in space to a concern with the narcissistic self. Shame makes us want to hide from our humanity, because "its reflex is to hide from the eyes of those who will see one's deficiency."[22] Emotions like compassion, guilt, anger, or fear, on the other hand, point outwards to a world of distinct others, and forward to a mature acceptance of our vulnerability and relatedness to others who have their own desires and life projects.[23]

There are a number of problems with this position. First, is it so clear that the emotions of guilt, compassion, and anger are so easily separated from an emotion like shame? Instead, I would argue that shame, guilt, anger, and compassion all need to work together to motivate individuals and polities to change themselves in response to actions that they deem unworthy of their own ideals. They need to feel guilt and compassion over what they have done to others, but also shame and anger at what they might have become by performing these actions. Although Nussbaum follows Kant in arguing that guilt is a salutary emotion connected with reparation and forgiveness, with agency rather than with thoughts about the self, and with treating other people as "separate beings with rights, who ought not to be harmed,"[24] this strict separation of shame and guilt falls apart when we examine the ways in which these emotions motivate us in our lives.

Moreover, these kinds of interconnections also occur in the case of the other emotions. The person whose sense of shame attunes them to a desire for the infantile omnipotence of the womb is the same person who will feel angry and lash out at those people who show them that they are vulnerable. Such a person will also fear this exposure in any of their social engagements and will feel compassion for those who share their desire for invulnerability. In other words, their fear, guilt, anger, and compassion will be no less "unreasonable" or attuned to the infantile desire for omnipotence and the need to hide from their humanity as would be the case with the person who is experiencing "primitive" shame.

Secondly, Nussbaum's view of shame assumes that our reaction to the moment of recognition—the moment when we realize that we are "abnormal" or have fallen below a standard or "other" which we hold dear—is always one of hiding. Here Nussbaum is criticizing not so much the cognitive content of feeling shame, but the ways in which we react to the painful and perplexing recognition of our inadequacy as this is revealed in the occurrent experience of shame. The reaction of hiding is only one of the possible ways in which a person might react. The other ways include either trying to contest the very standard by which one has been ashamed, or trying to transform oneself in accordance with the new insights for action that have come to light in the shaming situation. In fact, it is impossible to understand how anybody could ever move from the "primitive" shame that is supposedly characteristic of childhood to the more mature shame that Nussbaum describes unless one learns how to transform oneself in accordance with the new knowledge and situations one encounters. By dramatizing the process of learning about oneself and others through shame, Plato's dialogue both instructs and invites the reader to continually actualize such an education in his own public and private life in a way that is foreclosed by Nussbaum's treatise against shame.

Plato would argue that all the emotions discussed in this essay serve the necessary function of warning us about our mortality and vulnerability, but what makes them "irrational" or "primitive" depends on whether we try to cover up this insight with pleasant but false myths about our omnipotence, or whether we try to come to terms with our vulnerabilities in our mutual engagements with others. Indeed, if "primitive" shame really lingered in all of us to the extent that Nussbaum fears, it would be hard to understand how we could ever have moved towards more democratic and egalitarian institutions in which we all necessarily share in ruling and being ruled, shaming and being shamed in order to survive in an uncertain world.

1 Jon Elster, *Alchemies of the Mind: Rationality and the Emotions* (Cambridge: Cambridge University Press, 1999), p. 153; Martha C. Nussbaum, *Hiding from Humanity: Disgust, Shame and the Law* (Princeton: Princeton University Press, 2004), p. 183; Toni M. Massaro, "Show (Some) Emotions," in *The Passions of Law*, ed. Susan A. Bandes (New York: New York University Press, 1999), p. 89.
2 Barbara Koziak, *Retrieving Political Emotion: Thumos, Aristotle, and Gender* (University Park: Pennsylvania State University Press, 2000), p. 8.
3 For a full account of this, see Albert Hirschman, *The Passions and the Interests: Political Arguments for Capitalism Before Its Triumph* (Princeton: Princeton University Press, 1977); Stephen Holmes, *Passions and Constraints: On the Theory of Liberal Democracy* (Chicago: University of Chicago Press, 1995); Cheryl Hall, "Passions and Constraint: The Marginalization of Passion in Liberal Political Theory," *Philosophy and Social Criticism*, vol. 28, no. 6 (2002), pp. 727–748.
4 Hirschman, *The Passions and the Interests*; Hall, "Passions and Constraint," p. 733; Koziak, *Retrieving Political Emotion*, p. 8.
5 Hirschman, *The Passions and the Interests*, p. 33, p. 50; Hall, "Passions and Constraint," p. 733.
6 Holmes, p. 4, quoted in Hall, p. 733.
7 Michael Walzer, "Passion and Politics," *Philosophy and Social Criticism*, vol. 28, no. 6 (2002), pp. 617–633, pp. 619–622.
8 All translation are from Plato, *Gorgias* (Ithaca: Cornell University Press, 1998), trans. James H. Nichols, Jr.
9 H. G. Liddell and R. Scott, *Greek-English Lexicon* (Oxford: Clarendon Press, 1996), p. 531.
10 Dana Villa, *Socratic Citizenship* (Princeton: Princeton University Press, 2001), p. 3.
11 Martha Nussbaum, op. cit., p. 7.
12 Ibid., pp. 8–12.
13 Ibid., p. 192.
14 Ibid., p. 15, pp. 211–216.
15 Ibid., p. 15.
16 Ibid., p. 220.
17 Ibid., p. 16.
18 Ibid., p. 213.
19 Ibid., p. 6.
20 Ibid., p. 173.
21 Ibid., p. 191.
22 Ibid., p. 183.
23 Ibid., p. 69, p. 207.
24 Ibid., p. 209.

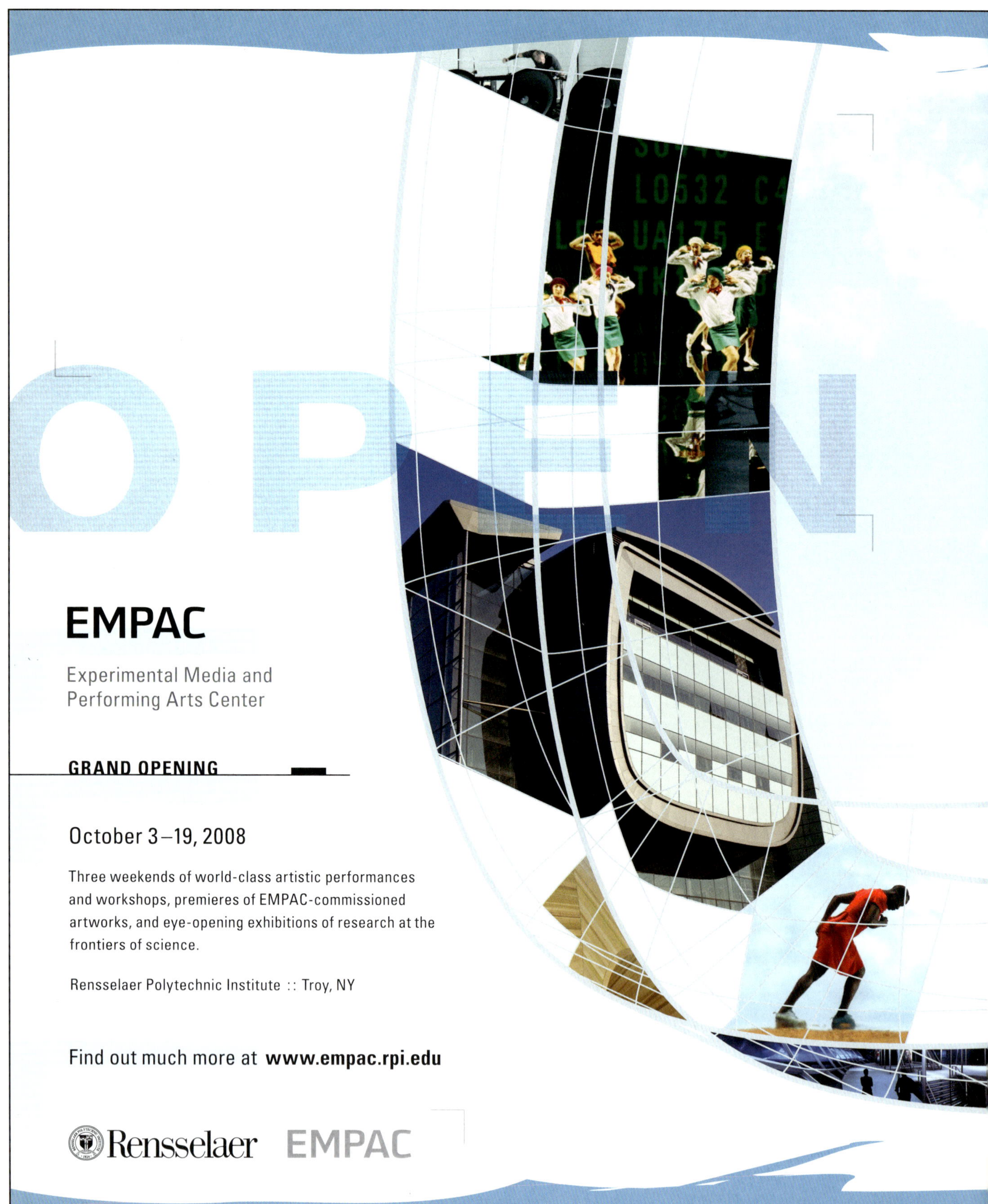
OPEN

EMPAC

Experimental Media and
Performing Arts Center

GRAND OPENING

October 3–19, 2008

Three weekends of world-class artistic performances
and workshops, premieres of EMPAC-commissioned
artworks, and eye-opening exhibitions of research at the
frontiers of science.

Rensselaer Polytechnic Institute :: Troy, NY

Find out much more at www.empac.rpi.edu

Rensselaer   EMPAC

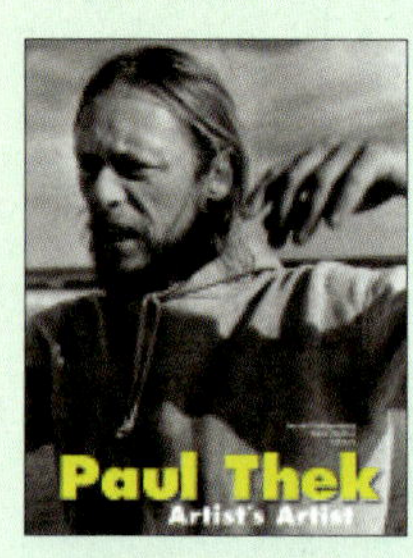

Paul Thek
Artist's Artist

edited by Harald Falckenberg and Peter Weibel

Images of more than 300 works by this groundbreaking artist document his journey from legendary outsider to central figure in many contemporary art movements.

Copublished with ZKM | Center for Art and Media Technology • 550 pp., 300 color illus., 200 b&w illus., $54.95 cloth

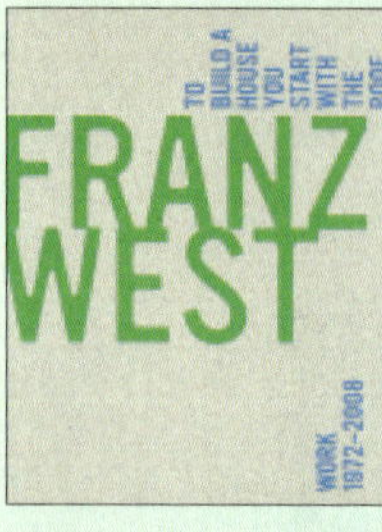

Franz West
To Build a House You Start with the Roof, Work 1972–2008

Darsie Alexander

with contributions by Rachel Harrison, Eric Banks and Tom Eccles

A book that makes clear why Franz West is not only Vienna's most influential living sculptor, but one of the most entertaining and cerebral contemporary artists anywhere.

Copublished with The Baltimore Museum of Art 288 pp., 160 color illus., $44.95 cloth

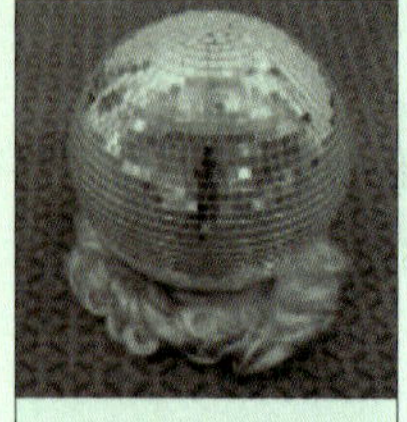

Martin Kippenberger
The Problem Perspective

edited by Ann Goldstein and Lisa Gabrielle Mark

Works spanning the legendary and prolific artist's twenty-year career, including many of his self-portraits, paintings, sculptures, works on paper, installations, and exhibition posters.

Distributed for the Museum of Contemporary Art, Los Angeles • 288 pp., 250 color illus., $44.95 cloth

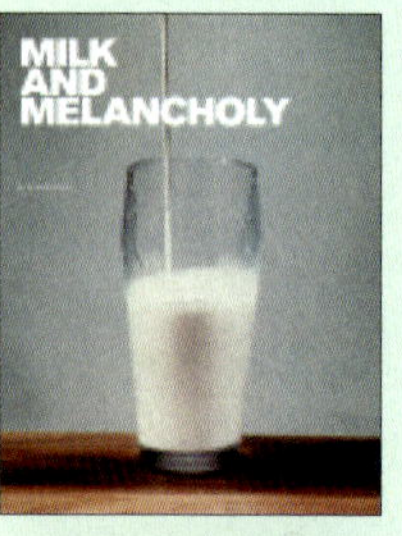

Milk and Melancholy

Kenneth Hayes

The first book on milk in art, from Harold Edgerton's drops to Jeff Wall's splash: a meditation with photographs.

Copublished with Prefix Institute of Contemporary Art, Inc. • 156 pp., 95 color photographs, 25 b&w photographs, $24.95 cloth

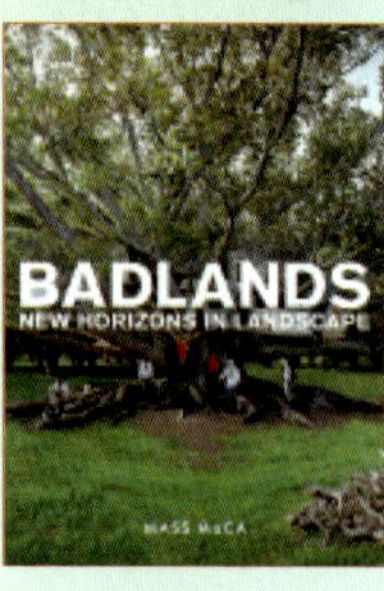

Badlands
New Horizons in Landscape

edited by Denise Markonish

foreword by Joseph Thompson

Contemporary art's new relationship to the landscape.

Copublished with MASS MoCA 232 pp., 151 color illus., 30 b&w illus., $24.95 paper

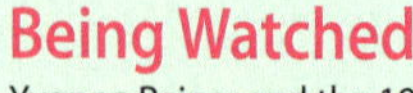

Being Watched
Yvonne Rainer and the 1960s

Carrie Lambert-Beatty

"A brilliantly vivid description of Rainer, Judson, and art making in the 1960s, *Being Watched* sets a new scholarly standard for dance and performance studies… *Being Watched* is an absolute pleasure to read." — Peggy Phelan, Stanford University

An October Book • 384 pp., 83 illus., $34.95 cloth

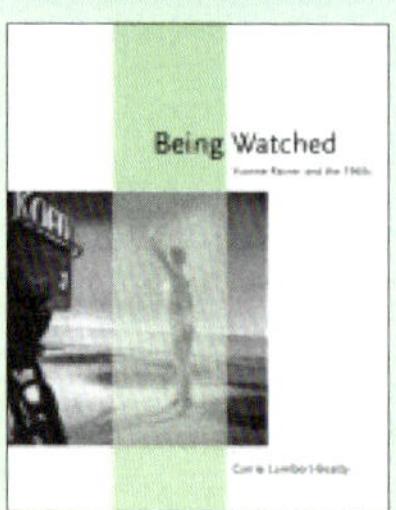

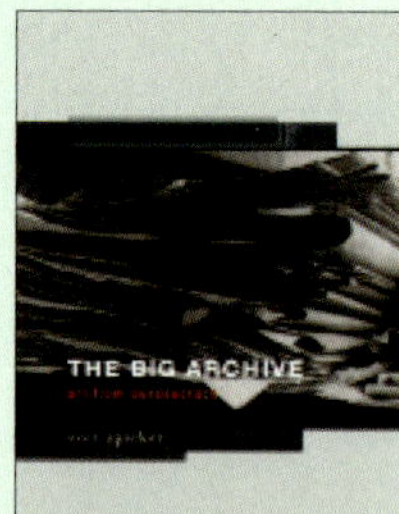

The Big Archive
Art From Bureaucracy

Sven Spieker

"This… book succeeds in transforming our notion of archive—from a rationally organized space in which monotonous, boring collections of documents are kept, to a place full of dark mysteries, hidden chaos and unexpected adventures. This non-fictional version of Umberto Eco's *The Name of the Rose* is indispensable reading for artists and scholars." — Boris Groys, Academy for Design in Karlsruhe, Germany, New York University, and author of *Art Power*

228 pp., 78 illus., $24.95 cloth

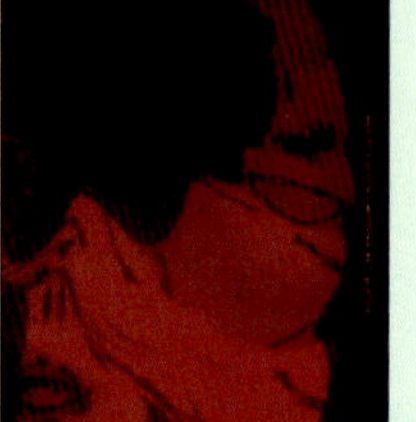

Anish Kapoor
Past, Present, Future

edited by Nicholas Baume

The first major American publication on this important contemporary sculptor.

Copublished with the Institute of Contemporary Art, Boston • 144 pp., 90 color illus., $29.95 cloth

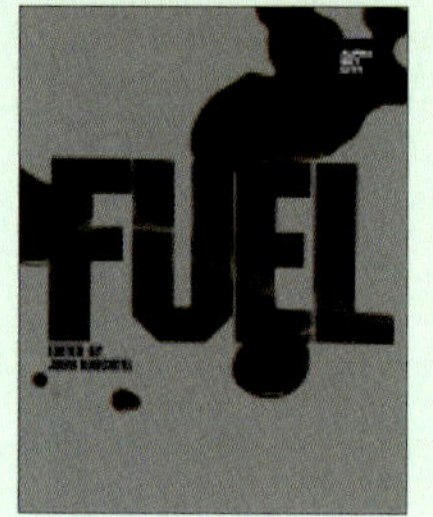

Fuel

edited by John Knechtel

Writers and artists imagine the transition to a carbon-free future and the radical reinvention of energy that would make it possible.

Copublished with Alphabet City Media 320 pp., 200 color illus., $15.95 cloth

NOW IN PAPER

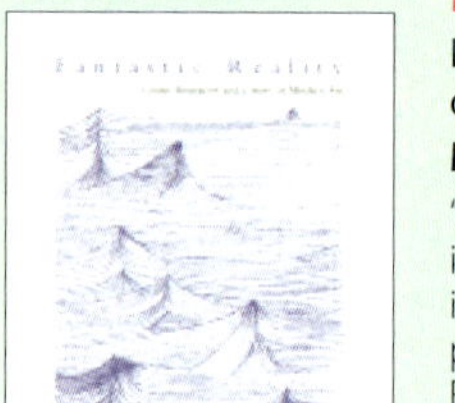

Fantastic Reality
Louise Bourgeois and a Story of Modern Art

Mignon Nixon

"In *Fantastic Reality*, Mignon Nixon not only illuminates the work of this revolutionary artist but rewrites the history of sculpture in the postwar years." — Linda Nochlin, Institute of Fine Arts, New York University

An October Book • 322 pp., 103 illus., $22.95 paper

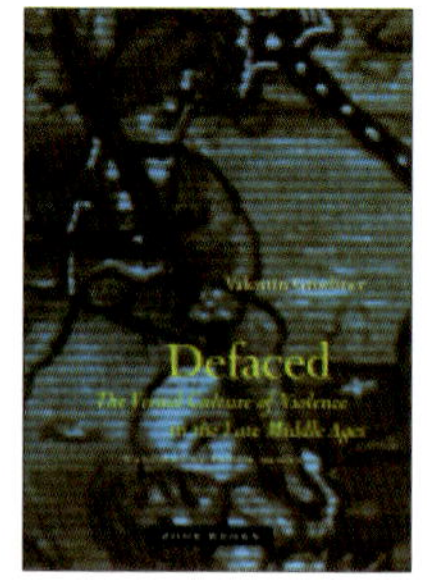

NOW IN PAPER FROM

ZONE BOOKS

Defaced
The Visual Culture of Violence in the Late Middle Ages

Valentin Groebner

translated by Pamela Selwyn

"Iconoclastic, yet humane, Groebner's compelling essays uncover the full spectrum of acts and images that, no matter how grisly or grotesque, formed part of a semiotics of savagery that continues to inform representations of law and order and the practice of compulsion and constraint well into the modern era." — Jeffrey Hamburger, Harvard University, author of *The Visual and the Visionary: Art and Female Spirituality in Late Medieval Germany* (Zone Books)

Distributed for Zone Books 199 pp., 27 illus., $22.95 paper

DAVID KRUT PUBLISHING

THE NEW YORK ART BOOK FAIR 2008
October 23-26, 2008
www.nyartbookfair.com

ARTIST BOOK INTERNATIONAL PARIS
October 24-26, 2008
www.artistbookinternational.com

David Krut Publishing
140 Jan Smuts Avenue
Parkwood, Johannesburg 2193
South Africa
t: +27 (011) 880 5648
e: bronwyn@davidkrut.com
www.davidkrutpublishing.com

David Krut Projects New York
526 West 26th Street #816
New York NY 10001 USA
t:+1 (1) 212 255 3094
e: info@davidkrut.com
www.davidkrut.com

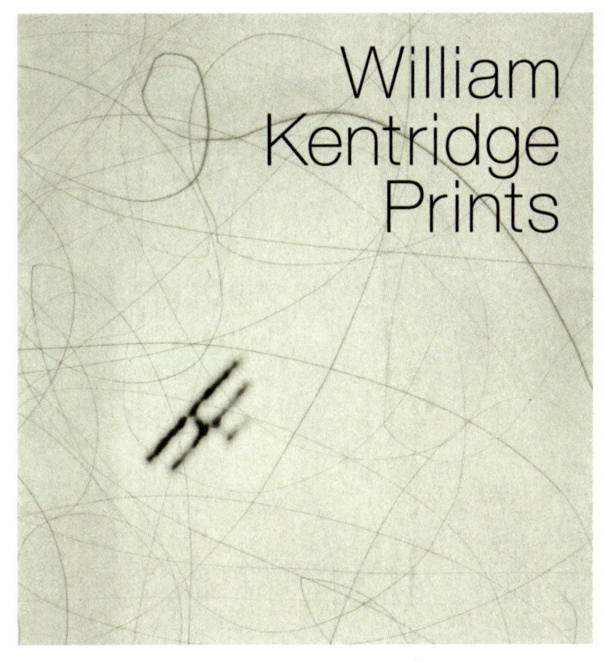

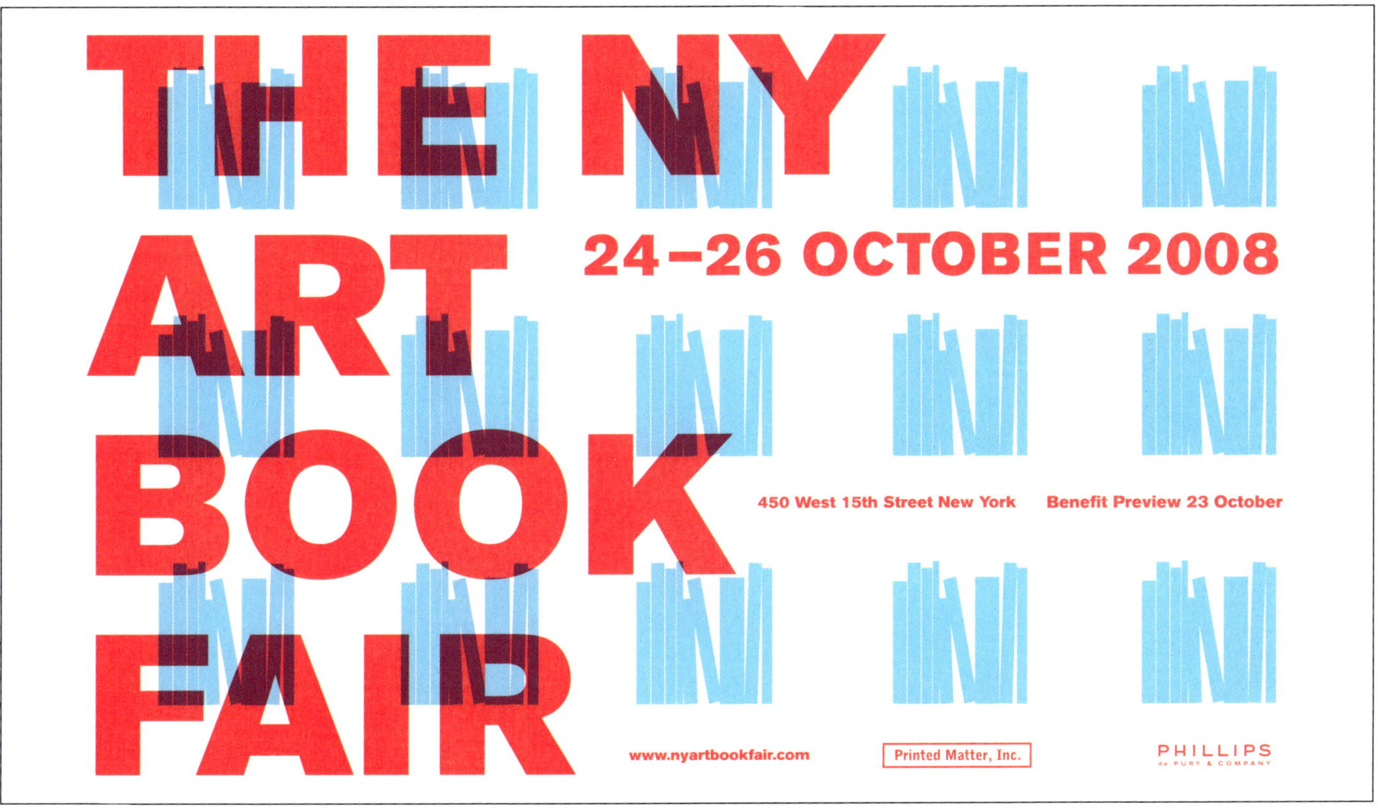

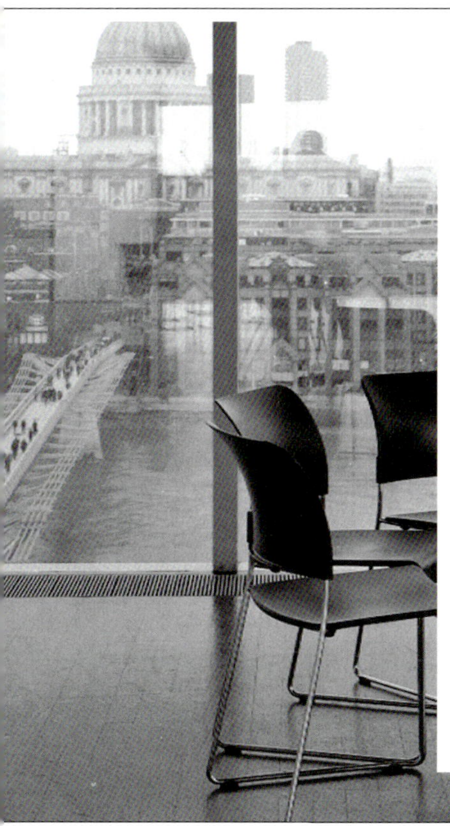

the london consortium

• • •

Multi-disciplinary postgraduate programmes in Humanities and Cultural Studies

The London Consortium offers innovative postgraduate programmes combining taught courses and individual research, theoretical exploration and practical insight.

The London Consortium offers:

– One year Master of Research (MRes) programme

– Three year PhD programme

– Degrees awarded by the University of London

– Innovative training in multi-disciplinary research through an ambitious series of core courses

– Expert support and input from some of London's most dynamic cultural and educational institutions

In association with:

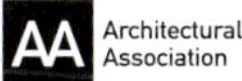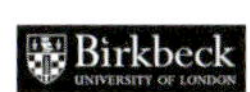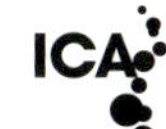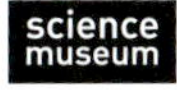

Full details online at www.londonconsortium.com or email loncon@ica.org.uk

©Leopold Kessler

LOMBARD-FREID PROJECTS 531 W 26TH STREET 2ND FL NEW YORK NEW YORK 10001

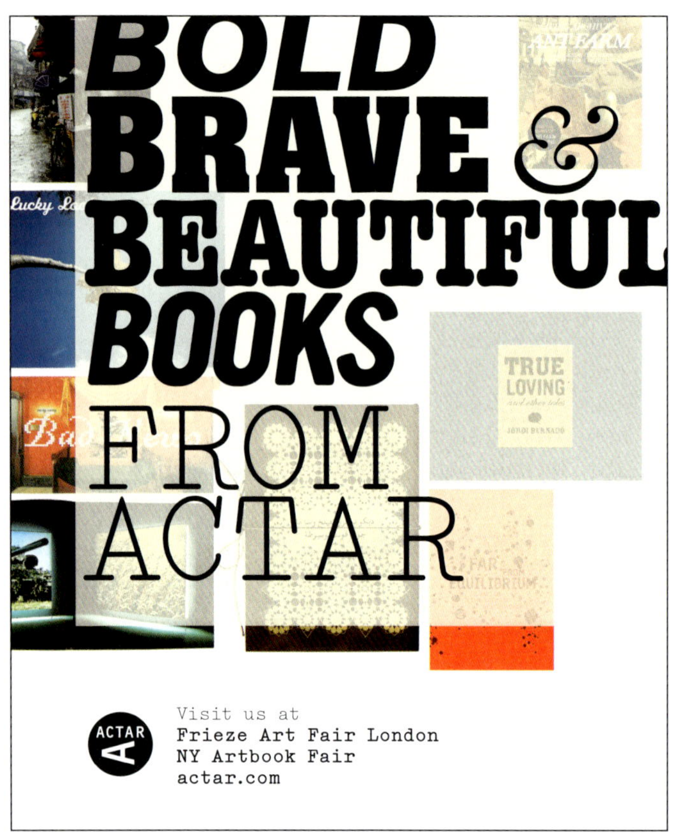

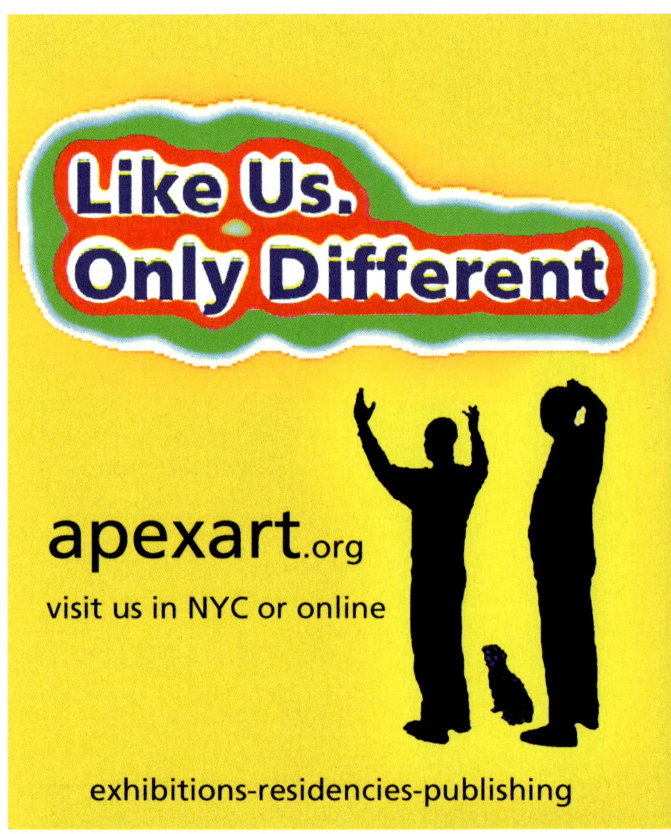

What Was Old Is New Again
A meeting of art and scholarship

November 21 to 23, 2008
ZKM, Karlsruhe, Germany
http://caeno.org/newagain/

Throughout history, belief systems have relied on music, theater, painting and other art forms to propagate accepted doctrines, and the arts in turn have shaped the articles of faith.

The CAENO Foundation, New York, is a non-profit organization established in 2000. It supports historical and physical research pertaining to the chronology of events, epochs and civilizations.

The ZKM Center of Art and Media, Karlsruhe, has a unique mission. Its work combines production, research, documentation, exhibition, and events pertaining to information technology. ///// ZKM Zentrum für Kunst und Medientechnologie Karlsruhe /

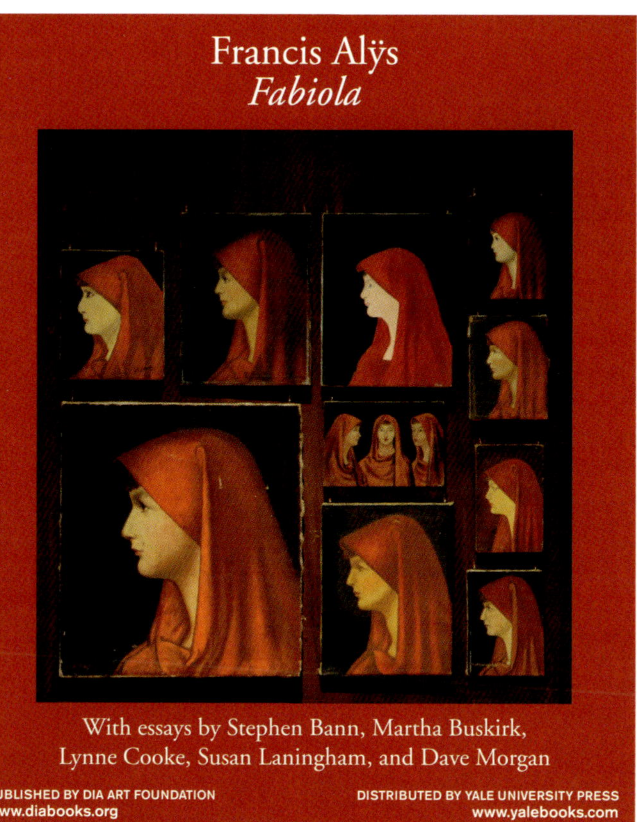

The Post Office has asked that we publish the following very interesting information.

STATEMENT OF OWNERSHIP, MANAGEMENT, AND CIRCULATION

Publication Title: Cabinet
Publication Number: 020-348
Filing Date: 10/01/08
Mailing Address of Office of Publication: 181 Wyckoff Street, Brooklyn, NY 11217
Contact Person: Sina Najafi @ 718-222-8434
Mailing address of Headquarters of Publisher: same as office of publication
Publisher: Immaterial Incorporated, 181 Wyckoff St., Brooklyn, NY 11217
Editor: Sina Najafi, 181 Wyckoff St., Brooklyn, NY 11217
Managing Editor: none
Owner: Immaterial Incorporated, 181 Wyckoff St., Brooklyn, NY 11217

EXTENT & NATURE OF CIRCULATION / AVERAGE NO. OF COPIES OF EACH ISSUE
DURING PRECEDING 12 MONTHS / NO. OF COPIES OF SINGLE ISSUE PUBLISHED
NEAREST TO FILING DATE (SUMMER 2008)

Total number of copies / 12,465 / 14,100
Paid/Requested Outside County Subscriptions Stated on Form 3541 / 3,399 / 3,581
Paid In-County Subscriptions Stated on Form 3541 / 0 / 0
Sales Through Dealers and Carriers, Street Vendors, Counter Sales, and other non-
USPS Paid Distribution / 7,911 / 8,858
Other Classes Mailed through the USPS / 538 / 592
Total Paid and/or Requested Circulation / 11,848 / 13,031
Free Distribution by Mail: Outside County as Stated on Form 3541 / 0 / 0
Free Distribution by Mail: In-County as Stated on Form 3541 / 0 / 0
Free Distribution by Mail: Other Classes Mailed through the USPS / 38 / 40
Free Distribution Outside the Mail / 85 / 80
Total Free Distribution / 123 / 120
Total Distribution / 11,971 / 13,151
Copies Not Distributed / 494 / 949
Total / 12,465 / 14,100
Percent Paid and/or Requested Circulation / 98.97% / 99.09%

Cabinet

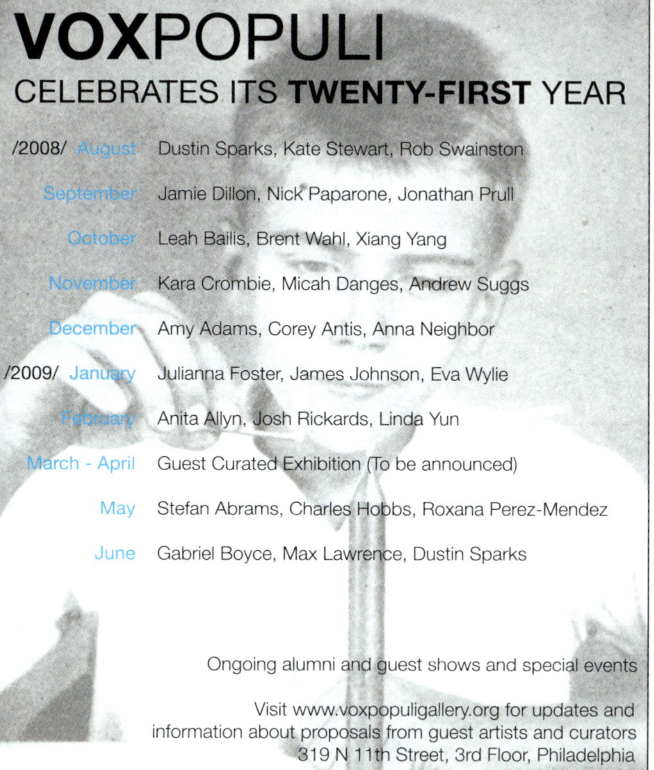

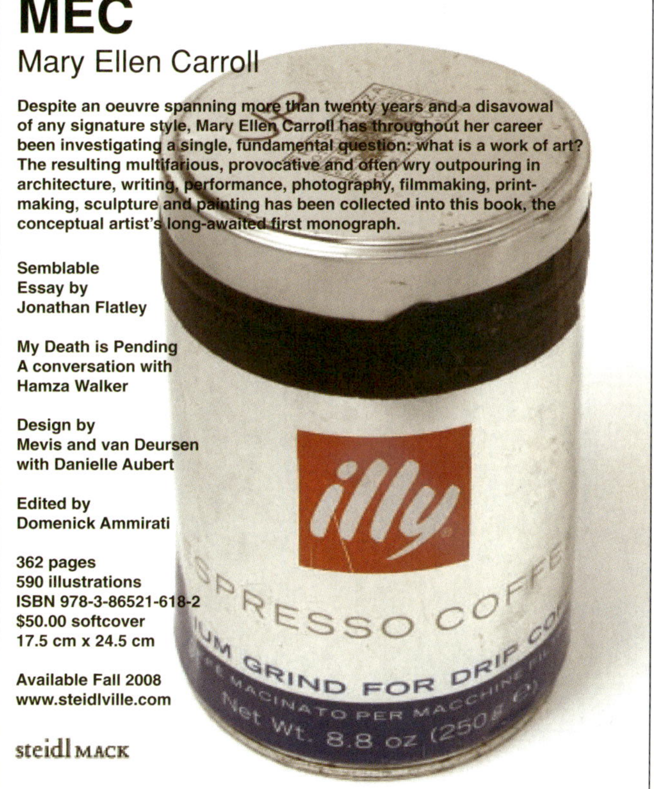

CABINET BACK ISSUES

Available back issues (pictured below) are $10 each + postage.
Postage rates: US $2.50 per issue; Canada & Mexico $9.50 for 1, 2, or 3 issues; Elsewhere $11.50 for 1, 2, or 3 issues.

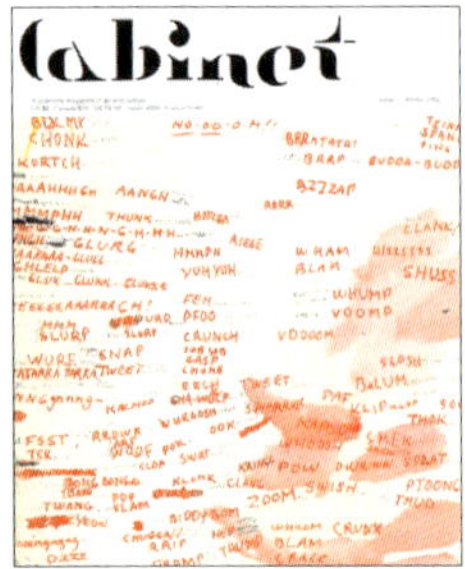

Issue 1 / **Invented Languages**

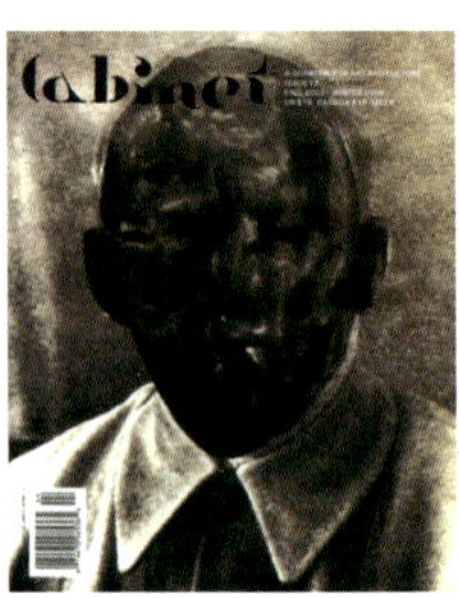

Issue 12 / **The Enemy**

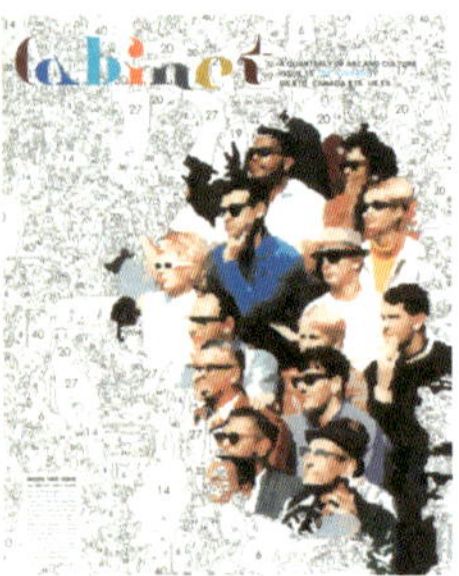

Issue 15 / **The Average**

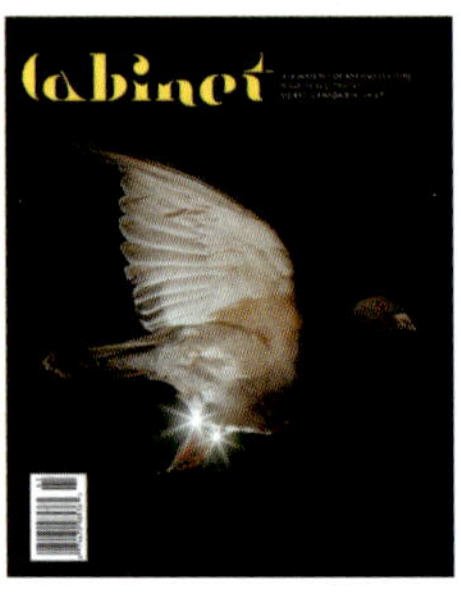

Issue 21 / **Electricity**

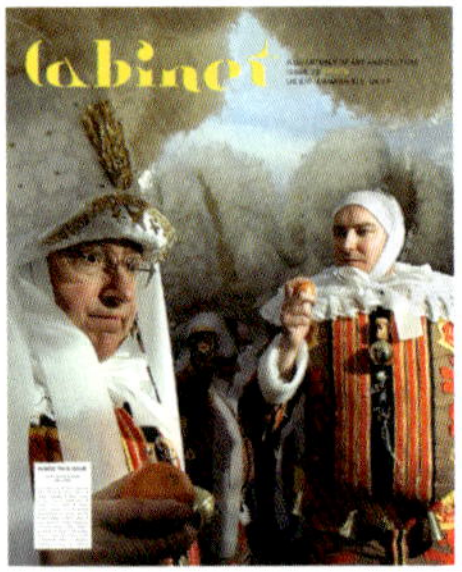

Issue 23 / **Fruits**

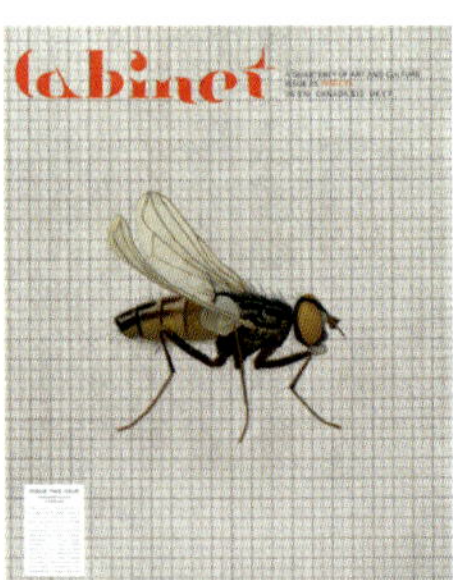

Issue 25 / **Insects**

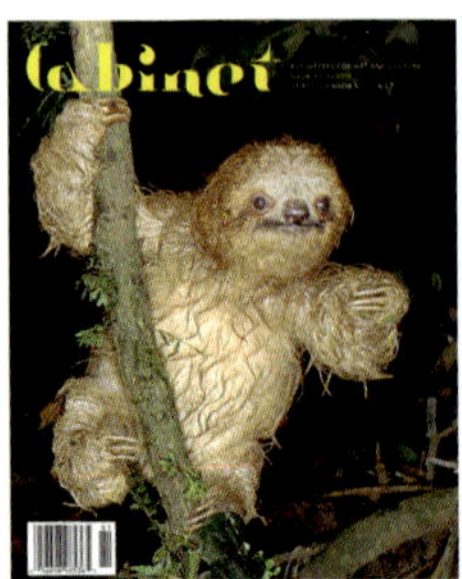

Issue 29 / **Sloth**

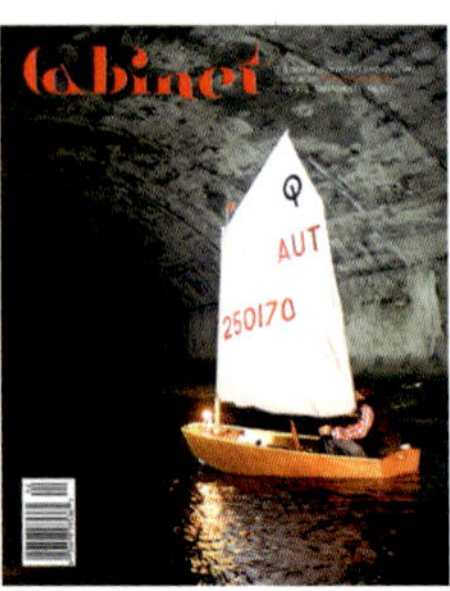

Issue 30 / **The Underground**

CABINET BOOKS

Prices in USD including postage.
Current subscribers: Take $5 off prices below.

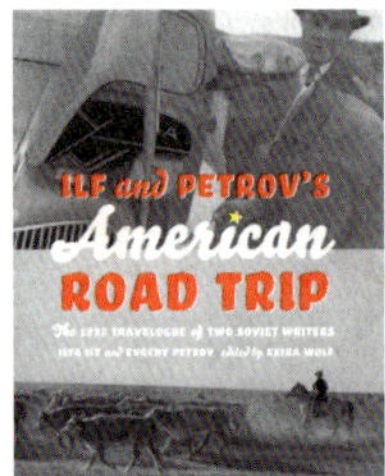

Ilf and Petrov's American Road Trip
The 1935 travelogue of two Soviet writers

US $18; Canada & Mexico $25; Elsewhere $27

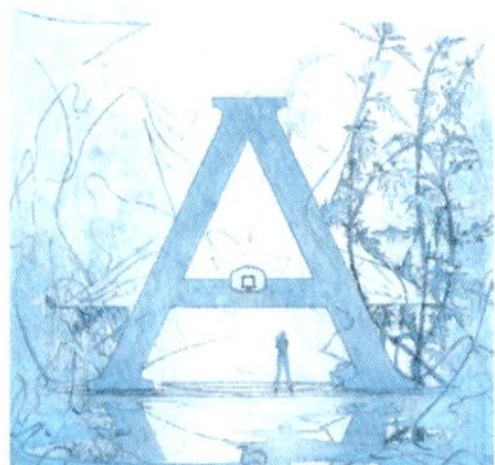

Letters from Mayhem
A large-format board book in the form of an ABC; Illustrations by Roger Andersson, text by Albert Mobilio

US $27; Canada $40; Mexico $45; Elsewhere $50

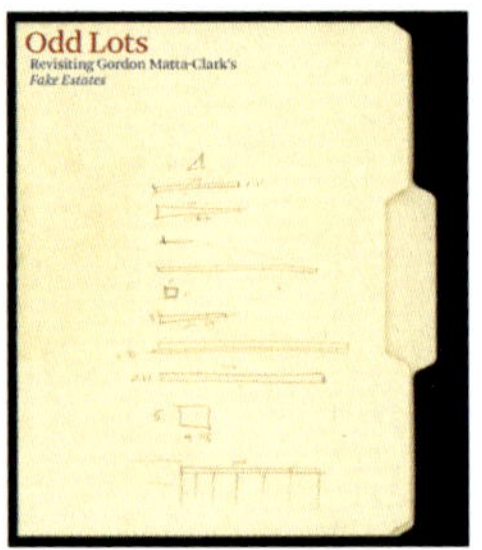

Odd Lots: Revisiting Gordon Matta Clark's "Fake Estates"
Essays and artist projects responding to Matta-Clark's seminal project from 1973

US $18; Canada & Mexico $22; Elsewhere $25

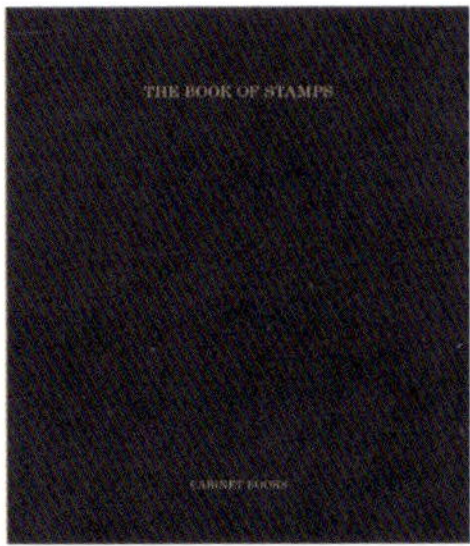

The Book of Stamps
15 detachable sheets of limited edition artist-designed stamps

US $23; Canada & Mexico $30; Elsewhere $33

HOW TO ORDER

1   Mail a check to Cabinet, 181 Wyckoff Street, Brooklyn, NY 11217 USA
2   Shop online at cabinetmagazine.org/shop
3   Fax +1 718 222 3700.
4   Call +1 718 222 8434.

Checks, made out to Cabinet, must be in USD and drawn on a US bank. We also accept Visa, MC, AmEx, Discover, and Paypal (paypal@cabinetmagazine.org) Prices and availability valid through 1 January 2009.

Visit cabinetmagazine.org to view our limited and unlimited editions, posters, and other tchotchkes.